Definitions of Art

Definitions of Art

Stephen Davies

Cornell University Press

Ithaca and London

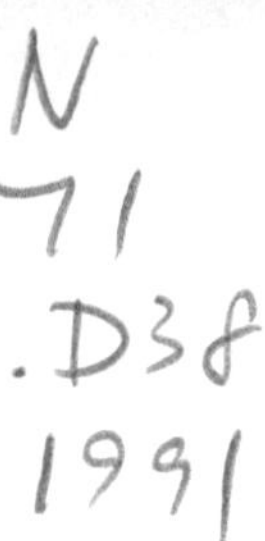

First published 1991 by Cornell University Press.

International Standard Book Number 0-8014-2568-9 (cloth)
International Standard Book Number 0-8014-9794-9 (paper)
Library of Congress Catalog Card Number 90-55756
Printed in the United States of America
Librarians: Library of Congress cataloging information appears on the last page of the book.

♾ The paper in this book meets the minimum requirements of the American National Standard for Information Sciences—Permanence of Paper for Printed Library Materials, ANSI Z39.48-1984.

Contents

Preface

In this book my primary aim is to describe and comment on the definition of art as it has been discussed in Anglo-American philosophy over the past thirty years. I bring to that discussion not a new theory but rather a certain perspective: I view the debate as revealing conflicting commitments to functional and to procedural accounts of art's nature.

My personal inclination is to prefer proceduralism to the other approaches I discuss. At the same time I am far from confident that the institutional theory's version of proceduralism is correct. It seems to me that much historical and sociological, as well as philosophical, work needs to be done if the institutional theory of the definition of art is to attain credibility. In any event, I am more concerned with the detailed development of the perspective on which I concentrate than with settling on a winner of the debate. Definitional questions are inextricably meshed with ontological, interpretive, and evaluative issues; their implications stretch in many directions and take many twists and turns. Where matters are as complex and fundamental as this, straightforwardly decisive arguments are not to be expected.

My second aim is to provide a resource for those who work in the area of philosophical aesthetics, in that I canvass the literature more thoroughly than is common (or usually necessary) and offer summaries and glosses of the wide array of proposals that currently hold the field. My intention is not so much to list who scored which points against whom but, rather, to locate the protagonists on the map I draw of the conceptual terrain. When much of the debate is confined to comparatively short pieces in scholarly journals, as is the case with this topic, I believe there is some value in the attempt to present an overview.

A section of the discussion of Chapter 2 appeared as "Functional and Procedural Definitions," *The Journal of Aesthetic Education*, 24 (Summer 1990); parts of Chapter 5 were published in "A Defence of the Institutional Definition of Art," *The Southern Journal of Philosophy*, 36 (1988): 307–324; a version of a brief argument found in Chapter 9 first appeared as "Feagin on Defining Art Intentionalistically," *The British Journal of Aesthetics*, 27 (1987): 178–180.

I am indebted to several people for their advice and insightful criticisms. In particular, I thank Donald Callen, Bob Ewin, Jerrold Levinson, and the first, anonymous reader for Cornell University Press, as well as the graduate students with whom I have worked at the University of Auckland. My gratitude also goes to John Ackerman, Carol Betsch, and Kay Scheuer of Cornell University Press, and to Lise Rodgers, my copyeditor.

STEPHEN DAVIES

Auckland, New Zealand

PART I

Introduction to Part I

Over the course of the following four chapters, I outline and develop a perspective on the debate in Anglo-American philosophy about the definition of art. I hope to demonstrate that this perspective is fundamental and insightful. I conceive of the debate as revealing a division between two approaches to the question of art's definition—the functional and the procedural. The functionalist believes that, necessarily, an artwork performs a function or functions (usually, that of providing a rewarding aesthetic experience) distinctive to art. By contrast, the proceduralist believes that an artwork necessarily is created in accordance with certain rules and procedures. At first sight these views appear to be complementary rather than exclusive. Where something is manufactured in response to some particular need, will it not be both (and inseparably) functional and procedural in its nature? Nevertheless, I believe that there are circumstances under which this question is to be answered in the negative, and I argue that the concept of art operates under just such circumstances. The relevant circumstances arise where the procedures under which a thing is created part company from the point of our having such things, from the functionality of the thing in question. I take this to be precisely the state of affairs with respect to much of the art (so-called) of the present era. When such a separation occurs, one might expect that the function, rather than the procedures designed originally to serve that function, would carry the day in determining the extension of the concept. Nevertheless, I argue that this is by no means inevitable and that some of our concepts are essentially procedural, rather than essentially functional. The question becomes, then, whether art is to be defined functionally or procedurally. Further, what differences are revealed by a commitment to the one view rather than the other?

To set up the problem of the definition of art, and because so much of the recent literature begins with it, in Chapter 1 I discuss Morris Weitz's seminal paper "The Role of Theory in Aesthetics." Weitz argued that art is a concept not amenable to essential definition on the grounds that there is no essence common to all and only artworks in virtue of which they are art. I pursue common lines of criticism against Weitz's position, although so familiar is much of this material that the chapter is intended more for students than for experts. Still, it would be a singular omission not to consider Weitz's views in the detail they deserve, because, although I judge his argument to be unsuccessful, not only did it motivate much of the work on which I concentrate in later chapters, it dramatically reoriented the attention of theorists from a search for intrinsic, exhibited, defining characteristics toward a consideration of complex, nonexhibited relational features of art. The definitions that have held sway in the debate since 1956 all have characterized the essential properties of art in such terms.

In Chapter 2, after a preamble about natural kinds and continua, I introduce the distinction between functional and procedural approaches to definition, outline the way in which functions and procedures may come adrift from each other, and provide some examples of what I take to be essentially procedural notions. At that point I turn to art. I consider the attitudes consistent with each of the two approaches on such issues as whether "hard cases," such as Marcel Duchamp's *Fountain*, are artworks, whether a definition of art will be essentially descriptive or essentially evaluative, and whether a definition of art should be expected to explain the place of art within the community. At this early stage I acknowledge, as I must, that there are approaches to the definition of art which, at first sight, fit readily into neither the functional nor the procedural camps.

In Chapter 3 I discuss the views of Monroe Beardsley in some detail, taking his theory to be a version of the functional approach to the definition of art. Beardsley is by no means a naïve functionalist, and there are respects in which he leans toward an intentionalist rather than a functionalist theory. Nevertheless, his account can be read as a predominantly functionalist theory unusual in its detail and depth. This chapter contains a discussion of the possible function of art which goes beyond (but probably complements) that offered by Beardsley. The chapter closes with a consideration of what I take to be a powerful objection to the functionalist approach—most important aesthetic properties of pieces are affected by those pieces' attaining art status, so it cannot be the case, as the functionalist holds, that a piece *qualifies* for art status only if it possesses the relevant properties.

I give a somewhat detailed consideration in Chapter 4 to the institutional theory of the definition of art developed by George Dickie, this theory being the most extended and sophisticated version of a procedural approach. As well as outlining the history of the theory's recent development and the detail of Dickie's version of the theory, I cover such topics as the circularity of his definition, his characterization of the role of artist, his views on artists isolated from social contexts, and so on. I am critical of some aspects of Dickie's theory (as I am also of Beardsley's), especially of the ahistoricism of his view and of his tendency to talk of status conferral as a type of action, rather than as an exercise of authority invested in a social role. Nevertheless, I believe that the institutional theory might be revised to accommodate many of the points made without compromising its approach to the definitional question. (This is not to say, though, that I take the institutional theory to win the day. Instead, my aim is to argue that the institutional theory could be more plausible than often is recognized.)

CHAPTER 1

Weitz's Anti-essentialism

Artists and philosophers have offered many characterizations of the distinctive nature of art. To mention just a few famous examples: for Plato art is imitation (or representation); for Wordsworth it is emotion recollected in tranquillity, and for Tolstoy and Curt Ducasse it is the expression of emotion; for Kant it is the interplay of forms, and for Clive Bell and Roger Fry it is significant form; Susanne Langer sees it as an iconic symbol of the forms of feelings.

Each of these theories seems plainly to fail as a definition. Either it does not distinguish artworks from other kinds of things—for example, tears are expressive of emotion but are not artworks—or it excludes from the realm of art pieces that indisputably are art—for example, at least some of Bach's fugues seem not be expressive of emotion.

Of course, a proponent of one of these theories might stick by it in the face of all opposition, insisting that the theory can accommodate any alleged counterinstance. In that case the defense saves the theory from falsity only at the cost of rendering the theory vacuous or meaningless (Lake 1954, Kennick 1958, 1964a). The theory becomes irrefutable, since no counterexample is accepted as such. If nothing is to be accepted as falsifying the claim, for example, that all artworks have significant form, what now can be meant by the notion of significant form?

Morris Weitz argues in a famous paper (1956) that the consistent failure of artists and aestheticians successfully to define art is no accident. Art is not susceptible to definition, he claims. The reasons he gives for his conclusion are philosophical, but no doubt a general dismay at the state of contemporary art might have pointed to his conclusion. When it looks as if anything at all might become (or be declared) art, the idea that something is an artwork because it shares with others of its kind a common essence looks to be implausible.

Weitz's Argument

The quest for an essential definition of "artwork" is a quest for a nontrivial specification of the jointly necessary and sufficient condition for "artworkness," where the realization of this condition is essentially and not merely contingently related to artworks' being artworks. Weitz's claim is not only that all past attempts to define art have failed, but that any attempt to provide an essential definition of art is doomed to failure for the reason that art has no essence—that no property is jointly necessary and sufficient for something's being an artwork. If we "look and see," he says, we will observe that there is no property common to all and only artworks.

Weitz might have accepted that there are both some necessary and some sufficient properties for artworkness; his point is that there are no jointly necessary and sufficient conditions for artworkness. In fact, though, Weitz goes so far as to deny that there is any property common to all artworks; that is, he denies that there is any necessary condition for something's being an artwork. He thinks that the possession of artifactuality is a necessary condition for something's being an artwork, if any property is. But he also holds that something can be made into an artwork without its also being made into an artifact. A piece of driftwood can be removed from the beach and becomes an artwork (without being artifactualized) in being presented as such within an art gallery. He concludes: not even artifactuality is a necessary condition for artworkness; so there is no necessary condition for artworkness.

Obviously if Weitz is right in this, he wins his case. If there is no necessary condition for something's being an artwork, it follows immediately that there can be no jointly necessary and sufficient condition for something's being an artwork, and hence, no essential definition of artwork.

Weitz does not rest his argument entirely upon empirical claims about what will be found when we "look and see," or about the legitimacy of the claim to art status of "Driftwood art" and the like; he makes what he takes to be a telling conceptual point. A definition of art would foreclose on future creativity. If art has some immutable essence, then the art of the future could not, in its essential respects, challenge, alter, subvert, or depart from the art of the past. But the history of art is the history of such a process, of an exercise of revolutionary creativity which time and again has turned the prevailing conception of art on its head and back-to-front. So art could have no unalterable aspect and, hence, no essential definition. Were we to find some property common to all and only artworks (which in fact we do not), that property would be bound to be an incidental, nonessential property, for it might always be rejected or ignored in the art of the future. (The point is made this way by Timothy Binkley 1976, rather than by Weitz, though Weitz would be bound to agree.) Indeed, such is the temperament of artists that the discovery of such a property would provoke a reaction against it!

The definitions of art offered in the past by philosophers are legislative rather than descriptive, Weitz says. Instead of characterizing the fixed essence of all artworks, each "definition" stipulates the range of properties regarded by its proponent as desirable in good art. What is no more than a recommendation in favor of some particular school is given the appearance of respectability in being presented as a definition objectively applicable to all art.

How, though, are artworks grouped together as such in the absence of a defining property? Weitz adopts the idea of "family resemblance" introduced in Ludwig Wittgenstein's *Philosophical Investigations* (1953). Just as the members of a family all resemble one another in some respect, though there is no single, pervasive respect in which each resembles every other, so too there are networks of similarity among artworks, despite the absence of a property common to all artworks. Just as the woven fibers of a rope can constitute a length of rope, though no single fiber runs through the full length of the rope, so too the complex web of resemblances among artworks groups them within a common, unified class. One piece is properly to be classed as an artwork along with other artworks by virtue of its sharing a family resemblance with them.

Weitz's Place in the Debate

Although Weitz's paper was to become more widely cited than any other, he is not alone in pursuing the line of argument indicated above. W. B. Gallie (1948, 1956b) argues that art has no essence and so is an essentially contested concept (as are ethical concepts also in his view, 1956a). He favors a conjunctive definition of art which lists its art forms, though he recognizes that such a list cannot be closed. John Passmore (1951) suggests that art has no essence, and that the dreariness of aesthetics follows from its futile pursuit of a definition. Paul Ziff (1953) is also an anti-essentialist who believes that artworks are classed as such in virtue of their resemblance to paradigm cases. William Kennick (1958) is another who dismisses the quest for a definition of art (for a discussion see Sircello 1973). Kennick (1964a) thinks that artworks are grouped by resemblance and analogy, and that general definitions that are not open-ended are bound to be stipulatory.

Also, Weitz has his followers: Haig Khatchadourian (1961, 1969) argues that art is a family-resemblance concept, and he favors the view (1974) that artworks are to be identified as such in terms of their resemblances to paradigm artworks. Arnold Berleant (1964) concludes that a completely unequivocal, demarcated account of the concept of art is both impossible and undesirable. Wladyslaw Tatarkiewicz (1971) accepts that an essential definition is bound to fail in trying to foreclose on creativity, and he believes that the only acceptable form for a definition would be an open-ended, disjunctive list of artworks, the intentions of artists, the effects produced by artworks, and so on.

Frequently anti-essentialist arguments are accompanied by the comment that, because we can make identifying references to art while lacking knowledge of its defining essence (if it has one!), a definition is unnecessary (see, for example, Mothersill 1961 and Tilghman 1989). Kennick (1958) makes the point by claiming that someone would know what to collect if asked to retrieve the artworks from a warehouse (= the world), but would be at a loss if told to bring from the warehouse all the items with "significant form" and the like. (For a modern version of this position, developed in conjunction with the causal theory of reference and suggesting that "art" is a rigid designator, see Carney 1975, 1982a, 1982b; Lord 1977; and Matthews 1979. For a powerful attack on their positions, see Leddy 1987—also see Kivy 1979.)

As they stand, such comments seem to be fair enough: it is true that, very commonly, we make identifying references to things without concerning ourselves with, or even knowing of, their defining essences. But the point is made by these authors in such a way as to suggest that they take it to reveal the total irrelevance, or even the impossibility, of one's providing an essential definition. There is, however, no reason to assume that the only interest a definition could have would lie in its making possible the identification of artworks as such. (Nor even a reason to suppose that a definition must be applicable in this way—Socrates perhaps set too strict a requirement in insisting that Euthyphro's definition of piety be directly and immediately useful in the identification of pious acts as such—see the Socratic dialogue *Euthyphro*.) Neither is there any reason to think that such ability as we have in identifying artworks bears upon the possibility or otherwise of art's having a defining essence.

Weitz held by his view (1973, 1977), refining it in some details but not responding seriously to his critics. And Weitzian anti-essentialism is common today. Indeed, some writers (Shusterman 1987, Bourdieu 1987, and Elgin and Goodman 1987) see the attack on definition as one of the very few achievements of analytic philosophy as applied to aesthetics. Many of the writers who offer a definition are very careful these days to emphasize that they aim to do no more than to characterize the concept's core, the paradigm art forms or artworks, and to characterize it in terms of necessary or sufficient conditions, but not in terms of conditions that are jointly both—see, for example, E. J. Bond (1975) and Beardsley (1982a).

Yet most philosophers who claim to have solved a perennial philosophical problem and who suggest that their colleagues turn their attention now to more fruitful concerns must surely speak with tongue in cheek. In the case of Weitz's paper, the attack on the possibility of the definition of art predictably provoked a heightened interest in the definition of art, and the topic received more attention than ever it had before. The reaction to Weitz's paper led to the development of new theories of the definition of art and to the much more detailed characterization of some of the older theories. Moreover, Weitz's arguments were subjected to close scrutiny. The remainder of this chapter is devoted to a critical examination of the adequacy of his arguments.

Criticisms of Weitz's Argument

Weitz has been attacked by Benjamin Tilghman (1973a) for misinterpreting Wittgenstein. (For a different version of the same complaint, see Moutafakis 1975.) According to Tilghman, Weitz concedes too much in denying that artworks share a common property, because in doing so he allows that Do artworks share a common property? is a meaningful question. And Weitz, in implying that we are concerned with classifying things as art or as nonart, fails to appreciate the unimportance of labeling within the rich social context of artistic life and practice. Like Kennick, Weitz fails to realize that the answer to Is it art? is strictly context-relative, and so he renders Is is art? meaningless by failing to specify a context within which such a question could make sense.

Tilghman's objections reject as altogether misguided the philosophical enterprise of which this book is an example, so it should not be surprising that I find them unimpressive. I do not accept, to use his examples, that whether or not something is a work of art depends on whether the question is asked in Miami Beach, San Francisco, or Philadelphia. I do accept that whether or not an item is an artwork depends on the history of art, the circumstances of its treatment, and so forth, but Weitz's discussion of Driftwood art suggests that this sort of relativity in the classification of artworks presents no problems for his position. I also accept that there is more of importance in aesthetics than definition, but do not see how this shows that questions of definition are entirely devoid of interest. There is a context in which the Is it art? question is not a request for definition but, rather, a request for a demonstration of the continuities between some alleged artwork and the traditions and purposes of art as the "art game" has been played prior to the arrival of the piece in question. Equally, though, there is a context in which the Is it art? question, as asked by Weitz, makes sense. The relevant context is that of a longstanding philosophical debate (which is not to say that the debate is confined to philosophers and the classrooms in which they teach—art making is such a self-conscious activity that the debate is pursued as much by artists and critics as by disinterested theoreticians). Tilghman (1984, 1989) asserts that, in the context of this debate, the But is it art? question is senseless, but I find no adequate support in his arguments for that assertion. That the question is not always to be answered by a definition (as Tilghman rightly recognizes) does not mean that it never is so to be answered.

Accepting the force of Weitz's argument, one might begin by trying to save the reputation of the writers attacked by Weitz. Many of them were interested only in indicating a typical or an important feature of art, or in offering a general theory; they were not attempting to offer an essential definition (Brown 1971, Snoeyenbos 1978b). Weitz suggests that these "failed definitions" are best to be understood as attempts to cloak with an air of objectivity opinions about the nature of good art, or about what art ought to be like, but this view may be unfair. It is not at all obvious that all or most of these writers were trying to smuggle anything past their readers. They were quite open about the evaluative judgments they made and never represented themselves as offering essential definitions.

Of course, this point, even were it to strike home, would leave untouched Weitz's central charge—that art has no definable essence.

Many writers have challenged the specific claim that not even artifactuality is a necessary condition for something's being an artwork. Against Weitz's example they argue either that Driftwood art is not art at all, or that, one way or another, the piece of driftwood is artifactualized in the course of its attaining art status. Those arguments are so interesting and important that I shall devote a full chapter to them later in this book. For the moment, though, the point to make is that Weitz might be mistaken in insisting that artifactuality is not a necessary condition for something's being art without his being mistaken in his main claim: that art has no jointly necessary and sufficient conditions.

The explanatory power of the idea of family resemblance has been called into question (Mandelbaum 1965, Manser 1967, Osborne 1973). The very example from which the notion takes its name points up the problem. People are not grouped together in families by virtue of the way in which they resemble each other. Typically they are grouped in families in terms of genetic relationships. (This is the common, but careless, way of putting the objection. Spouses, adopted children, in-laws, and so forth are not usually genetically related but are family members for all that. The objection could be put more carefully, however, without its force being undercut.) The recognition of a resemblance among family members presupposes, and does not explain, the basis for that membership.

More than this, in the absence of some way of specifying a restriction on the class within which resemblance is to be sought, or in the kinds and degrees of resemblances that are to be counted, resemblance is a notion that is useless as a basis for classification (Diffey 1973, Osborne 1973). Anything might resemble any other thing in some respect. (Germs resemble galaxies in that both are mentioned in this sentence, both have names beginning with *g*, neither can be seen by the unaided eye in daytime, neither has the same weight as any emu, and so on.) If resemblance is to provide a basis for classification, there must be some restriction on the type and/or range and/or degree of resemblance which is relevant. Now, though, the specification of criteria of relevance for resemblances (as bases for classifications) will lead unavoidably to an essential (and probably disjunctive) definition that Weitz's talk of family resemblance was intended to render otiose. We get something like this: an artwork is anything that resembles any paradigm artwork in not less than nineteen of the following fifty-two respects . . . and a paradigm artwork is one that. . . . (This point may lie behind the charge made in Zerby 1957 that Weitz himself is offering an essential definition of art as an open-ended concept united by a web of family resemblances.)

This objection applies not only to Weitz's account but also to that of Ziff (1953). Ziff rejects the idea that artworks possess some essential property and defines art both in terms of its paradigm instances on the one hand, and in terms of a similarity between its paradigms and other artworks on the other. He recognizes that there may be no feature common to all and only paradigm artworks, so probably he feels that the paradigms are to be enumerated, and not defined. In any event, the idea that new artworks can be identified as artworks by virtue of a similarity that holds between them and paradigm artworks is empty without a specification of criteria for relevant similarity, and the search for that specification must reopen the question of essential, versus inessential, types of resemblance or sources of resemblance. (A similar line is taken against Khatchadourian 1974 by Beardsley in 1982a.)

To return to Weitz: George Dickie (1984) has produced a further objection to Weitz's appeal to family resemblance. He notes that family resemblance could never explain how the very first artwork qualified as an artwork. Even if most artworks are artworks in virtue of their similarity with earlier art, still there must be some original artworks that lack artistic predecessors. The explanation of the qualification of these early artworks for art status cannot rest on resemblance. A recursive definition in terms of resemblance (*X* is an artwork if it resembles the artworks of the past) is incomplete unless a different account of the art status of the earliest pieces is included (and the first artworks were artworks—or can be seen, retrospectively, as artworks—because . . .). So, at best, Weitz's appeal to family resemblance provides an incomplete explanation of how things become art.

Now there is a general problem that arises in connection with priority, with "firstness"—which came first, the chicken or the egg? There is a problem in accounting for a first mover, a first cause, and a first existent, as is outlined in the first three of Aquinas's Five Ways of arguing for the existence of a god who is self-moving, self-causing, and necessary in itself. There is equal difficulty in accounting for something's being the first sentence of a language. This problem about firstness is such a general one that it would be unfair, perhaps, to appeal to it in objecting to Weitz's argument. So we might ask, is Dickie's objection of the general kind, or is it an objection more specific to Weitz's treatment of the issues? It seems to me that Dickie's point is of the latter type, and hence that it is fairly posed. Accounts of art status in terms of resemblance lead inevitably to recursive criteria for art status, and recursive criteria cannot help but highlight the importance of the first elements in the chains of resemblances. Weitz's approach, whether he means it to or not, gives a special importance to the art status of the earliest artworks, and so his methodology specifically invites the objection raised by Dickie. (Note that historically founded definitions, such as those considered in Chapter 7, might deal with such an objection by characterizing the art status of the earliest works as being achieved retrospectively. The point here simply is that Weitz is open to Dickie's objection—not that the objection must be insurmountable.)

One further difficulty with the claim that resemblance provides the basis for classifying items as artworks is posed by Duchamp's readymades, Driftwood art, and many instances of Conceptual art. Duchamp turned one urinal indistinguishable from others of its type into an artwork without thereby affecting the nonart status of those other urinals. If two urinals are alike in their appearance (and alike also in the causal history of their manufacture), how could the resemblance between artworks and one of these urinals explain how that urinal is an artwork without its showing the other urinal to be an artwork also? And again, one piece of driftwood resembles another piece of driftwood more closely than either resembles the vast majority of artworks, so how could resemblance explain how the one piece might be an artwork and the other not? (Of course one might challenge this objection by questioning the status as art of readymades, driftwood pieces, and the like, but that course is not open to Weitz since he accepts that pieces of driftwood actually can become artworks.)

Notice, however, that, if these criticisms are decisive, they show only that Weitz's *positive* account, his account of how we group artworks together, is mistaken. They do not show his main *negative* point to be in error; that is, they leave untouched the claim that artworks are not grouped together in terms of a common essence, since they have none.

Weitz (following Wittgenstein) exhorts us to *look and see* that art lacks an essence. That instruction is importantly misleading, for it suggests that Weitz's views are based on empirical observation rather than on conceptual analysis. But there is little evidence that Weitz has spent much time on an empirical investigation—for instance, he does not discuss many examples (Snoeyenbos 1978b). It is worth noting that what one perceives, while it may not be theory determined, is much affected by what one believes and by theories to which one subscribes about the way the world is. It is only within the context of a great many systematically organized beliefs that I can see, for example, that the government is in trouble, that the flashlight batteries are low, that there is a valid proof of a Pythagorean theorem, and so on. For this reason Weitz's argument should be seen (!) as resting mainly on a conceptual point and not on anything that might be revealed uncontroversially through an empirical study.

Dickie (1980, 1984) has objected that Weitz is too liberal when he "looks and sees," in that Weitz accepts all uses of the word "artwork" as equally legitimate and so fails to distinguish the literal, classificatory use of the term from uses that are evaluative, metaphoric, ironic, and so on, as well as from those that simply are in error. Dickie's point is that we can hardly expect to find the essential core of art if, as well as considering the *Mona Lisa* as an artwork, we also count Aunt Flo's scones, my love's ear, and so on, as works of art. Further, Dickie notes that if just any use of the term "work of art" is to be accepted as legitimate, then conflicting judgments about what is and what is not art also will be equally legitimate, in which case the appearance of disagreement will be illusory because such judgments will amount to no more than expressions of personal taste.

Is Weitz guilty of the fault imputed to him? He may be, though I am not certain that he is. Anyway, Weitz's position does not rely for its plausibility on any such sleight of hand. It is arguable that not even art's paradigm instances share a common property. What intrinsic, perceptible feature is common to Shakespeare's *Hamlet,* a *Song without Words* by Mendelssohn, Donne's *Hymn to God the Father,* Picasso's *Guernica,* Austen's *Pride and Prejudice,* Michelangelo's *David?* It is not obvious that there is any perceptible, aesthetic property common to them all.

Weitz's main conceptual point is that an essential definition of art would determine the character of yet-to-be-made artworks in a way that would rule out art making as a creative activity. From this claim he concludes that it must be impossible to give an essential definition of art, since art making necessarily and inescapably is a creative activity.

A number of writers are unconvinced by the allegation of an incompatibility between creativity and the availability of necessary and sufficient conditions for art status (Sibley 1960; Mandelbaum 1965; Brown 1969; Sclafani 1971; Bywater 1972; Snoeyenbos 1978a, 1978b; Margolis 1980), and rightly so, I think. After all, that it is made by a creative person might be a part of the essence of an artwork, might be something mentioned in its definition. (Some such condition is specified in Todd 1983). How could such a definition foreclose on future creativity, since it does not tell artists what to do, although it insists that, whatever they do, they do it creatively? Moreover, why think of rules as restraints instead of as means facilitating one's actions, including one's creative actions? It is not chess I am playing if I do not play by the rules that map the limits of the game itself, and I can play creative, innovative, radical chess only within the framework of those rules.

There is a common view that dates back to Kant (and no doubt much further) according to which artists are geniuses unconstrained by rules and the artworks that result from their actions are valuable and interesting only insofar as they are unique and resistant to description in general terms. (A recent work on this wavelength is that by Mothersill 1984.) Now, if we see definitions as formulas or rules, it will be natural for us to share Weitz's conclusion that creativity precludes definability.

This argument (whether or not it be Weitz's) rests on several common (but mistaken) assumptions about the nature of creativity, of rules, and of the usefulness of definitions. The conception of the artist as genius and of creation as the unfettered expression of the intellect, emotions, or spirit is a peculiarly nineteenth-century, European one that sits ill with the character and the style of creation of such artists as J. S. Bach, who worked to order and with strict deadlines. Equally unacceptable is the view that an adequate definition must be usable as if it were a recipe (thus obliterating any distinction between art and craft). To return to the above example, how could a definition of artworks as the product of artists' creative efforts serve as a mere formula for the production of art?

A more important issue here, I think, is the implied view of rules as inexorably carving a straight line into the future, so that to follow a rule is to have the outcome of one's actions determined in advance and in a fashion that is quite independent of what one does and judges, or what others do and judge. Wittgenstein, in 1953 (within a few pages of discussing family resemblance), was the first to challenge this conception of rules and to emphasize not only that no rule determines its own interpretation, but also that what counts as following or applying a rule is determined in connection with patterns of communal behavior and judgment (Leich and Holtzman 1981,

Wright 1981, Kripke 1982). The intention to follow a rule does not guarantee that one will follow the rule correctly. But this lack of a guarantee does not indicate that the individual's actions count for nothing in a world in which the outcome of all applications of the rule are settled in advance of a consideration of what people do and judge. It indicates, instead, that the individual's actions must be cast against the background of the wider, communal practice.

The point is this: that one is following a rule is no bar to one's doing what is new. This is true even in the most mundane instances of rule interpretation. Wanting to obey the injunction that I not walk on the college's lawns, and faced with a track worn to the ground by the passage of others across an area of grass, I must, in applying the rule, reach a judgment about whether the pathway cuts across a single lawn or now divides two lawns (which may once have been one lawn). If the path divides two lawns, I will not be breaking the rule in taking it, but if it cuts across a single lawn, I should not take the path. In adhering to the rule, I do not merely discover the answer to my predicament as something laid up in advance within the rule itself. What I do is make a judgment rather than discover something that was waiting unsighted all along, because what is to count as the correct application of a rule to a case is not determined by a statement of the rule. Where the dilemma has been faced by others, and a body of practice or official rulings have dealt with it, the burden of judgment might be removed from my shoulders. Many cases, however, call for a new or novel application of a rule (or might reasonably be judged to require one), and where this is so, I cannot avoid deciding how the rule is to be applied to the case in hand. My judgment alone does not determine what is to count as the correct application of the rule, since my coming up with an answer is not what makes that answer correct, but my decision contributes to the communal practice of applying the rule in question, and it is that practice, coupled with the judgments of the practitioners, which determines what is to count as a correct application of the rule. (In my example it may be that someone has the authority to make a ruling on the matter. That is not true of all rules and, even where it is true, does not affect the point that the person in authority must exercise his or her judgment in deciding how the rule applies to the given case.) To call me a "rule follower" is misleading in implying that the rule has been there before me, so to speak—what we are is "rule appliers" or "rule interpreters." When we are seen in these terms, there is no reason to oppose the notions of creativity and of rule following.

A defender of Weitz might concede the previous argument and yet continue to hold that, in much if not all art, the norm is rule breaking rather than rule applying. Many artists of the past and yet more in the present set out deliberately to challenge the rules and conventions that seemed to govern their predecessors. Art often is reflexive in taking its own former self (its former practices and its former rules) as its present subject matter. In continually dissociating itself from itself, it transcends its past and the rules and conventions that typified that past.

I find this reply unconvincing—if anything, it shows that the rules applied by artists in creating art can be changed, and not that there are no such rules. A change in first-order rules is perfectly consistent with the continuing application of second-order rules about how and to what degree first-order rules might change, so change is not itself antithetical to rule application. Indeed, if what artists do is to be correctly understood as a new way of making art and not to be seen merely as a new way of indulging or amusing themselves, then some link with the past practice of art making must be preserved (Levinson, 1979, 1989; Carroll 1988). If I create a new form of art, and not merely a new style of fruit picking, or paper folding, or house building, then there must be something about my fruit picking, paper folding, or house building—something about its intentional context, its consequences, its function, or whatever—which separates it from all non–art-making acts of fruit picking, paper folding, or house building and unites it with other acts of art creation. Artists cannot be so free that they leave all constraints behind them, because if they were, there would be no reason to think that what they are doing is creating new art, as distinct from creating mere new junk, mere new buildings, mere new pastimes, and so on.

Weitz concerns himself at first with openness with respect to the border between present and future art. Later (1973) he recognizes that openness might take many forms—suffice it to say that he recognizes the difficulty of tracing the borderline between present art and nonart, as well as between present art and future art. On the one hand, there are any number of controversial or otherwise "hard" cases where something alleged to be art is in most respects indiscriminable from nonartworks or seemingly is not worthy of the status of art—Duchamp's readymades, Driftwood art, Chimpanzee art, Minimal art, Conceptual art, Environmental art, and so forth. On the other hand, there are many pastimes and entertainments the products of which are not usually classed as artworks but which seem worthy of that appellation—musicals, break-dancing, joinery, fine-point sewing, pottery, scrimshaw, and so on. One way in which the concept of art might be open is in the absence of any clear border between what is and what is not to be classified as an artwork.

Even if we accept for the sake of the argument that there is no clear border between some artworks and some nonartworks, it is not obvious that the possibility of an essential definition of artwork has been ruled out. Two accounts of this type of openness are possible, and either is compatible with the giving of an essential definition. (Some concepts might best be approached the one way, others the other. In what follows I make no attempt to consider which is the better approach to the concept of art.) In the first type of case, the openness of the concept indicates an epistemic difficulty we have in deciding just where the boundary of the concept lies. In this view the concept does have a clear boundary, and so any given item really is or is not an artwork, but because we cannot be sure or cannot agree on where the boundary falls, we cannot always be certain what is and what is not an artwork. In that event it will also be the case that we cannot be certain which of several plausible candidates is the correct, essential definition of artwork. But that we will then have a difficulty in demonstrating to everyone's satisfaction which is the correct definition does not show to be incoherent the notion that there is a correct definition. In the second type of case the borderline vagueness is ontological; it is characteristic of the way the concept is instantiated in the world and is not simply a reflection of the uncertain basis of our knowledge of the world. Cases are hard to determine precisely because there is at the borderline no definite, correct answer as to whether or not something is an artwork. But again, that a concept is indefinite in some respects is no bar to its being defined. An adequate, essential definition of the concept will record the limits of the area in which the application of the term is equivocal. If it is part of the essence of the concept that it is indefinite in some ways and/or at some places and/or at some times and/or under some conditions, then the dimensions of this indefiniteness will feature within an essential definition of the concept.

Weitz's instruction to *look and see* if artworks share a common, essential property indicates that he thinks an essential property (were there to be one) would be a property perceptible within each and every artwork—to put it crudely, that all and only artworks are red, for example. The same assumption is indicated by the conflict he postulates between creativity and definition, because these two most obviously would clash if the definition specified that the artwork, to qualify as an artwork, must possess a perceptible property, such as a particular type of form or content. (Even if artists might be creative in working within such constraints, the history of art making suggests that they do not see themselves as restricted to operating within such a framework.) These indications suggest that, in denying the possibility of an essential definition, Weitz is denying the possibility of an essential definition in terms of particular sorts of properties; that is, in terms of the perceptible properties intrinsic to artworks. Of course, he may be right in thinking that no internal, perceptible property is essential to something's being an artwork, while being mistaken in the claim that he actually makes—that no essential definition of art is possible.

The first commentator to put forth this powerful objection was Maurice Mandelbaum (1965). Instead of concluding (from the fact that there is no essential property perceptible within all and only artworks) that an essential definition of art is impossible, Mandelbaum points out that it would be as or more plausible to conclude that the essential property for art is some imperceptible property, such as a relational property between certain sorts of objects, practices, and people. Weitz cannot find an essential property for art only because he looks for that property in the wrong place. Mandelbaum does not go on to spell out a definition, but he does indicate the direction in which one is to be sought. He suggests that what all and only artworks might have in common is a particular function. (Functional analyses of family-resemblance concepts were also recommended in Khatchadourian 1958 and Manser 1967.)

Many commentators agree (rightly) that Mandelbaum's objection is the most serious of those considered so far; but they also (wrongly) concur that it is fatal for Weitz's position. In fact, there is a reply to Mandelbaum's objection which, though it seems obvious, few people acknowledge. (One person who does so is von Morstein, 1986.) It is: if you "look and see," just as you will notice that there is no intrinsic property common to all and only artworks, equally you will find that there is no extrinsic property common to all and only artworks. There is no relational property the instantiation of which is essential to a thing's being an artwork. The shift of attention from perceptible to relational properties provides no guarantee that the difficulties that arise with respect to definitions citing the former will not recur with respect to definitions citing the latter.

This move is successful in staving off the immediate collapse of a Weitzian position, but as a long-term strategy it does not look to be promising. Weitz's claim that there is no property common to all and only artworks appears highly plausible when we confine our attention to the perceptible and/or intrinsic properties of artworks but is far less plausible when extended to cover all the possible types of properties an artwork might have. For there are many properties that seem to be both important and common to a great many artworks, if not to them all—for example, that artworks are chosen, shaped, or created with certain sorts of purposes and effects in mind. Even if it is not self-evidently true that some relational property is essential to something's being art, it is by no means ridiculous to argue toward such a conclusion.

Be that as it may, Weitz held by his account in the face of all objections, although he did revise some of its detail. What was the effect of Weitz's paper, apart from its kindling an interest in the definition of art which he had hoped to scotch? Even if it did not convince everyone that definition is impossible, it did at least persuade many that artworks could not be defined in terms of their perceptible, intrinsic properties. In particular, the definition of "artwork" in terms of artworks' being objects with certain aesthetic properties, such as beauty, seemed to be abandoned. Instead, those who pursue the definition of art turned their attention to the complex, extrinsic, relational properties possessed by artworks. They began to concern themselves with the historical and social context within which art is created, presented, interpreted, understood, and enjoyed and, in wider terms, with the function played by the production and consumption of art in our lives. This shift of focus was a radical departure from the preoccupations of traditional aesthetics, and a measure of responsibility for that most rewarding of reorientations belongs undoubtedly to Weitz.

CHAPTER 2

Functional and Procedural Definitions

If the world contains demarcated natural kinds, we can define those kinds by describing the world's seams. That is, we can delineate all and only the members of a natural kind by tracing divisions within the world's structure, and provided that those divisions arise as a direct consequence of the essential nature of those kinds, such a method of classification will provide a definition. Moreover, in the case of natural kinds, the defining properties will be internal to the members of the class being defined, rather than external, relational properties.

The most obvious candidates for natural kinds are the elements (such as calcium, mercury, helium, and gold), chemical compounds (such as salt, or the carbonates, sulphates, sulphites, and chlorates), and biological species (such as the aspidistra and the zebra), genera (such as eucalypts, monotremes, and hawks), or phyla (such as birds and mammals). Even in these cases the natural divisions might not be so exact as to facilitate definition. Isotopic forms of the elements break the neat symmetry of the periodic classification of elements according to their subatomic structure, and the line between biological species is blurred by hybridization, mutation, and throwbacks. To the extent that differences between the elements or species are gradual, and to the degree that such gradual differences relate to their various essences, doubt would be cast on their claim to be natural kinds.

If parts of the world are differentiated across continua (that is, with each part grading imperceptibly into the next and, hence, not being clearly demarcated from the next), then the way in which we categorize those parts of the world reveals as much about us as it reveals about the world's structure. Rather than discovering the world's natural boundaries, we, as observers, impose our own divisions upon its continuities. The colors are not natural property kinds (and, of course, neither are they natural substance kinds such as those just mentioned). Although yellow and violet are quite different colors, the color spectrum contains within it no discontinuities to mark a natural boundary between the two. Because color classifications are made by us and are not merely discovered in the world, they do not simply map its natural divisions. The number of colors into which we divide the range reveals something of the perceptual discriminations of which we are capable and something of the importance that color discrimination plays in the conduct of our lives. Our classification of the world's colors is not indifferent, as it is supposed to be in the case of natural kinds, to the fact that we are (have been/might be) present in the world as describers of it. Accordingly, the defining properties of colors will be relational, since what makes a color what it is is a function of the properties of observers as well as of the properties of light wavelengths and the like. The relational character of the definition will be more or less emphasized in accordance with the particularity or universality of the relation. On the one hand, if all human beings discriminate the primary colors, for example, then the relation drops out of account. If something is red to everyone (under standard conditions), then it is red and not merely red-to-me. On the other hand, if the color distinctions being drawn are finer than is usual and/or are tied to interests not universally shared (such as those of a person producing a photographic catalog of the paintings in an exhibition), the relational element must be treated with more care. This would be the case if we were to try to define the meaning of "magenta" for example.

The pitch continuum provides both a clear illustration of these points and an interesting contrast to the color continuum. We experience the pitch continuum as divided into segments at the interval of the octave; it seems to be a brute fact about human hearing that at the octave we hear the same notes again, so we experience the pitch range as if it were like a color range in which some eleven rainbows are laid side by side across the continuum. (Although I say this is a "brute fact," I do not mean to suggest that no explanation of the phenomenon is possible. Pure sine waves are without overtones, but most of the notes we hear do have overtones, and the first and most prominent among these is the octave. The overtones affect the timbre of the note and are not usually heard as such; that is, we hear a note played by a trumpet or a flute, say, and not a timbreless chord in which the higher notes are weaker than the lower ones. The acoustic properties of tones explain the affinity we recognize between notes at the octave, but our recognition of this affinity is a "brute fact" in that its explanation comes after and presupposes the fact of the recognition.) An element in the experience of the pitch range is an awareness of "sound-space" in terms of which one occurrence of a note is distinguished from an occurrence of the same note at a different octave. For some cultures the spatial terms are "high" and "low;" for others they are "big" and "little" or "thin" and "fat." So familiar is this secondary use of spatial terms that a pianist who is asked why the one note is higher might reply that it must be higher since the hand moves *up* the keyboard to find it, this being illustrated by a movement of the hand which is sideward. Different cultures divide the continuum within the octave in different ways, and so work with different musical scales (though most if not all peoples employ the perfect fifth and fourth in at least one of their scales). The way in which we divide up the octave, our scales, is more revealing of our cultures than of the world's structure. (Although musicologists sometimes have attempted to justify the "correctness" of one scale or another by reference to the notes of the harmonic series of overtones, their efforts are refuted both by the variety of scales used across the world and by the deviation of all scales, including the just and well-tempered major scales, from the pitches of the higher overtones.) By contrast, all peoples preserve the sanctity of the octave as the standard, fixed unit of "sound-space." The sameness of octaves reveals something of the world's structure and not merely something about us.

Why are octaves not natural kinds? Because their sameness is a sameness between experiences of things rather than between the things themselves. But how do we draw that distinction? It might be argued that no likenesses are independent of experiences of likeness, and such an argument might be used either to suggest that octaves are natural kinds or, more likely, to attack the idea that there are any natural kinds as such (that is, observation-independent divisions in the world's structure). To pursue this dispute would involve a consideration of the debate between realists and antirealists, and that debate lies far beyond my present concerns.

The Point of Concepts

Fortunately it is not necessary that I consider whether or not there is a distinction between our describing the world's structure as (sometimes) discontinuous and our describing the world's differences as merely inherent in our mode of experiencing the world's continuities. This is not necessary because my concern lies with a much more radical type of relativity than is at issue in this debate. Many of our classifications arise not so much from an attempt to describe the way the world is as from the quite deliberate imposition upon the world of a structure that derives directly from our needs, interests, and desires. The point of many of our concepts obviously relates to our needs and concerns. For example, we have the concept of food because generally we value our lives, and the maintenance of our lives depends upon our nourishing ourselves in a deliberate, ongoing fashion. Indeed, if a wide enough view is taken of our interests (so that we are seen as creatures with a need for complete, systematic categorizations), it is arguable that all our concepts have points that reflect our concerns.

I mention two illustrative examples. Because we do not wish to die or be harmed, we have a need to pick out and avoid things that might have such effects upon us, and we have a further need to distinguish those dangerous things which might be self-inflicted by accident and so on. Moreover, because we sometimes wish to kill some things and not others (for example, weeds but not flowers), we are interested also in the ways in which nonhuman things are liable to harm. This is the point of our concept of poison. The point of the concept of kindness, on the other hand, reflects our social, rather than our personal, needs. Kindness makes social life smoother and more pleasant than otherwise would be the case, and it is for this reason that there is a point to our marking off the quality of character exemplified in kind acts. Given the way the world is, anyone, through no fault of his own, might sometimes need help, freely given, in meeting his obligations within the cooperative enterprise. In turn, each person will be more likely to act with kindness as a result of seeing the prevalence of kindness in others. The fact of kindness's being a virtue depends upon the demands of social life. Kindness facilitates the cooperation without which life with others is impossible.

Of course, I do not mean to imply that there can be no more than a single point for any given concept; nor that the point or points of a concept might not alter through time.

Concepts Defined with Respect to the Functionality of Their Instances

If it is true that there is a point to our having each of the concepts we do have, it might be expected that we could define instances of that which falls under the concept in terms of the concept's point. That is, it might be thought that what makes a thing an *X* is its serving (or, in some cases, its being intended to serve) the point of the concept of *X*. In some cases this is so, but in others it is not. Where it is the case that what makes a thing an *X* is its functional efficacy in promoting the point of the concept in question (or, in the case of concepts that mark harms, its functional efficacy in avoiding the point of the concept), then I shall say that *X* is to be defined *functionally.*

The notion of a poison is to be defined functionally. What makes something a poison is a matter of its deleterious effects when absorbed, injected, ingested, breathed, and so forth, and it is just because of our desire to avoid or to inflict such effects that we have the concept of poisons. Because we are vulnerable in many ways and to many kinds of things, and because those things we might want to kill vary both in their character and in their vulnerabilities, and because not all poisons have the same causes or consequences, the only thing common to poisons is their functional significance.

Once the concept of poison has a public use, there might be very good practical reasons for introducing conventions, procedures, and institutions with respect to poisons. For example, we might adopt as a standard symbol for poisons a stylized representation of a rearing snake; that is, we might adopt a convention with respect to marking poisons. The convention is designed to serve the purpose for which we have the concept of poison in the first place—to warn us that a substance is dangerous in a certain sort of way. Provided that the convention runs side by side with, and as a servant of, the function by virtue of which we have the concept at all, it might even be possible to define "poison" in terms of the convention followed with respect to poisons, provided that the definition is accompanied by a rider that points to the tie between the convention and the concept's point. A definition in those terms is "operational." Operational definitions are usually designed to serve some special purpose; for example, hunger might be defined for the purposes of an experiment as the rate at which a rat will push a bar to obtain food. So operational definitions usually are parasitic upon the primary, established meaning of the term; unlike essential (or real) definitions, operational definitions frequently presuppose rather than analyze the nature of the concept so defined. (The exception to these points is the case in which the notion being defined is itself essentially operational, as is the concept of measuring.)

By contrast, the notion of food is not be defined functionally (or, at least, is not to be defined solely in terms of its primary point). Not all things that could nourish us or other creatures are classed as foods. In New Zealand seagulls are not food, though it would generally be recognized that they are edible and might serve as food under extreme conditions or in societies with different conventions. The uneaten portion of a meal which is scraped from the plate ceases to be food when it has fallen into (what may be a perfectly clean) rubbish sack. That a concept *has* a function does not mean that it is *of* a function.

Of course, under different circumstances, or in different subcultures, or with respect to different animals, edible material found in rubbish sacks counts as food. And the uneaten portion of a meal which is scraped into a doggie bag continues to be food, despite the similarity between that bag and a rubbish sack. Such cases, rather than counting against the claims I have made, illustrate my point. Whether or not something is food is not determined solely or simply by its capacity to nourish the creature in question; that is, not everything that serves the primary function of food is food.

Similarly, and in a rather striking fashion, it is clear that kindness is not to be defined functionally. Kindness derives its importance for us from the social good that is the consequence of kindness in general—kindness in general facilitates and encourages the sort of cooperation upon which social life depends. But if an act is *aimed* at the point of kindness, at smoothing the course of social life, then it is not an act of kindness, even if it does smooth the course of social life. A kind act is one that flows from a desire to assist someone *simply* because he needs the help (with the proviso that the action must be suited to meeting the other's need). Accordingly, a particular act of kindness still would be an act of kindness if it happened, on this occasion, to disrupt the course of social life. Kindness is its own reward in the sense that the motivation essential to an act's being kind excludes the possibility of the act's being aimed at anything other than the good of the person helped. An act directed at contributing to the social benefits of kindness in general could not be a kind act because it lacks the appropriate motivation. If I act with the intention of smoothing the course of social life, I may reveal an admirable quality (say, a pronounced sense of civic duty or pride), or a moral virtue (such as conscientiousness), but I do not in that act reveal myself to be a kind person. Many motivations might lead one to act as a kind person would do, but a kind act is one performed for no reason other than the recognition of another's need. Wishing to be a good person, I might ask myself what a kind person would do and act accordingly, or wishing to be thought a kind person, I might do what the kind person would do, but in neither these nor similar cases do I show myself to be kind. We would not have the concept of kindness were it not for the social consequences of kind acts in general, but kindness is not a consequential, not a functional, notion. (For a fuller discussion of the complex relation among the moral virtues and of the respects in which morality is functional without its being the case that moral concepts are concepts of the functionality of their instances, see Kovesi 1967 and Ewin 1981.)

Frequently items are manufactured with a purpose in mind because nothing occurring naturally serves that purpose or serves it as we would want it to be served. It is as likely that one is to define an instance of that thing as much in terms of the procedures, rules, formulas, recipes, or whatever by which such things are generated as by the functional significance that gives point to the relevant concept and that the mode of production was instituted to serve. The more standardized and regular are the methods for producing items of the type in question, the more likely is this to be the case. That is, it may be that what falls under the concept is to be defined procedurally rather than functionally, or is to be defined in jointly procedural and functional terms.

When fixing carpets to the floor became fashionable, it also became necessary to find a method of cleaning carpets effectively and efficiently. Someone designed a vacuum cleaner for the job. Of course, soon part of what made a thing a vacuum cleaner was that it came out of the factory that made Vacuum Cleaners (or out of different factories making vacuum cleaners under a different brand name). What makes a thing a vacuum cleaner is partly the fact of its being made to a certain design (or type of design) and not simply that it cleans carpets by the use of air suction or even that it cleans carpets efficiently at all. If a new species of animal were discovered tomorrow which lived by sucking dirt from lichens, then it would not be a vacuum cleaner despite the fact that it might perform the function for which vacuum cleaners were invented more effectively and efficiently than does any vacuum cleaner. The creature could not be a vacuum cleaner because the creature is not a machine of any type, let alone a machine of the right type. The creature could be used *as if* it were a vacuum cleaner, and it could do the job of a vacuum cleaner, but none of that would make it a vacuum cleaner.

The example is one in which a brand name that marked where and how a thing was made became the name of that kind of thing (and following that, the name of an activity, as in the gerund "hoovering"), so that type of thing came to be definable both in procedural and in functional terms. The point being illustrated does not depend solely on whether a brand name comes into general use. Whether that happens might depend upon a judge's ruling in a case in which the original manufacturer sues another. The point is not so specific as that. Simply, it is this: where the things that have functional significance for us are made by us in accordance with stock procedures, it is perhaps likely that the concept is to be defined procedurally as well as, or instead of, functionally.

Concepts the Instances of Which Are to Be Defined Procedurally

Social institutions and conventions sometimes are created with particular purposes in mind. Once established, they have a tendency to take on a life of their own, as it were, and in this way to drift apart from the function they were intended to serve. In time the stylized representation of a rearing snake first used to mark poisons might, when placed on signs standing beside bush tracks, come to signify the presence of snakes, rather than of poisonous things as such. This might happen because most people cannot tell poisonous from nonpoisonous snakes and so have a reason to avoid all snakes. Alternatively, the import of the sign might be generalized in a different way to cover potentially dangerous but nonpoisonous things, such as barbed wire or corrosive liquids. Indeed, the conventions might become independent of the purpose for which they were instituted to such an extent that the conventions can be used in ways that conflict directly with that purpose. The sign of the snake might come to indicate only that something is purchased from a pharmacist's shop, and not that it is dangerous at all.

Under what circumstances do procedures and functions tend to separate? I can think of several ways and I list them in no special order. (1) As I said before, procedures tend to take on a life of their own and so to depart from their function. They have functions of their own. As conventions they must be public, widely applicable, and comprehensible. Moreover, the very existence of one convention might create a need for some other. The reason for establishing a committee might be that its members would otherwise be the only team members not already on a committee. (Our being able to joke that people join the firm in order to find a marriage partner or that the last place you would go to get an efficient coffee maker is a factory that manufactures percolators, suggests that the phenomenon is a familiar one.) (2) It may be convenient sometimes to establish a single procedure simultaneously to serve many different functions, which, because they are not otherwise united, might tend to drift apart from each other and their common procedure. Once it was thought that the best procedure for training people for life in its varied aspects was to teach them the classical languages. Perhaps both mathematical skills and the capacity to fill one's leisure time with nondestructive pastimes have become more important in life than once they were. Perhaps their being trained in classical languages fits people well for the one activity and not at all well for the other. (3) In what may be a variant of the preceding, it may be that there is a gap between the efficacy of the procedures and the realization of the function in question, so that any procedures are bound to be functionally inadequate. There might be a point to foretelling the future, but the rules for divination might in various ways fail sometimes in their predictive power. (4) Perhaps, once the procedure is in place, it might easily be adapted or appropriated to perform a function other than the one for which it was designed. The procedure might become separated deliberately from the function it was first designed to serve. The factory established to make coffee percolators might, at a time of war, be converted to the manufacture of mortar casings. (5) As a variant on the previous type of case, the procedures might actually be used with the aim of *opposing* their original function. Legal devices instituted with the aim of protecting the rights of the accused in order that justice might be done could come to be used in certain cases not to protect those rights but, rather, to found a defense on technicalities precisely in order that justice not be done.

Where procedure and function come to be separated, it might be thought obvious that an interest in definition would be bound to focus on the point of the concept rather than on the procedures instituted to serve that point. If the procedure takes its own course, then the procedure could not be a defining part of the concept. Poisons are to be defined in terms of the point of our distinguishing them from other types of things, and not in terms of procedures that are not tied to that point. In the end, what makes a thing a poison, what is essential to its being a poison, is not the matter of its being labeled with a stylized picture of a rearing snake.

The earlier discussion of kindness, however, suggests that the above view may be misguided sometimes—by no means are all our classifications essentially consequential. When conventions and the point of the concept they were instituted to serve part company, it may be revealed that instances of the concept in question are to be characterized in terms of the conventions or procedures giving rise to them and not in terms of the concept's point. In other words, sometimes that which falls under a concept is properly to be defined in procedural, rather than in functional, terms. Accordingly, although there is a point to our having a concept of such a thing, one cannot tell whether or not one is regarding an instance of the thing in question merely by observing if it might serve the relevant function, because not all things of that type will or could perform that function.

Three examples:

Presumably the notion of speeding derives from a need to distinguish dangerously fast motion from its safer, more sedate forms. Once, to say that someone was speeding was to say that they were driving or riding dangerously fast. But in time the notion became conventionalized in law, and now it is the case that one is speeding if one is exceeding some fixed limit. It is not difficult to see why the notion came to be procedural rather than functional in this way. First, the function is respected in the procedure that has been adopted, since the procedure is designed with an eye to the point of the concept. Second, there is a need for a widely agreed on and understandable public standard by which to judge whether or not someone is speeding, since the matter must fall under the law and the law cannot serve its point unless it can be (seen to be) interpreted publicly and impersonally. This second reason suggests that there is a functional point to our making the notion of speeding a legal, procedural one, but this fact does not undercut the force of the example—what now defines one's action as speeding is one's driving at sixty miles per hour in a forty-mile-per-hour zone (not that sixty miles per hour is a dangerously fast speed given the conditions, the car, the driver, and so on).

There is a function to the giving of knighthoods—(supposedly) they are awarded in recognition of outstanding personal achievement and/or social service. They are given to people in the business world who have climbed high on the ladder of success, to mountaineers who have peaked in their chosen pastime, to politicians who are over the hill, to military men who have ordered others over the top, and the like. Nevertheless, what makes one a knight is not the fact that one deserves this form of public recognition, or even public acknowledgment that one deserves the title. Rather, what makes one a knight is the fact of one's being dubbed as such under the appropriate circumstances by someone with royal authorization to confer the title. This, I think, is the way it has been for a very long time. In the past the conferring of knighthoods served a different function—the title went to those who exhibited the proper sense of chivalry or displayed militaristic skills or political faithfulness or whatever. Even then, however, what made one a knight was neither that one merited the title nor that one performed the job of a knight, but that the title was conferred upon one in the proper manner. Knighthood is a useful example just because it is apparent that what has remained constant in the creation of knights is the procedure by which the title is conferred, rather than the function performed by knights or the point of awarding knighthoods. "Knighthood" names a concept with a point, but the meaning of "knighthood" is to be defined procedurally rather than functionally.

I offer one further, more controversial, example. The notion of property derives (at least part of) its point from the fact that people have in common basic needs for certain goods and, given that we do not live in a world in which there is a superabundance of that which would meet those needs, a further need for security in our access to those goods. Some set of procedures for the acquisition and transference of rights over goods was established or evolved to meet these needs. Of course, many different sets of procedures might have been (and have been) adopted to serve that end. The procedures actually adopted in any given community determine who owns what in that community. In unforeseen ways the continued application of those procedures might result in a social condition in which one person acquires in the appropriate fashion so many goods that others in the society cannot obtain ownership of that which they need to meet even their basic needs. Indeed, that person (perversely) might have been motivated by a desire to bring about just such a circumstance. That is to say, the rules of the institution of property might apply over time in such a way as to create a circumstance in which their continued application is at odds with the very point of the concept of property. Even where this occurs, until the rules are changed, the perverse individual is the owner of the property that she has acquired in accordance with those rules. What defines the notion of property are the rules that regulate the institution and not the point of the concept—even though the rules might have been chosen or might have evolved in the first place in recognition of that point.

Of course, I accept that, for concepts defined procedurally as that of property is, one might look to the point of the concept to justify a change in the procedures where the current rules have ceased to serve that point. However, I do not accept that, before the rules have been changed, the rich and perverse individual does not really own the property she has acquired in accordance with the established procedures. That is, while I acknowledge that the procedural rules defining the concept of ownership are ultimately answerable to the point of the concept, I nevertheless deny that this shows that one can define what property is by reference to the concept's point.

Morals to Be Drawn from the Preceding Discussion

Sometimes (perhaps always) the point of our distinguishing some type of item from all other things in the world is that it meets some need or needs, and not because it reflects some aspect of the world's structure. Nowhere is this more obvious than in the case in which we design and manufacture a thing for a purpose since nothing naturally present in the world serves that purpose. When it comes to defining the nature of that which falls under a concept, it may be found either to be essentially functional or to be essentially procedural, or to be essentially both. When it is possible that the procedures do not clearly and efficiently produce items that serve the point of the concept, the question of whether or not those items instantiate the concept is a real one. When the evolution of the procedures leads to the use of those procedures in ways that go so far as to conflict with the point of the concept (so that the concept cannot be defined in jointly procedural and functional terms), the question of whether or not items of the type in question are to be defined functionally or procedurally is crucial. It will not do to say that, in some respects, the concept operates functionally and, in other respects, is procedural. If the procedures are at odds with the function, then the definition must settle on one or the other as giving the essence of the concept's instances. If the two are in conflict and the concept is essentially functional, then only those things which meet the function instantiate the concept, and items produced in accordance with the standard procedures but which do not meet that function do not instantiate the concept. On the other hand, if the concept is essentially procedural, then all those things produced in accordance with the given procedure instantiate the concept, whether or not they also serve the function that those procedures originally were set up to meet.

Are Instances of Art, Artworks, to Be Defined Functionally or Procedurally?

After this preliminary discussion we can return to the topic in hand, the definition of art. It should be apparent that artworks do not as a class form a natural kind; neither does the concept result from an attempt to impose order upon some natural continuum. Rather, the classification of things as artworks would seem to reflect a need or concern that we have. Moreover, many if not all artworks are manufactured with that interest in mind. Artworks might be made for many reasons, but many are made with the intention that they do a job specific to art. The fact that only a comparatively few natural items are appropriated and presented as art, and that only a comparatively few items that were manufactured as nonart are appropriated and presented as art, indicates that a thing's efficacy as art commonly and centrally depends upon its intentional creation as art.

At the close of the previous chapter, I suggested that the search for the definition of art would do well to focus on external relations between artworks and other things, rather than upon artworks' exhibited, internal properties. By now the reason for that advice should be clear, quite apart from the earlier consideration of Weitz's arguments. Artworks do not form a natural kind; typically artworks are manufactured with the specific intention that they be artworks. And the variety of the forms and categories of art suggests that there will be no intrinsic, exhibited property that all and only artworks share. These considerations are bound to lead one to expect that the defining essence of art will consist either in a relation between certain items and their (intended) functional effects and/or uses or, alternatively, in a relation between certain objects and the procedures in terms of which they come to be created (or are intended to be created).

How is the definition of art to be approached? The character of much modern art and the attitude adopted toward it by the public is symptomatic of a separation between the point of art and its works (that is, the products of the procedures in terms of which art status commonly is taken to be conferred). There is a tension between both the forms and approaches of modern and of more traditional art. For this reason the otherwise attractive option of defining art in jointly functional and procedural terms seems not to be viable. Equally unattractive, I think, is the option of defining art disjunctively—as either functional or as the product of certain procedures. Such an approach deals with the tension I have identified only by ignoring its existence. It is perhaps not surprising, then, that contemporary philosophies of the definition of art split into basically functional and procedural camps. So the question becomes: Is art to be defined functionally or procedurally? The reply to that question is by no means obvious. In the remainder of this chapter, I explain what I take to be at issue between the two views and illustrate the way in which their protagonists beg the question against each other by their failure to appreciate the difference between the two approaches to defining art.

The most convincing attempt at a functional approach to the definition of art has been offered by Monroe C. Beardsley (especially 1958, 1982a, 1983); the most convincing version of a procedural approach to the definition of art is the institutional account developed and defended by George Dickie (especially 1974, 1984). At this stage I am not interested in the detail of their positions; instead, my concern lies with the difference in their approaches and in what it reveals about the types of definitions they favor. Already some of the differences between their positions will be inferable. A proponent of the institutional definition of art need not deny that many artworks play an important role as art in our lives, even if some particular artworks do not and could not play that role successfully. Nor need that person deny that the fact that a piece would admirably serve the function of art (for example, in being rewarding and enjoyable when viewed as art) is a reason for conferring upon it art status (cf. Wollheim 1980). Moreover, a supporter of the institutional theory can allow that there are defeating conditions that count against the activation of the conventions by which art status normally is conferred. But the defender of the institutional view of the definition of art holds that, whether or not it meets the point of art in general, a piece is or is not an artwork in accordance with its having that status conferred upon it by someone with the authority to do that conferring. Whereas a proponent of the functional view of the definition of art holds that only a piece that could serve the point of art could become a work of art, whatever procedures were followed and whatever the artistic authority of the person following them.

The difference thus described will lead to disagreement over the approach to be adopted to "hard cases"—"hard cases" being putative artworks that in one way or another fall into the gap left by the separation of the function of artworks from the procedures used in their creation. (For a different account of hard cases, see Battin 1988.) The most famously discussed hard cases are the piece of driftwood, which seemingly qualifies for art status in terms of purely formal procedures, since it is presented as art within a gallery (although it may be no better at meeting the function of art than many other damp sticks stuck in the sand), and Duchamp's *Fountain*, a urinal perceptually indistinguishable from many other urinals, which was offered by him to the Artworld (to use the term coined by Arthur Danto in 1964) as an artwork. Equally hard, in a different way, are works that are in many respects perceptually indistinguishable from other artworks—such as Duchamp's *LHOOQ Shaved*, which closely resembles *Mona Lisa*, as well as *LHOOQ*, in which Duchamp added, among other things, a beard to a picture postcard of *Mona Lisa*.

These graphic examples do not always have clear counterparts in the other art forms. However, John Cage's *4′33″*—a work in which the audience is invited to listen to whatever sounds happen ordinarily to be occurring in the concert hall during a period of four minutes and thirty-three seconds which is marked by the opening and closing of a piano keyboard—is one case of a musical equivalent to the driftwood case, adding to it the idea that the artist who "selects" the driftwood might be blindfolded at the time. A work such as Gerald Hoffnung's quartet for vacuum cleaners would correspond to *Fountain.* Composers, such as Olivier Messiaen, who make extensive use of bird song, come close to creating equivalent works, although Messiaen treats the song more as a medium than as a content. The same may be true of those composers who have included typewriters in their works and those who have used taped natural sounds in their *musique concrète.* Conceptual dramas along the lines of *All That Happens in the Philosophy Department of Auckland University on April 1, 1991*—a work as notable for its verisimilitude as are *Fountain* and Andy Warhol's *Brillo Boxes*—are not uncommon. Meanwhile the notorious "performances" of the Portsmouth Philharmonic are perhaps not dissimilar from *LHOOQ Shaved,* and Jorge Luís Borges has produced a famous fictional example in his story of Pierre Menard of one literary work being word-for-word identical to (part of) another. What is true, I think, is that there is no bar to the creation of counterparts of the examples I have given in other art forms. The dawn chorus or the sounds of a working foundry might be presented by a Stockhausen as musical works, given the appropriate use of "framing devices."

If art is to be defined procedurally, we could not expect a definition to give us any grip on the puzzlement caused by hard cases. Hard cases will be "hard" not because their status is in doubt, but rather because they set up a tension between the point of the concept of art and actual instances of art. The philosophical interest will not be found so much in the definition of art as in a discussion of the attitude appropriate to that tension. If, on the other hand, art is to be defined functionally, hard cases will be "hard" as a matter of determining their possible status as art. Candidates for the status of art will qualify as art or not to the extent that they serve the point of art. An artwork will be (whatever else is involved) worthy of its status as a result of its serving the point of the concept.

The disagreement about the status as art of puzzling cases might be characterized this way: many works of the avant-garde seem to challenge the very traditions and conventions upon which the point of art might be supposed to depend—for example, by attempting to break down the barrier between art and reality, as Duchamp tried to do with his readymades. Now according to the view that sees art as a concept to be defined procedurally, it is (thought usually to be) beyond question that such "hard" pieces are artworks. They are created by artists or others who have earned the authority to confer art status; they are discussed by critics; they are presented within the context of the Artworld as objects for (aesthetic/artistic) appreciation; they are discussed by art historians; and so forth. Such works could perhaps not have been artworks in the past (even had they been created by established artists of the past), in that both the Artworld and the artist had to be "ready" for this new use of the conventions for conferring art status. Nevertheless, such pieces are held undoubtedly to be artworks where they have been created in accordance with the "rules" used to confer art status (at a time and under conditions where those rules can so be employed). But, this view continues, to the extent that such works undermine the very point of art, they do call to account the usefulness of that general classification. The status of such works as art is dubious only in the sense that they call into question the status of all art by pursuing a use of the conventions of art creation which is at odds with the point of art. According to this account, we might regard the activities of such avant-garde artists as counterproductive in that their works undermine the status of art in general, although the status (as *instances* of art in general) of the artworks they produce is not in doubt. Whereas, according to the view by which art is a concept to be defined functionally, pieces such as these are controversial in their claim to be artworks. In this view works that seem to undermine the point of art could not automatically qualify as art. What is controversial is their claim to art status, rather than the way in which they reflect generally on the classification of pieces as art. Such pieces, at best, have not validated their claim to art status. So, accordingly, the frequently asked question But is it art? is not to be parsed as a question about the merits as art of the piece but is to be understood literally as asking if the piece qualifies for elevation to the status of art at all.

Quite apart from the way in which the two approaches to the

definition of the concept of an artwork are to be applied to the matter of hard cases of possible art, they differ in two other striking respects.

It is not uncommon to find in the philosophical literature disagreement over whether the classificatory use of "artwork" is essentially descriptive or evaluative. This debate arises, I believe, out of the difference between functional and procedural approaches to the definitions of the term. In either view artworks will be evaluated as such in terms of the point of art in that good artworks will be pieces that would serve that point. According to the view that art is to be defined procedurally, the proper classification of pieces as art will be purely descriptive. Once they are classified, artworks then will be evaluated with respect to their success or otherwise in serving the point of art. Works that qualify in meeting the descriptive criteria will then be subject to evaluation, and works that tend to function in a way that undermines the point of art in general will, thereby, be bad. (In this respect, if not with respect to the definitional issue, the proceduralist nods in the direction of functionalism.) Whereas, in the view that art is to be defined functionally, the act of classification is itself evaluative, since only works that do not undermine the point of art will qualify as such. There is a threshold of merit, where merit is measured in terms of the efficiency of a piece in promoting the point of art, which a work must meet before it qualifies as an artwork. Then, within works so classified, a further evaluation might be attempted as a measure of the extent to which a particular artwork exceeds the threshold of merit that qualifies it in the first place for the classification (Pepper 1962, Barrett 1971/72, McGregor 1979, Beardsley 1961—but in 1983 Beardsley allows that a value-neutral classificatory use of "artwork" is possible and necessary; also see Zemach 1986 and, for a reply, Levinson 1987b). A piece that does not attain the threshold level of merit (for example, because it challenges the point of art) will not qualify as art. A piece that does attain the threshold will qualify as art, but if it does not exceed the threshold it will be bad art relative to those artworks which do exceed the threshold. (Of course the functionalist may be willing to concede that the appreciation of a particular artwork takes place under conditions that help us to identify the objects worthy of aesthetic attention and, in this respect, if not with respect to the definitional issue, nods toward proceduralism.)

Harold Osborne (1973) implies that functionalists on the definition of art simply are confused in failing to appreciate that evaluation presupposes a prior basis for classification, since evaluations are class relative. As the following discussion reveals, they are not confused in the way that Osborne suspects. Classification might depend upon a threshold of merit along some dimension even if subsequent evaluation of class members is made also in terms of that dimension. (For a different attempt to bridge the gap between classificatory and evaluative definition, see Bachrach 1977.)

Tilghman (1984) makes clear that the distinction between classification and evaluation is not an easy one to draw. He distinguishes three readings of the question But is it art? The first is a straightforward question about the work's credentials, about whether the piece was made by an artist, belongs in a gallery, and so on; the second is a question about how good as art the piece is; and the third is a question about whether or not the piece meets the point of art. This third question is asked by someone who accepts the piece's formal credentials as art (for example, who knows that the piece is made by an artist who was funded by the Arts Council, that the piece is insured as art, and so forth) and who is not yet in a position to evaluate the piece as art because she cannot see how to approach the piece as art. Tilghman points out that this person does not want to be told how the piece belongs within the institution, because that story is a story about its credentials. To approach the piece as art, according to Tilghman, is to see how the piece can function as art.

Tilghman's three questions show up the issue at stake. A functionalist on the definition of art is not someone who crudely confuses classificatory questions with "ordinary" aesthetic evaluation. The functionalist makes two measures of the work against the function of art. The first, the classificatory move, considers whether or not the piece has the potential to engage at all (or to a sufficient degree) with the point of art. The evaluative move comes second, if it comes at all.

A piece that has been classified as art is judged to be good or bad art relative to its success in serving the point of art. The functionalist allows for the possibility in which a piece is technically an artwork in that it has the right "formal" credentials, without its being approachable as art, and hence, without its really being art.

Insightful though Tilghman's approach is in showing how the functionalist dodges the accusation of confusedly running together classificatory and commendatory judgments about art, he shows little grasp of the proceduralist's position. A proceduralist on the definition of art argues that art status is no more and no less than the possession of the appropriate credentials. Tilghman seems to think that this is an unacceptably crude view just because it brushes aside the real, practical difficulty posed by modern art to the person genuinely interested in art and its appreciation. Tilghman sees the issue this way, however, only because he begs the question against the proceduralist in thinking that a thing achieves art status only by its engaging with the point of art. Whereas in fact a proceduralist on the definition of art is not someone who crudely sees no problem in approaching difficult cases as artworks. Rather, the proceduralist differs from the functionalist on the definition of art in suggesting that the problem does not follow from, or correspond to, a difficulty about the status of the item as an artwork.

There is another respect in which the two approaches differ, the matter of whether a definition might be judged to be satisfactory or not in accordance with its providing a way of accounting for the place that artworks fill in our lives. A functionalist on the matter of the definition of art will judge a definition to be adequate only if it explains the point of our distinguishing art from other things. (Although there need be no one-to-one correspondence between concepts and nouns in the language, in this case the question might reasonably be put as: Why do we have the word "artwork" in our language?) That is, even if artworks interest us as financial investments, a satisfactory definition must characterize the interests met by art which justify our classifying artworks as art and not merely as financial investments, doorstops, and the like. By contrast, a proceduralist on the matter of the definition of art will see no reason to expect that a successful definition should account for the place of art in our lives. She might concede that no adequate *theory* of art could leave that matter undiscussed, but would go on to deny that a definition must be substitutable for a complete theory if it is to be acceptable.

The differences described above between the two approaches to the definition of art are nicely revealed in Dickie's theory (1974, 1984) and the criticisms it has attracted. In presenting his definition he has next to nothing to say about the point of art, and his proposed definition pays no heed to the role that gives art its significance in the cultural life of a community. He thinks that Duchamp's readymades (for example) undoubtedly are artworks and sees it as a virtue of his definition that it includes such works. He also accepts that some artworks are at odds with (indeed, might set out deliberately to undercut) the point of art. He states explicitly that, in its primary (classificatory) use, "art" is a purely descriptive term. (In the preface to his recent book on evaluating art—1988, ix—Dickie writes that the lack of connection between his institutional theory of art and his present book "should not be surprising, for the institutional theory of art is supposed to be a *classificatory* theory of art—a theory that explains why a work of art is a work of art. Why a work of art is valuable or disvaluable is an additional question.") Predictably, Dickie's opponents (not all of whom, it must be admitted, are functionalists) have attacked his theory for its failure to reveal the point of art (Lipman 1975, Beardsley 1976, Schlesinger 1979, Diffey 1979, Wollheim 1980, Osborne 1981, Sparshott 1987); for its identifying as artworks pieces that are controversial in that they challenge the very point of art (Cohen 1973, Silvers 1976, Dziemidok 1980, Crowther 1981, Nash 1981, Fletcher 1982, and Humble 1984); and for its assumption that a descriptive as opposed to an evaluative definition is possible (Morton 1973, Aagaard-Mogensen 1975, Beardsley 1976, Shusterman 1987, Krukowski 1987—interesting observations on this issue are made in Kjörup 1976 and Wieand 1981a; also see Werhane 1979).

(By contrast, Graham McFee, in 1989, believes that the close connection between something's being an artwork and its being worthy of attention might be used as evidence in favor of an institutional definition, but he seems not to allow for the possibility that the procedures by which art status is conferred have broken free of the point of art. Jeffrey Wieand, in 1983, who is criticized by McFee, more obviously does allow for this possibility but doubts that the practice of putting forward artworks for appreciation could long continue where such a break has occurred.)

Functionalist-type and institutionalist-type arguments miss each other in this way because neither side makes explicit why it holds that art must be defined the one way as opposed to the other—functionally or institutionally. Perhaps such "deep" disagreements are irresolvable and so should be kept hidden; perhaps if the argument were lowered to this foundational level, it could consist of no more than empty rhetoric. If so, the line I shall take is misguided, because I hope to draw out the difference between the two approaches and not only to attack the functional approach to the definition of art, but also to defend the procedural approach. Of course, a debate of this sort is bound to be played out on a grand stage. Any theory that settles the difference between these two approaches to an analysis of the concept of art must cohere with a wide spread of intuitions about the terms in which art is discussed and interpreted. It cannot rely on a narrow match between its claims and a single critic's comments about some particular, controversial work of possible art.

There is a moral to be drawn here about the quest for a definition of art. Probably most people look to a definition of art in the hope of finding an account of the value and importance of art. The interest and worth of the philosophy of art lies in its facilitating just such an account. In the preceding discussion I have suggested that the institutional definition of art is not necessarily faulty in its failure to be enlightening in this respect. Suppose that the institutional theory is correct in its account of the definition of art. This will not mean that the theory is ultimately without interest or importance. It will show, however, that not too much should be expected from the enterprise of definition, and that more fertile areas for inquiry lie elsewhere. Indeed, it is possible that the general air of dissatisfaction expressed by aestheticians in connection with the institutional theory of the definition of art reflects the unreasonableness of their expectations as to the revelatory importance of definitions of art and does not reflect a lack of satisfactoriness in the definition offered by the institutionalists. That there is more to philosophical aesthetics and to art than could be captured by the institutional theory might indicate only that there is more to aesthetics than the determination of a definition of art.

Other Approaches to the Definition of Art

It might be objected that, in trying to narrow the field to only two contenders, I have excluded from consideration other different but nonetheless perfectly respectable approaches to a definition of the concept of an artwork. It seems to me that I have excluded four approaches to the definition of art—aesthetic property, aesthetic attitude, historical, and intentional accounts. The first of these four approaches has received already as much consideration as it will get. That is to say, approaches aiming to define artworks as those items which possess some distinctive type of aesthetic property, where that property is an internal, exhibited property (as usually it is assumed to be), have been rejected already. More sophisticated versions of such definitions will be subsumable under the other three types of definition, I think.

Historical approaches to the definition of art might be either functional or procedural, since both the function and the procedures originally designed to serve that function might have their own interesting, changing histories. The same remark might be made about the intentional account—art makers' intentions might be oriented either with respect to the procedures in terms of which art is created, or with respect to the function of art creation. In Chapter 7 I consider some examples of both theories. I suggest that such theories fail insofar as they remain uncommitted to one or another of the functional and procedural approaches to the definition of art. The main argument for this suggestion is taken up in the final two chapters, in which I discuss the status of artists' intentions as it reflects not only on the intentionalist approach to the definition of art, but also on differences between the functional and procedural approaches.

To forestall a possible confusion, I should at this stage point out that neither Beardsley nor Dickie are intentionalists as I use the term, although they both mention as a *necessary* condition for something's being an artwork that it be produced in accordance with certain intentions. Intentionalist theories are, in my view, ones that treat the artist's having the appropriate intentions as a *sufficient* condition for the artist's products being artworks. An intentionalist might allow that the relevant intentions are motivated by functional or procedural considerations but does not regard such considerations as among the necessary conditions governing a piece's attaining art status. Admittedly Beardsley came close to endorsing such a view in his later writing on the subject (1982a, 1983), but I regard him as a functionalist both because his earlier writings are functionalist and because I doubt that he abandoned the Deweyan strain clearly present in his earlier work (1958—see, for example, 1979). In other words, I believe that, for him, functional efficacy remained a necessary condition for something's attaining art status. In my interpretation Beardsley's emphasis on the necessity of artists' having the appropriate intentions in the creation of artworks was aimed not at cutting adrift the functionality condition but, rather, at insuring that the intentionality condition should be seen as no less important than the functionality condition.

Aesthetic-attitude approaches to the definition of art fall into a different bag. The idea that there is such an attitude has been attacked by George Dickie. Much as I agree with Dickie's criticisms that there is no psychological state identifiable in terms of its introspectible qualities as an aesthetic attitude, and that neither is there a mode of aesthetic perception (a kind of "seeing as") which is distinctively aesthetic, I am inclined nevertheless to defend an account of the aesthetic attitude according to which an aesthetic interest is an interest in something for the sake of the pleasure that comes from regarding it as a work of art (if it is one) or as if it were a work of art (if it is not). The upshot of my view is this: while I am happy to defend a qualified version of an aesthetic-attitude theory, I am inclined to regard that attitude as characterizable only in the light of some prior identification of artworks and of the attitude appropriate to them, from which it follows, of course, that I do not regard the aesthetic attitude as providing a basis for any definition of artworks. These and related matters are covered in Chapters 3, 7, and 8.

CHAPTER 3

Beardsley's Functionalism

Before considering whether or not the instances of art are to be defined in terms of the point of art, it is important to consider what that point is. Plainly art cannot be defined in terms of the concept's point if it has none. Yet it is hard to see how the concept could never have had a function, both because "art" standardly names a manufactured item, rather than a natural kind, and because there would have been no reason for our distinguishing art from nonart (or for our making art as such) if that conceptual distinction had not been useful in indicating some use or function served by artworks. Of course, art might have long since lost its original function. On the one hand, however, if art in general has taken on some new function or functions, then it serves as a functional concept and might be definable in terms of its function or functions. And on the other hand, if our classifying things as art no longer acknowledges any point served by art in general, it becomes difficult if not impossible to explain why art (qua art, and not simply qua investment or whatever) plays so significant a role in the lives of so many people.

It is perhaps fashionable to deny that art in general has a point; for example, both Osborne (1973) and Dickie (1984) deny that art serves any single or pervasive need. How could this view be correct in its observation if it is also true that art is to be defined functionally? This would be possible, in the first instance, if not everything that is called "art" literally is art. "Work of art" is an epithet that can be bestowed on an item in a metaphoric or ironic manner. There is nothing surprising about the fact that nonliteral uses of the word "artwork" are uses that pay no heed to the function of art in general. In the second instance, even when we confine ourselves to literal uses of the term, it is clear that misapplications of the term (whether intentional or not) will refer to items that need stand in no close relation to the point of art. But when no mistake is obvious, it remains true that many pieces (or perhaps modern artworks in general) seem not to serve any point. At this stage the debate about the functionality of art takes a new turn. As I indicated in Chapter 2, those who would define art functionally claim that many things that are taken to be art are not really art because those things are not functional in the appropriate way, whereas those who would define art procedurally would defend the status as art of the works in question.

The point I wish to make here is about the procedural approach. It could be true that art in general has a function even if art status is to be defined procedurally; that is, it could be true that the concept of art has a point even if it is equally true that what makes a thing an artwork is not its functionality (Sparshott 1987). A proceduralist on the definition of art need not deny that art in general has a function. A proceduralist on the definition of art is not committed to denying that the concept of art has a point, even if he recognizes that, because function and procedure have come adrift, many artworks are not functional in the appropriate manner. Some proceduralists, of whom I take Dickie to be an example, seem to believe mistakenly that proceduralism is antithetical to the view that art in general is important to us because it serves a distinctive function. My point is that this may be too strong a line to take. What are opposed are the two accounts of how art is to be defined. A procedural approach to the definition of art is compatible with the view that art is functional (if not with the view that art is to be defined as functional) and that we have the concept, originally at least, in recognition of this fact.

Beardsley's Theory

A proceduralist who confines his attention to the matter of the definition of art need not be concerned to characterize the point of the concept of art, so it is perhaps not surprising that proceduralists often do not set out to characterize any function of art. By contrast, a person who would define art functionally must be prepared to characterize the point of the concept, since what makes something an instance of art is (necessarily if not sufficiently) its serving that point. Artworks might serve a great many useful functions—as paperweights, investments, topics of conversation at boring parties, and so on—but here the question is: What *distinctive* function (or functions) is served by artworks? In what way are (or were) artworks important enough to us that we feel (or felt) the need to mark them off as a class of their own?

In this chapter I consider the views of Beardsley as illustrating the functional approach to the definition of art, since his theory is the most detailed and sophisticated of those available. (Similar views are stated in Schlesinger 1979, Humble 1984, and Tolhurst 1984. For criticism of Tolhurst, see Carroll 1986 and Dziemidok 1988, and for criticism of Schlesinger and functionalism of the type considered here, see Dempster 1985. For a detailed discussion of Beardsley's views from the perspective of a different concern, see Dickie 1988.)

Beardsley characterizes an artwork as either an arrangement of conditions intended to be capable of affording an aesthetic experience with marked aesthetic character, or (incidentally) an arrangement belonging to a class or type of arrangement that is typically intended to have this capacity (1982a, see also 1979, 1983). The intention to which his definition refers is an intention to provide a possible source of aesthetically qualified experience. Once such intentions have been executed often enough that an art kind has been established, artworks might then be created by their relation to the established art kind. At times (1979, 1982a) Beardsley has thought that genre membership by virtue of similarity makes the piece an artwork even though it was not intended to be a possible source of aesthetically qualified experience, but at other times (1983) he has said that the fact of a work's belonging to what indubitably is an artistic genre warrants the inference to its having been created with the appropriate artistic intention.

To the definition given above, Beardsley adds: a piece has aesthetic value if it has the capacity to afford, through the cognition of it, an experience that has value on account of its marked aesthetic character (1979). He defends at length the claim that pieces can be evaluated from an aesthetic point of view and that such judgments may be objectively defended (1979).

To avoid circularity in the proposed definition, it must be the case both that an account can be given of an "experience with marked aesthetic character" and that an account can be given of the kind of value which attaches to such experiences, without appeal being made to the notion of an artwork (or of an art kind, which for Beardsley is a notion derivable from that of an artwork—see 1982a, 1983). Beardsley explicitly acknowledges his need to show that (1) there can be an aesthetic character to experience and (2) that character is a valuable feature of such experiences (1958, 1979).

In response to (1) he outlines five phenomenal features of aesthetic experience (1979)—(*a*) it is directed toward an object; (*b*) what comes has the air of being freely chosen; (*c*) the object is emotionally distanced; (*d*) there is active discovery of connections, etc.; (*e*) there is a sense of integration between oneself as a person and the object of interest. He states that (*a*) is a necessary condition and that any four including (*a*) are sufficient for an experience's being aesthetic. (For a similar list see 1983, where Beardsley says that an experience has an aesthetic character if it has some or all of these phenomenal characteristics.) In providing an account of aesthetic experience, Beardsley was returning to what was for him a recurrent theme. His earlier accounts were less phenomenological and were more concerned with the relation between the experience and the properties of its object. In section 28 of 1958 he says that an aesthetic experience is one that is object directed, possesses some intensity, and displays unity, both in that the experience has coherent continuity and in that it is usually complete in itself. He there characterizes a good work of art as a work capable of producing an aesthetic experience of great magnitude. In 1969 he states that an aesthetic experience is a unified and pleasurable experience that results from the concentration of one's attention on the formal and regional qualities of a sensuously presented or imaginatively intended object. In 1970 he describes the aesthetic point of view as an interest in whatever aesthetic value the object of interest possesses—and defines the aesthetic value of *x* as the value *x* possesses as a complex whole, when correctly and completely experienced, by virtue of its capacity to provide gratification obtained primarily from attention to its formal unity and/or regional qualities.

On the matter of (2)—why the character of aesthetic experiences is valuable—Beardsley answers that the value derives from its giving rise to valuable effects. He denies (1958, 533–542) that *anything* is valuable simply in and of itself but says that some things are valuable means to so many ends that we give them a privileged and protected position among the values of life. He acknowledges the difficulty in providing a complete list but mentions with approval (1958, 573–576) seven effects on consumers of art noted by Shelley, I. A. Richards, and John Dewey. Aesthetic experience (*a*) relieves tensions and quiets destructive impulses; (*b*) resolves lesser conflicts within the self and helps to create an integration, or harmony; (*c*) refines perception and discrimination; (*d*) develops the imagination and along with it the ability to put oneself in the place of others; (*e*) is an aid to mental health, but more as a preventive measure than as a cure; (*f*) fosters mutual sympathy and understanding; (*g*) offers an ideal for human life.

In his later writings Beardsley's answer to (2) followed, perhaps more tentatively, along similar lines. He writes that a consideration of the valuable effects of aesthetic experience "calls for consideration of profoundly difficult questions about the nature of human goodness, what constitutes a good life, happiness, well-being and well-doing, and perhaps the meaning of life—though even if we differ in our answers to those questions, we may be able to agree that it is good for us to experience, at least occasionally, and to a degree seldom made possible except by artworks, the immediate sense (say) of inclusive self-integration and complex harmony with phenomenal objects" (1979, 743).

Elsewhere Beardsley emphasizes both that art enriches life by integrating and reconciling us to our world and that it can serve this function only because of its autonomy, its separateness, from our more mundane transactions with the world:

> If we are looking for distinctive roles for art to play in human life . . . at least part of the answer, I believe, is one that makes no reference to signs at all, and does not require that artworks belong to semiotic systems in order to fulfill their function. . . . The fictive character of artworks distinguishes them from the works of nature and objects that are merely tools or machines: and this enables them to feature, to flaunt, the expressive or aesthetic qualities that are in a *special* way our mark on the world around us—for they are the human regional qualities we give to things. In creating works of art we humanize the earth as we can in no other way, we warm it for ourselves, make it a place where we belong, far more fully and significantly than technical objects can do. . . . But individual artworks cannot carry out this function, cannot serve us in this unifying, reconciling way, unless we grant to them a measure of independence and autonomy, a sphere of influence all their own, in which they can be respected as individuals. (1982c, 368–370)

Beardsley lists the virtues (as he sees it) of his definition and so reveals what he takes to be the requirements of an acceptable definition (1982a, 1983). A definition of what an artwork is should be of the greatest utility to inquirers in fields other than aesthetics (especially to those who work in art history and anthropology), because art making is a fundamental, practically universal, and highly important cultural phenomenon, even if the natives of some cultures have no name for art as such and mix their art making with other culturally important activities (such as religious observances). Moreover, Beardsley insists, the definition should acknowledge a tie between art and the aesthetic. Even if not all artworks are aesthetically successful and not everything that is aesthetically interesting is an artwork, still our concept of the aesthetic derives from and gets its significance from our experience of artworks.

Equally, Beardsley is happy to enumerate what some might see as weaknesses in his account (1982a, 1983). His definition does not cover everything that has been classed as art. It excludes anti-aesthetic art (into which category fall all works lacking aesthetically interesting sensuous properties, such as the Conceptual work *All That I Know but Am Not Thinking of Now* and Duchamp's *Fountain*). It excludes all pieces created merely by an act of titling or indexing (such as Duchamp's *Fountain*), since the genuine work of art has aesthetically relevant (formal and regional) properties for which someone can take responsibility. (Whether or not Beardsley means to exclude so-called Driftwood art in this way is not clear to me, since such pieces are presented in order to attract attention to their aesthetic merits, and they do resemble works in an established category of art—sculpture.) Artworks are produced, even if the process of production is so modest as to cover the artist who brings snowflakes into the house to let them melt as they will (1983). Because artworks are produced to be art, Beardsley holds that an artwork is an artwork from its beginning until its end; arthood is not a status that can be acquired in midlife (1983). And finally, his definition excludes works designed to shock (or whatever) but which do not involve (even at a subordinate level) the intention to produce something with the capacity to provide aesthetic gratification. (Once again Beardsley cites *Fountain* as an example of such a work.)

Beardsley is not embarrassed by the fact that much avant-garde art is excluded by his definition because he is happy to deny that such so-called art really is art at all. Although Beardsley does think that such so-called art produces an aesthetic experience of not much value (1969), his view is not that it is *bad* art; rather his view is that only that which could engage with the point of the concept of art and is intended to do so is art. He holds that art making necessarily has a point—that its product gives rise to an experience valuable for its marked aesthetic character—and that there is no point, or no such point, to indexing one's anxieties, for example, as art (1982a). Duchamp's readymades are not properly to be classified as artworks, says Beardsley (1983).

The Value of the Effects of Aesthetic Experience

Beardsley's account of the valuable effects of aesthetic experiences of great magnitude—that is, his account of the instrumental value of aesthetic experience—might seem strange in two respects. First, one might wish to claim that aesthetic experience, or some aspects of aesthetic experience, simply are valued for themselves and not as means to further ends. Dickie (1988) has offered just such a criticism, suggesting that the experience of (some) aesthetic properties is intrinsically pleasurable and, to that extent, intrinsically valuable. Second, one might wonder if the effects listed by Beardsley could justify the importance attached to art. The point is not that the effects he mentions are unimportant but, rather, that the experience of artworks would seem to be an extremely indirect and perhaps inefficient means to such effects. Such effects could be aimed at directly—counseling might relieve tensions and destructive impulses more directly and effectively than does a reading of *The Brothers Karamazov*. So even if artworks do produce experiences that lead to such desirable effects, could we explain the introduction of art into communal life as being aimed at the realization of such human goals and aspirations?

I believe that both of these points miss the character of Beardsley's analysis. He says: "Aesthetic objects differ from . . . directly utilitarian objects in that their immediate function is only to provide a certain kind of experience that can be enjoyed in itself" (1958, 572). In view of this remark I suggest that Beardsley holds that the value of art in general should be seen as distinct from the way in which we value particular artworks. The experience engendered by artworks, where that experience has great magnitude, is valued for itself in that we do not treat art merely as the means to long-range, indirect effects, but, nevertheless, art would not have the value it does were it not for its having such desirable long-range effects. Typically, in other words, we value artworks for themselves and not for the sake of the valuable effects that come from an interest in art in general (that is, an interest in a sufficient number of unspecified artworks). Indeed, an interest in particular artworks merely as means to the valuable effects of an interest in art in general would be a nonaesthetic interest, since such an interest treats the individual work as a member of a series that has no specific membership because the series' importance derives from its members' number and not their individuality. However, although our concern usually focuses on the pleasure that follows an interest in the aesthetic individuality of the artwork, art in general would not be valued as it is were it not for the fact that it gives rise to beneficial effects of the type outlined above.

This account is similar to that offered of kindness in Chapter 2. Particular acts of kindness are not aimed at the beneficial effects of kindness in general. Indeed, they would not be acts of kindness if they were motivated solely by a desire to smooth the course of social life and hence not motivated by a desire to help people simply because they need the help. Nevertheless, kindness would not be the virtue it is were it not so that kindness in general has beneficial social consequences (see Davies 1987a).

In this section I offer my own, speculative, account of the experience of art and of the way in which value attaches to that experience. The views presented are my own, rather than Beardsley's, but I believe that what I have to say complements Beardsley's theory by providing a way of replying to the two puzzles noted above—that aesthetic experience sometimes is valued for itself, rather than as a means to valuable effects, and that an interest in art is not an efficient means to the effects identified by Beardsley as giving art its value.

Typically and characteristically we interest ourselves in artworks neither out of a sense of duty nor as a means to the pursuit of some independently specifiable practical goal but, rather, simply for the pleasure we take in them. I might read *War and Peace* in order to please my parents, since I am a dutiful son; or I might examine a painting in order that I might pass an examination in art history or in order to discover how people dressed at the time the painting was done. But such motivations would not be standard. More frequently a person takes an interest in art because the contemplation of art (or of this work, or of art of this kind, or whatever) is (usually) pleasurable for the person.

(Of course some people earn their living from art, and for them art is a matter both of duty and of a means to prosaic ends. A point perhaps to make is this: such people tend to earn their living in that way because, usually, they already have an interest in art, an interest that would not disappear if they failed to get a job in the arts, for example. For them the interest does not arise out of the job, but vice versa. For the less common case in which the interest in art does arise out of employment in the arts, the interest still is not the same thing as the job.)

This account of aesthetic experience invites two questions: In what way is the experience pleasurable? and, Why is the experience pleasurable?

There is no single way in which the experience of art is pleasurable. The experience, or an element within it, may be simply sensuous (and even sensual)—an experience of brittleness, starkness, lushness, coldness, or whatever. The colors are enjoyed for their warmth and vividness, the sounds for their timbre, the textures for their feel or look, the words for their sounds, and so on. It is common to overrate this "natural" dimension of aesthetic experience, but, for all that, it would be an error to deny its importance. Additionally, the experience may be variously and complexly cognitive, and the pleasure that goes with the experience is the pleasure of understanding a pattern, of solving a puzzle, of grasping connections. This latter experience is the more common and, for most artworks of most cultures, the most appropriate form of aesthetic appreciation. In case I am misunderstood, I should emphasize that, in describing the experience as cognitive, I do not in any way mean to imply that it is dry, feelingless, academic, technical, or theoretical, neither that all artworks have some hidden, deep significance from which we might infer the meaning of life, the universe, and everything. What I mean is that the experience is a thoughtful one rather than a mindless one, and that artworks are appropriately to be viewed as possessing significance (as do actions, utterances, thoughts, and the like) and, hence, as inviting understanding. And again to avoid being misunderstood, I should emphasize that this concern with patterns is not purely or simply formal. The distribution of pieces on a chessboard displays a form, but chess players view the pieces on the board more as fields of force with potential for different, dynamic resolutions. So too the patterns of art are appreciated as dynamic rather than as static structures, as interacting to generate the work's possibilities, some of which may be the more significant for their not being realized explicitly. These patterns may be formal and abstract, but equally they may be representational, semantic, or narrational.

Typically, then, the audience's experience of an artwork involves an attempt to understand or to come to terms with the work, and this attempt cannot be pursued mindlessly or passively. The audience interacts with the work—looks for patterns, design, relationships; looks for connections and contrasts among formal, semantic, and whatever other elements there might be; looks at the work under one aspect, then under another, and so on. Kant's account of the aesthetic experience as involving the "free play" of the imagination and the understanding is recalled to mind, but I am reluctant to claim Kant as an ally, so difficult do I find his ideas to understand.

The pleasure afforded by art accompanies this exercise of the intellect. That is, the pleasure goes not just with the understanding reached but also with the very business of engaging with the work in order that it be appreciated.

Why do we return with pleasure to a familiar work?—because artworks are rich and complicated, so that more might always be discovered within them. Yet further, art is created in the light of art, so that the more one learns about other works, the more one can find in any particular work. Both the works that precede and those that follow the work in question might draw one's attention to certain of its features as artistically relevant, and in the light of an appreciation of these other works, one might return and see the older piece anew.

Now to the second question: Why do we find this process of understanding and appreciation pleasurable? It is hard to answer without indulging in a little speculative sociobiology.

One answer might be this: we take pleasure in the way in which an interest in art develops and hones skills that have a general evolutionary payoff in making us more constructively analytical, more aware of the world of others, and so on. That is to say, we take pleasure in the way in which an interest in particular artworks is a means to the beneficial consequences of an interest in art in general.

Now these claims may be true. There is no incompatibility in one's being aware of the valuable benefits achieved through an interest in art in general and one's being interested in artworks "for their own sakes." (A person might be aware of and take pleasure in the benefits of marrying a millionaire, even if the marriage is founded on a love of the person for her own sake.) Even if this first answer is true as far as it goes, it falls far short of a full explanation because the pleasure comes more from an appreciation of the individuality of the object of interest than from a concern with the beneficial, but indirect, consequences of that interest.

A more complete answer might take this form: certain talents and characteristics, like curiosity, have an evolutionary payoff. And what really pays off is our having those talents as such, not our having them as rigidly tied to the pursuit of some particular goal. We find the exercise of those talents pleasurable in its own right; pleasure goes with the exercise of those talents, and not simply with their successful use in producing the desired goal. That is the kind of creature we are. Being like that, we use those talents in all sorts of contexts where they have no direct payoff; the use of the talents is an end in itself. Those talents are used both in the production of things for our own amusement and in our taking an interest in what others produce. It would not be surprising that people who show the ability to stimulate the use of others' talents are encouraged to do so, given that those others find the use of their talent enjoyable for its own sake and will value the occasion for its use. To mention just one kind of example: it is perhaps not surprising in a social species, such as ours, which is concerned with successful communication and for which there can be no guarantee that any particular attempt at communication will not fail, that what facilitates communication becomes valued for its own sake, apart from the worth of the contents it helps to communicate. Thus we have an interest in the medium of the message for its own sake, in the meanings of words and the connections between them, in the techniques and effects of different styles of narration, and so on (Davies 1987b).

Art is a spin-off, rather than a means to an end. The reward does not lie primarily in what one gets out of an interest in a sufficient number of artworks; the reward becomes a matter of what one gets out of each particular work approached with a concern for its individuality. The value of aesthetic experience resides in the pleasure produced, the pleasure being taken in each individual work.

(In the foregoing discussion I reject a distinction discussed in Diffey 1982, Stecker 1984, Lord 1985, and Dickie 1988 between an "instrumental" view of aesthetic value, according to which artworks are valued as a means to some nonaesthetic end, such as knowledge of the world, and the view that art is "autonomously" valued for its aesthetic qualities. Like these writers I believe that these two sorts of interest in art are compatible.)

Criticism of Beardsley's Account of Aesthetic Experience

There are several grounds on which Beardsley's account of aesthetic experience might be attacked. I am doubtful that aesthetic experience has a phenomenally distinctive character and suspect that it can be identified as aesthetic experience only by reference to its being the kind of experience preeminently provided by artworks, or by things viewed as if they are artworks. (Perhaps Beardsley had reservations too on this point. At times he allows that aesthetic gratification is *aesthetic* gratification in being the type of gratification characteristically provided by paradigmatic artworks—see 1970, 1982a.) Moreover, I think that there may be an inconsistency between Beardsley's holding that artists' intentions are not essentially relevant to the interpretation of their works and his holding that art is to be defined intentionalistically. (A similar worry is expressed in Grossman 1983.) Beardsley has rejected this objection (1982a, 1982b), saying that identification does not involve interpretation and, hence, that the two issues are separate.

Finally, I believe that the notions of "correctness and completeness" to which Beardsley appeals in characterizing the aesthetic point of view are problematic. They are there on the one hand to exclude the case in which a person's perceptual capacities are affected by a hallucinogenic drug, and on the other to explain how one might justify the high value one attached once to cheap novellas as arising from the selectiveness of one's youthful response. But when attention is restricted, as it is in Beardsley's account, to the level of the individual responder, any line drawing would be arbitrary. Can I use opera glasses at the opera? And 3-D glasses at a 3-D film? How many gins may I drink in the interval? Is my youthful enjoyment of Edgar Rice Burroughs's novels to be explained so easily as selective, so that I failed to notice the faults of the work and overemphasized its modest aesthetic merits, or rather, is it that my judgment of what is a fault has changed?

I agree with Beardsley that some normative standard for "correctness and completeness" of regard is necessary, but I doubt that one can establish those norms simply by attending to aspects of the individual's experience and attentiveness. Rather, I believe the relevant norms to be established socially; that is, the wider practice of members of the Artworld, and the conventions articulating that practice, set a standard against which the actions of the individual may be judged for "correctness and completeness." Beardsley, in concentrating on the aesthetic experience of the individual, may appear to lose sight of the extent to which the approach to, and experience of, art is structured in terms of historical factors and social conventions that are "external" to the narrow sphere that encompasses the artwork as object and its observer. (This appearance could be misleading—elsewhere he acknowledges social norms as background conditions for the existence and experience of art—see 1976.)

Beardsley's Formalist Leanings

Beardsley always has been criticized as a formalist, and this criticism was raised again with respect to his final paper on the definition of art (Grossman 1983, Konstan 1983). Whether this criticism is deserved could be disputed. Beardsley identifies the aesthetically relevant properties of artworks as formal unity and "regional properties." He includes among "regional properties" not only formal properties but also the vast array of human (expressive) qualities, and he allows for the aesthetic relevance of the propositional content of literary works. He accepts also that knowledge of a work's social and historical context is necessary for its proper interpretation. In these respects his position is not a formalist one.

On the other hand, Beardsley does regard artworks as autonomous, as "standing on their own," and resists theories that attempt to assimilate aesthetic experience to cognition. In general he sees artworks as affected by, but not as inextricably embedded in, their sociohistorical setting. Moreover, he tends to discount the relevance to aesthetic experience of knowledge of details of the artist's life and of the artist's private wishes, thoughts, and intentions. For him factors of this sort are relevant to a work's aesthetic appreciation only if they affect the interior properties of unity, diversity, complexity, and intensity. Usually it will be unnecessary to consider such matters since the internal properties will unambiguously announce their significance in the experience of the work (provided that it is approached with the appropriate knowledge of its artistic and historical context).

Whether or not the description of Beardsley's views as formalist is an unfair caricature is an issue that I need not adjudicate so long as it is recognized that Beardsley's alleged formalism comes from his general theory of art and is not presupposed by functionalism itself. A functionalist on the matter of the definition of art might easily allow that whether or not some piece will meet the function of art in such a way as to become an artwork is intimately affected by the relation in which the work stands both to the history of art and to its social context (for example, see Eldridge 1985). Such a theorist accepts (as Beardsley may also have done) that the aesthetic properties some given item has, and in virtue of which it merits creation as an artwork, depend for their existence and character on the history of prior artworks and, in general, on the work's sociohistorical setting.

A functionalist of this persuasion could allow for the following cases: Schönberg's opera *Moses and Aaron* could not have been created as a musical work had it been produced in 1800, but it could be created not just as an opera but as a good one when Schönberg wrote it. Stravinsky's opera *The Rake's Progress* is Mozartian in flavor but probably would not have been accepted as an opera had it been written in 1790; and, if it had been written and accepted then, it could not have been enriched, as Stravinsky's opera is, by its referring to musical clichés of the eighteenth century (precisely because then it would have been *using* those clichés without also *quoting* them as Stravinsky does). Stravinsky's opera has a mannered charm through its near mimicry of Mozart and Rossini, but the effect of Mozart's quoting from himself and his contemporaries within *Don Giovanni* is quite different. (For an interesting discussion of the issues and for different examples, see McFee 1980. For a corrective to McFee's excesses, see Levinson 1988; also see Godlovitch 1987.)

The historically minded theorist accepts that a thing qualifies as an artwork mainly by its being equipped with the properties that allow it to perform (at least to some minimally acceptable level) the function of art. Typically the piece will be made to have those properties just as, and at the same time, it is produced as an artwork. It earns its status as art by virtue of its possessing the functionally efficacious properties and if, for some reason, the attempt at production had resulted in an item lacking such properties, the attempt at art creation has failed. (Of course, a functionalist might require that other necessary conditions be met as well—for example, that the functionally efficacious properties be intentionally produced.) A formalist who was also a functionalist would differ from the historically minded theorist in her description of the nature and determinants of the aesthetically relevant properties, but not in the account of the role of those properties in securing art status for the item in question.

The Main Criticism of Functionalism

Here I wish to raise another objection, which, so far as I know, has not previously been leveled at functionalist accounts of the definition of art. If this objection is successful, it calls functionalism in general (including the historicist version mentioned above) into question. The objection rests upon an argument advanced by Arthur Danto, though the application made here of Danto's argument is mine.

The objection is this: the aesthetic properties of pieces are affected by their being given art status. That is to say, aesthetic properties depend on the categorization of the objects in which they are instantiated as art or nonart (and within those categorized as art, on the genres, periods, and so forth to which they belong). A piece may have some aesthetic properties prior to its attaining art status, but on attaining art status and as a result of doing so, a piece takes on many other aesthetic properties. These newly acquired properties may be of a quite different order from those it possessed prior to its acquiring art status (or from those possessed by an otherwise indistinguishable object that lacks art status and also from those possessed by an otherwise indistinguishable artwork created at a different time). Moreover, the aesthetic properties by virtue of which the piece meets the point of art are those it acquires on attaining the status of art rather than those it possesses prior to its attaining that status.

So while a piece may display aesthetic properties prior to its becoming art, it does not merit elevation to art status on the strength of those properties. Rather, it has aesthetic properties that allow it to meet the point of art only because it has acquired art status, and not vice versa. The functional view of the definition of art, according to this objection, holds that aesthetic properties exist mainly prior to, and provide the basis for, a piece's attaining the status of art. It is apparent, however, that it is art status that is prior to, and a determinant of those aesthetic properties of artworks by virtue of which they serve the function of art.

(Some writers distinguish between "aesthetic" properties—such as daintiness—and "artistic" properties—such as irony. That distinction does not affect the argument here, because functionalists, including Beardsley, would see both types of properties as serving the function of art. Nothing need hang, therefore, on the choice of terms.)

In explicating this objection I develop points made by Arthur Danto (1981 and "The Appreciation and Interpretation of Works of Art" in 1986b; the following page references are to the former work). Danto claims that artworks have aesthetic properties not displayed by their "real" (possibly perceptually indiscernible) counterparts, and that it is only when artworks are rightly recognized as art that they take on these properties. As a urinal Duchamp's *Fountain* shares its properties (including aesthetic properties) with other porcelainery; as an artwork it shares its properties with marble statues (94). The aesthetic properties it may have prior to its attaining art status are properties it shares with countless other urinals that do not merit that status. But as an artwork it takes on many aesthetic properties other urinals lack (for example, it refers to the history and techniques of sculpture). Furthermore, if *Fountain* is successful in meeting the point of art, its success is owed to its having aesthetic properties gained as a result of its attaining art status, and not by virtue of aesthetic properties it shares with other urinals that do not have such status. Taste is not a matter of discerning aesthetic properties that were always present, since learning that a piece is a work of art entails recognizing that the piece has properties its untransfigured counterparts lack (99). This point is brought out in several less controversial cases: a chained sculpture of a cat may be indistinguishable from a sculpture of a chained cat, yet clearly the latter will have aesthetic properties that the former does not have, and these properties will be apparent only to someone who can "constitute" the artwork; that is, to someone who knows on some basis other than that of the straightforwardly discernible aesthetic properties common to both pieces what is included and what excluded from the artwork (102–104). Similarly, if an artist sculpted a piece (perchance titled *Can Opener*) just as his inventive neighbor made the first can opener (which happened to be perceptually indistinguishable from the sculpture), then the two pieces would have very different aesthetic properties, and the difference would depend upon the status as art of the one piece and, hence, its location within an art-historical tradition of sculpture (29–30).

Danto believes that this point is obscured by the fact that the same words often are used in describing the aesthetic properties of nonart (or pre-art) and the aesthetic properties of artworks. A barbarian with no conception of art might appreciate beauty (in men or women, for example) but would not necessarily appreciate the beauty of an artwork (103–107). Where a judgment that a painting is a beautiful painting of *X* licenses the judgment that there is a painting of a beautiful *X*, the barbarian would be at home. Standardly this is not the case with artworks, which can be seen as beautiful only when they are known to be artworks. (A beautiful painting often is not a painting of a beautiful subject.) In the same way, to describe an artwork known to be an artwork as empty is not to say that it is empty in the way in which an unfilled box is empty, even if the artwork happens to be an unfilled box (2). And the barbarian's judgment that a painting is "black and white paint and no more" differs from the similarly worded judgment of an art critic who realizes that she is describing a painting. The critic's remark is one about the artist's return to the physicality of paint through an atmosphere of artistic theory and history (133). Although this difference in judgments is obscured by the form of expression in some cases, in others it is explicit. Neither flowers nor mere splotches of paint on canvas could be powerful, but a painting of flowers may be (156–158). This is a function of the painting's being an artwork, and not merely a representation, for artworks use the means of representation in a way that is not exhaustively specified when one has exhaustively specified what is being represented. Ordinarily the medium of representation is transparent to its content, but, in recognizing that a representation is an artwork, one recognizes that a thought about the content is expressed. A diagram is neither expressive nor inexpressive; an artwork in the form of a diagram expresses something about the represented content, because the medium of representation is never merely incidental to the appreciation of the artwork's aesthetic properties (147–148). A diagram *displays* a style without having one; artworks must necessarily be appreciated and judged as having a style that interacts with, and does not merely superintend on, their content (197–204). Even if an artwork "says" that it is no more than that which it represents, it differs both from what it represents (since that exists without asserting its own existence) and from other forms of representation (since they can be understood as performing their representational function without commenting on their doing so) (see 87). Mere representations *re*-present their subjects, whereas artworks are *about* their subjects; when artworks are understood as such, they are understood not only as indicating what is seen but also as revealing a way of seeing. To use Danto's often-repeated simile: artworks stand to their real (including representational) counterparts as actions stand to mere movements and persons stand to their bodies (5, 103, 202–203).

If the spirit of Danto's arguments is accepted, then they show that, whatever aesthetic properties artworks may share with their real counterparts (should they have them), they take on other aesthetic properties when seen properly as artworks falling within artistic traditions. There is no doubt that Danto regards such properties as different in kind, and not merely in degree, from those possessed by nonart (or pre-art). To appreciate such pieces as artworks is to appreciate them for such properties. It is just by virtue of their possessing such properties that artworks have value for us as art. So art status must be conferred as a prior condition of the generation of the very aesthetic properties in terms of which art is valued as such.

The Functionalist's Reply

A functionalist on the matter of the definition of art might concede many of the points just made. He need not hold that anything that might meet the point of art thereby qualifies as an artwork. For example, even if the Grand Canyon would have been a fine work of art had it been created by an artist, a functionalist on the definition of art need not claim that it is an artwork. That is, a functionalist is likely to accept that various conditions must be met, beyond the mere possession of aesthetic merit, before a piece can attain the status of art. (For Beardsley, for example, it is a necessary condition for art status that the putative artwork be created by an agent.) So a functionalist on the definition of art is not committed to denying the distinction between artworks and aesthetically pleasing natural objects. Moreover, he can accept that the products of agents' actions are bound to possess aesthetically relevant qualities, such as representational properties, which natural objects could not possess. Yet further, a historically minded functionalist can allow that the fact that an agent acts within an art-historical tradition affects the aesthetically relevant qualities of her products. So neither need a functionalist on the definition of art be committed to denying a distinction between artworks and other aesthetically pleasing artifacts. That is, the functionalist may concede that the production of (some of the) aesthetically relevant properties of a piece might depend upon the artist's acting against the background of an Artworld and, to the extent that the Artworld is an informal institution, upon her acting within an institutional context. Much art might possess the properties by virtue of which it meets the point of art only because it was created within the institutional setting of the Artworld. To sum up: a functionalist on the definition of art might concede to the objection everything but its conclusion.

The objection, in drawing its conclusion, assumes the following model of art creation: a piece that is not an artwork exists with some aesthetic properties. Without modifying it in any other way, an artist confers art status on the piece. This conferral of art status alters the work's aesthetic properties, so that it now has aesthetic properties it previously lacked. The piece serves the function of art by virtue of its possessing these new properties. This "chronological" model of art creation obviously derives from a consideration of such cases as Duchamp's readymades but is intended, in some nonchronological version, to cover also the orthodox case of art creation. The model counts against the definition of art as functional in suggesting that art status exists logically prior to the generation of the aesthetic properties in terms of which artworks meet the point of art and, hence, in implying that arthood is not a status merited as a result of a piece's performing the function of art.

In denying the objection's conclusion, the functionalist on the definition of art must reject this model of art creation. Commonly a work of art is created as a work of art, without its having a chronologically prior existence. This is true, for instance, of *Can Opener,* one of Danto's examples. *Can Opener* has aesthetic properties its "untransfigured" counterpart lacks, and *Can Opener* serves the function of art by virtue of its exhibiting those properties. This is not to say that it gains those properties merely as a result of an act of status conferral with no more than institutional significance. Rather, *Can Opener* is *made* by the artist to have those aesthetic properties, and there is no sense in which its acquiring art status predates its acquiring those properties. Its achievement of art status coincides with its gaining those properties, and had the generated properties not merited art status, *Can Opener* would not be a work of art, despite its creation within the Artworld setting and the dependence of its properties upon its creation within that setting. The institutional setting within which *Can Opener* is produced is irrelevant to *Can Opener*'s status as art (or its failure to attain that status) in that, while its aesthetic properties are determined in part by that setting, the setting alone does not guarantee the creation of aesthetic properties that merit art status.

In what may be the most passionately polemical piece of writing he ever penned, Beardsley appeals to this argument in rejecting the claim to art status of Duchamp's readymades:

> The fuss that has been made about Duchamp's *Fountain* has long amazed me. It does not seem that in submitting that object to the art show and getting it more or less hidden from view, Duchamp or anyone else thought of it either as art or as having an aesthetic capacity. He did not establish a new meaning of "artwork," nor did he really inaugurate a tradition that led to the acceptance of plumbing figures (or other "readymades") as artworks today. If there was a point, it was surely to prove to the jury that even their tolerance had limits, and that they would *not* accept anything—at least gracefully. This small point was made effectively, but the episode doesn't seem to me to provide the slightest reason to regard the aesthetic definition [that is, Beardsley's functional definition] as inadequate. Many objects exhibited today by the avant-garde evidently do make comments of some kind on art itself, but these objects may or may not be artworks. To classify them as artworks just because they make comments on art would be to classify a lot of dull and sometimes unintelligible magazine articles and newspaper reviews as artworks, and where is the advantage of that? To classify them as artworks just because they are exhibited is, to my mind, intellectually spineless, and results in classifying the exhibits at commercial expositions, science museums, stamp clubs and World's Fairs as artworks. Where is the advantage of that? To classify them as artworks just because they are called art by those who are called artists because they make things they call art is not to classify at all, but to think in circles. Perhaps these objects deserve a special name, but not the name of art. The distinction between objects that do and those that do not enter into artistic activities by reason of their connection with the aesthetic interest is still vital to preserve, and no other word than "art" is as suitable to mark it. (1983, 25)

Tilghman's approach (1973a, 1984) to such cases is similar. Instead of asking if such pieces are good enough to be artworks, he asks, What is the point of calling these things artworks? (which is to be understood as a request for an account of how they are to be seen as continuous with past practices of art making and art appreciation). An unfunny joke has amusement as its point, though it serves that point poorly; something that did not, or could not, serve the point of amusement could not be a joke at all. Likewise, Tilghman reasons, to ask of Duchamp's readymades if they are art is not to ask if they are good art but is, rather, to ask if they serve the point of art.

P. N. Humble, in 1982 and 1984, also doubts that the readymades could, or were intended to, serve the point of art. William Tolhurst in 1984 allows, by contrast, that the readymades are artworks—because they were "placed," if not made, by an artist—but doubts that such pieces as *LHOOQ* or *LHOOQ Shaved* could be art—because he doubts that they lend themselves to aesthetic appreciation.

The Rejection of the Functionalist's Reply

Beardsley and Tilghman are correct in holding that assuming that the readymades are artworks begs the question against a functional definition of art. But their replies in turn beg the question against the alternative view. To insist, as Tilghman does, that one establish the art status of the readymades by showing how they serve the point of art is to reject out of hand the proceduralist's approach of showing how Duchamp's actions are continuous with the use of the institutionalized conventions by which art status has been conferred in the past. Tilghman assumes precisely what is at issue: that art status is functional. It will not satisfy Tilghman to show how Duchamp's actions are continuous with uses of the institutionalized conventions for art-status conferral. The only answer Tilghman will accept is one that shows that Duchamp's readymades serve the point of art as do their less controversial predecessors. To put the issue this way simply is to assume what the institutionalist rejects—that art is a functional concept and that one discovers whether or not something is an artwork by considering whether it meets the point of art, at least in the minimally required manner. If the point of art is to provide aesthetic satisfaction (let us suppose), then the question for Tilghman is, Does *Fountain* qualify as a candidate for appreciation? where qualifying as such is not a matter of meeting the institutional requirements and is instead a matter of being suited to the function. Any approach, such as Tilghman's, which assumes that the question is to be settled by considering the functionality of the object begs the question against the institutional theory of the definition of art in that it refuses to countenance the possibility that arthood might have drifted free from its own function. Tilghman has no argument as such; his is a rejection of the enterprise, rather than a commentary on the moves made within it. He admits that he has no *proof* that *Fountain* is not an artwork, but he thinks that the burden of proof lies with his opponents.

As I pointed out in Chapter 2, hard cases, such as that presented by *Fountain*'s claim to art status, mark the point of disagreement between the institutionalist and the functionalist on the matter of the definition of art, so we cannot settle the dispute between protagonists of these two views by prejudging the status as art of such pieces. As it stands the previous objection to the functionalist approach is question begging, but so too is the reply offered by Beardsley and Tilghman. So on whom does the burden of proof lie? It seems to me that it lies with the functionalist, and that this conclusion can be demonstrated in a way that reveals the decisiveness of the objection given formerly to the functional account of the definition of art.

Fountain is generally credited as being Duchamp's work, even if he did not make the urinal he appropriated in creating that work. Art historians and critics talk about the piece; it is constantly pictured and referred to in books on the history of modern art and in courses on recent art history. Moreover, artists have been influenced by Duchamp's readymades and frequently allude to them, not only in their manifestos but also in their own artworks. In brief, *Fountain* and its kin are treated as artworks (indeed, as important artworks). While it may be true that some works in the past have been similarly treated, only to have their art status revoked or seriously questioned at a later time, the conditions under which this reversal has occurred (for example, upon the discovery that the piece in question was forged) seem not to be applicable to the case of the readymades. For this reason—that is, for the reason that their approach cuts across the prevailing practice in a way that would appear to be legislative rather than descriptive—the burden lies with the functionalists on the matter of the definition of art to prove that the readymades are not artworks after all.

It is implausible to think that the functionalists could seriously deny the impact of Duchamp's efforts on the theory, history, and practice of art. How then might they concede these facts while denying art status to such pieces? It might be pointed out that many things, such as technological developments in the production of paint, have had an equally dramatic impact on the history and development of art without thereby qualifying for art status. Clearly, though, this reply is inadequate, for Duchamp's works do not enter into the history of art in anything like the way in which such developments, or other accoutrements of the Artworld, such as gallery catalogs, do. Accordingly the functionalist is forced, I think, to concede that Duchamp's works are pseudo-art, are works that have been given an honorary status, as it were, without their meriting that status in the orthodox fashion. As Paul Windeatt has argued (in an unpublished paper), the functionalists must see such works as having been accorded the "rights" of members of the institution without their having fulfilled the "obligation" of meeting the point of art. But then, how does the functionalist answer the charge that *Fountain* and its counterparts have more than paid back the Artworld for the rights accorded to it? Perhaps *Fountain* is an honorary artwork. But this assertion implies that there are two ways to be an artwork and that the functionalist is mistaken in believing that an ability to serve the point of art is a necessary condition for something's being an artwork. In the end it is not obvious that a functional definition of art can claim to be aimed at capturing our concept of art rather than at legislating a new and conservative meaning for the term "art," if the functionalist acknowledges (as surely he is forced to do) the importance that Duchamp's works have attained within the history of art.

This is not to deny that the readymades and their avant-garde equivalents in the other forms and categories of art are hard cases. As I noted before, those who adopt a procedural approach to the definition of art have a way of explaining why these are hard cases without at the same time accepting that their hardness lies in the authenticity of their art status. They are hard cases precisely because they challenge and perhaps even undermine the function of art. They are hard cases because they fall into the gap left by the separation of the function of art from the procedures, or the use of the procedures, in terms of which art status is conferred.

In order to give the functional approach to the definition of art its most convincing form, I have confined myself in the preceding discussion to a consideration of cases that would be widely acknowledged to be hard. At this stage it is perhaps worth observing that a great many works, the art status of which is not in doubt on any account, pose problems for the functionalist. Many artworks are boring or, at best, evoke indifference. To insist that such works are poor works of art, as the functionalist does, avoids the problem of questioning their status only at the cost of raising a serious doubt as to the feebleness of the minimum standard that, according to the functionalist, must be attained as a necessary condition of something's being an artwork. The standard must be set very low if the theory is to account for such works' attaining art status. But now, the standard seems to be so low that it becomes difficult to see how anything's meeting *that* standard could have much bearing on its serving the point of art. I doubt that the functionalist's standard can be as low as the existence of very bad art indicates while also allowing an explanation of the importance attached to art within the life of the community.

Of course, this objection need not apply to an intentionalist who pays regard to the function of art only as an appropriate motivation for the art-defining intention. For such an intentionalist what matters is not that the threshold of functional efficacy is attained, but that it is aimed at—secondarily, if not primarily. Very bad art then might qualify as art because it was intended to be better art than it turned out to be. At the close of Chapter 2, I acknowledged that Beardsley might be interpreted as having abandoned the functionalism of his earlier views in favor of an intentionalist approach. If he did so, he would not be subject to the foregoing objection—but the price paid would be the rejection of functionalism as such. (How big a price that would be depends upon one's assessment of the importance retained by functional considerations as motivating, but not as defining, conditions for art status.) Although that interpretation of Beardsley's position is a plausible one, I believe that the alternative is equally plausible. In the context of an overview of his writings, I am inclined to believe that, in coming to draw more attention to the importance of artists' intentions, Beardsley did not intend to abandon the necessity of the functionality condition.

On the other hand, the existence of very bad art poses no special problem for the procedural account of the definition of art, because the proceduralist sets no lower limit on the aesthetic value of artworks. So long as some artworks meet the point of art in a way that marks them as great, and so long as there is no prior guarantee about which new artworks will be great, the proceduralist can readily account for the special place accorded to the production of art in face of the fact that so much art is less than mediocre in its aesthetic worth.

CHAPTER 4

Dickie's Institutional Theory of the Definition of Art

I turn now to a consideration of an example of a procedural definition of art. The most powerful so far presented is the institutional theory. According to it, something is a work of art as a result of its being dubbed, baptized, or honored as a work of art by someone who is authorized thereby to make it an artwork by her position within the institution of the Artworld. Usually artworks achieve their status in the course of their being manufactured, but now it is possible (as once it was not) for an artist to confer the status of art on something without her making that something.

When the theory was first presented, it struck some people as preposterous, as involving an elementary mistake. The theory entails that things are artworks by virtue of their being placed within the appropriate institutional context, whereas normally we would think that it is because they are art that it is appropriate so to place them. Melvin Rader (1974) and Donald Walhout (1986) express a common view in holding that the institutional theory gets thing back-to-front, as it were (just as Euthyphro allegedly reversed the proper order of things in suggesting that acts are pious because they are loved by the gods, instead of recognizing that the gods love pious acts because those acts are pious).

The institutional theory of the definition of art faces some obvious difficulties: if artworks can be created by artists who never show their creations to the public, then it would appear that the institutional context is not necessary for the creation of art. If not everything hung inside the door of an art gallery (for example, an artist's raincoat) thereby becomes an artwork, then the institutional context is not sufficient for the creation of art. It is possible to see something of the shape that an institutional theory must take if such objections are not to be fatal. It must characterize the institution widely enough that "artist" (and "public") name roles within the institution, so that the lonely artist acts as an agent of the institution despite his lack of an official office within it. Accordingly the Artworld must be seen as broadly reaching and as informally structured in at least some of its parts. It must also describe the Artworld as structured (if only on an informal basis) so that outwardly similar actions might be seen as having quite different imports because of their institutional contexts. The acts of hanging up a raincoat and hanging up a painting in the gallery might differ in their significance because the one act is performed within the context of one role, and the other act is performed in the context of another. In the same way, although anyone may utter the words "I release you from your debts," not just anybody can thereby release me from my debts, and not everybody who could thereby release me from my debts under some given circumstances could so release me under different circumstances.

This, the briefest of sketches, will serve my purposes in this book. My concern lies not with the detail of any particular version of the approach, but instead with the general shape that such a theory must take if it is to be convincing. In the following discussion I concentrate on George Dickie's account, since that is the most fully articulated version of the institutional theory, but I am not concerned with the detail of his account except insofar as the discussion of detail becomes important in replying to the more serious and general of the objections faced by such a theory.

A Short History of the Institutional Theory

No doubt cynics have always suspected that the distinction between the arts, on the one hand, and crafts, entertainments, and hobbies, on the other, has no firmer basis than the mere declaration of its existence by some institutionally entrenched, protected, and isolated elite who wish to distinguish their concerns and pastimes from those of their slaves or the hoi polloi. Provided that those cynics saw the actions of the elite as structured by their place within an institution designed by them (or evolved from other of their practices) for the creation and appreciation of "art," then those cynics are proto-institutionalists on the matter of the definition of art.

Although philosophers who have argued for an institutional account of the definition of art sometimes have been accused of elitism (for example, see Goldsmith 1983), the more broad-based is the institution of the Artworld as they describe it, the less liable to the charge of elitism do they appear to be. In fact, Arthur Danto, Terry Diffey, and George Dickie have characterized the Artworld, the republic of the arts, the art institution, or whatever one calls it, in a way that is, or might be, democratic. Either most people are said to be members or they are said to be capable of joining should they choose to do so. (But see Wolfe 1976 for some interesting figures on the numbers who are actively involved in buying, criticizing, and promoting modern art. Similarly, see Carrier 1987, chap. 5.) These theorists, unlike the cynic mentioned above, do not see the function of art as essentially, or even primarily, political and so do not characterize the structure of the Artworld in political terms.

The charge that the institutional theory is elitist is a serious one. It arises, I think, when a critic accepts that the Artworld is institutionalized and then argues both that many artworks do not fall within this official Artworld and that many art makers do not identify with, and hold no position within, the official Artworld. In this view the notion of art is a broader one than is encompassed by the institutional theory, and so the theory is unacceptably elitist. Other critics accept that the Artworld is democratic and then argue that the democratic principles and practices constituting the Artworld are not institutional in character. That is, whereas the first group of critics identify the Artworld with the institutionalized character of art, the second group of critics do not. At heart the objection raised by both types of critics is the same—an institutional definition of art is too restrictive to encompass the notion of art, whether or not it is too narrow adequately to characterize the Artworld itself. This is a crucial objection and one to which I devote attention in the following discussion. There I tend to consider it in terms of the second rather than the first approach, but as I have indicated, the objection might be developed in either fashion.

The notion of the Artworld was presented by Danto in 1964. His idea was that artworks are surrounded by "an atmosphere of theory" which the eye cannot descry. To recognize and understand a work of art as such one must be able to locate it within a historical and social context. That context, or atmosphere, is generated by the changing practices and conventions of art, the heritage of works, the intentions of artists, the writings of critics, and so forth. Taken together, these constitute an Artworld.

There is nothing in Danto's account to suggest that he believes the Artworld to be structured to a degree that might make it to be viewed plausibly as an informal institution, and he has explicitly rejected Dickie's institutional theory as not addressing the questions that interest him and that are, in his view, the important ones (1981, especially 92–94; 1986b). Danto always has been interested in the fact that artworks refer to other artworks and the practices of art creation, and in the way this reference generates a history of art such that works that could not have been created as art in the past become creatable as the art of the present slips into the past.

Danto's discussion of the Artworld shifted attention from the artistically relevant properties of artworks to the social context without which they could not take on and present such properties. That shift of attention prepared the ground for an institutional account of the definition of art. For that reason it is not surprising that Danto has been taken to be a proto-institutionalist to be discussed in the same breath as Dickie. Even if this view of Danto does not do justice to the richness of his interests, it is surprising to find him claiming to have a rival definition quite different in kind from that offered by the institutionalists (1981). One would expect his views to be compatible, if far from identical, with the institutional approach.

Danto attacks the institutional theory on the grounds that it is concerned only with the mechanics of the context in which art is created, whereas he is concerned with a definitional question of more substance: that of how art status might be merited. In fact I believe Danto to be running together two distinct issues: (*a*) how a piece might deserve to have art status conferred upon it, and (*b*) how a work with art status might merit appreciation and understanding in a way its indiscernibly similar, "untransfigured counterparts" might not.

I find (*a*) could be anti-institutional if it implies that status conferral is an unnecessary formality; that what really makes something a work of art is the aesthetic qualities it has "prior" to its receiving the imprimatur of the Artworld, "prior" to its being baptized as an artwork. Whereas (*b*) is concerned not so much with how a thing comes to be an artwork, but instead with how its being an artwork affects its aesthetic/artistic properties. Now even if there is a relation of logical dependence between a thing's acquiring art status and its taking on new aesthetic properties, its taking on certain specific aesthetic properties may be logically independent of its becoming an artwork. A consideration of (*b*), where the focus falls on the specificity of artistic properties, need not involve any interest in definitional matters. Moreover, even if a sufficiently general consideration of (*b*) is bound to reflect on definitional issues, still there is no reason to think that what will be revealed opposes the institutional account rather than complementing it. So it is not true that someone interested in (*b*) thereby is offering a theory of the definition of art such as might be opposed to the institutional account.

For all that Danto sometimes claims to be dealing with (*a*), there is no doubt that it is (*b*) on which he concentrates—and it his discussion of (*b*) which I have used in Chapter 3 as the basis of an attack against the functional definition of art. Therefore, there is no reason to see his concerns as threatening an institutional account such as the one given by Dickie. However, what is true, I think, is that Dickie's version of the institutional theory pays insufficient regard to the important issues raised in a consideration of (*b*). I take this insufficiency to be what lies behind Danto's criticism of the institutional approach.

Diffey (1969) was perhaps the first to defend a thoroughgoing institutional view. He argues that arthood is a status conferred by the "republic of art," and he recognizes that such an account presupposes the need for a description of a structured institution and of the distribution of authority within the institution. One respect in which his position strikes others (Beardsley 1976, for example) as counterintuitive is in his claim that pieces not submitted to, and accepted by, a public could not be artworks. In his view the status is conferred by the public rather than by the artist alone. Subsequently Diffey moved away from the spirit of the institutional theory (1973, 1977), which he came to renounce (1979) on the grounds that it violates common sense, confuses treating a thing as an artwork with its really being an artwork, and offers nothing by way of an account of what the status amounts to (as opposed to how it is generated).

Dickie also produced the first statement of his theory in 1969, revising and refining that statement (1971, 1973a, 1973b) until it received a fully articulated presentation in 1974. For the better part of the decade that followed, Dickie ignored the theory's critics (exceptions being 1975b, 1977, 1979). Then he produced a new version of the theory (1983, 1984) in which he discusses some, but by no means all, of the objections the earlier account attracted. He supplements and modifies the detail of his theory to accommodate what he takes to be his critics' better points. This latest version of the theory has provoked a strong response, as did its predecessor. Dickie has remained aloof from the debate apart from a few brief replies (1987, 1989a, 1989b).

Dickie's Definition

Dickie (1974) defines "work of art" as (1) an artifact (2) a set of the aspects of which has had conferred upon it the status of candidate for appreciation by some person or persons acting on behalf of the Artworld. Each of (1) and (2) is necessary, and jointly they are sufficient for something's being an artwork. He has modified and refined this definition (1984) so that now it reads: (1) an artist is a person who participates with understanding in the making of an artwork; (2) a work of art is an artifact of a kind created to be presented to an Artworld public; (3) a public is a set of persons who are prepared in some degree to understand an object that is presented to them; (4) the Artworld is the totality of all Artworld systems; (5) an Artworld system is a framework for the presentation of a work of art by an artist to an Artworld public. Again, each of (1) through (5) is necessary, and jointly they are sufficient for something's being an artwork.

In the remainder of this chapter, I develop an extended objection to Dickie's account. It is my claim that Dickie too often discusses the conferral of art status as if it were a kind of action, like shaving, rather than an exercise of authority vested in socially defined roles, with the result that he has no useful explanation to offer of who can confer art status on what and when. Accordingly he fails to characterize the structure of the informal institution that is the Artworld, he fails to consider the factors limiting and defining the boundaries of the roles that comprise that structure, and he pays insufficient heed to the history of the institution as affecting that structure and those rules.

As should be apparent from these remarks, my aim is to criticize Dickie for failing both to deliver a truly institutional account of art and to reveal how such a theory would counter, rather than invite, the objections faced by his version of it. My aim, in other words, is to defend the institutional theory from its chief protagonist as much as from its critics.

Is Everyone Equally an Artist?

Dickie maintains that artists confer art status within the institutionalized context of the Artworld, and that each member of the Artworld is (or might be) an artist. In his view what distinguishes Duchamp's offering a urinal for appreciation and a urinal salesman's doing the same thing in the course of his employment is the institutional context in which the two acts are performed. The urinal salesman did not create an artwork (as Duchamp did) because he did not act within the context of the Artworld. There was no institutional bar preventing the salesman's having done what Duchamp did. That the salesman did not do what Duchamp did was only the result of his own limited imagination or courage. He might have been successful in creating *Fountain* as was Duchamp had he acted within the appropriate institutional context. That is, the salesman was as much an artist, *within the context of the Artworld,* as Duchamp.

This view is implausible (Sclafani 1973). Even if the salesman might have created artworks—for example, paintings—it is not obvious that he could have acted in so radical a fashion as did Duchamp and succeeded as Duchamp did in conferring art status on a urinal. The point is not about the Artworld's acceptance or rejection of the salesman's attempt to confer art status on a urinal, had he made it prior to Duchamp's. The institutional theory does not suppose that only that which is accepted by the Artworld public as art is art. The conferral of art status, where it is successful, occurs before the piece is submitted to the public, if it ever is. Rather, the point to be made is about the salesman's authority to alter, as Duchamp did, the conventions by which art status might successfully be conferred. To accept that just anyone is (or might be) an artist seems to undercut the institutional theory in that it deprives of any substance the notion of role differentiation, on which such an account must rely if it is to be convincing (Morton 1973, Blizek 1974, Wieand 1981b, Welsh 1981, Simpson 1986). Roles that are occupied by everyone are not roles of the sort that characterize social institutions. Such institutions are structured in terms of differences in roles and differences in the authority that accompanies such roles. If everyone always has been equally authorized to confer art status, then the notion of authorization is empty, as is the claim that such authority marks the limits of an institutionally defined role.

This objection counts powerfully against the institutional theory as presented by Dickie. Why does he leave his account open to it? Perhaps because he recognizes that the creation of artworks does not depend on formal training or formal qualifications, so that, other things being equal, anyone with a conception of art—and who among adults would not have such a conception within our society?—might create art. Many people paint as a hobby. Sometimes they display their works for sale in the foyers of shopping malls and the like, but often they do not. It is not absurd to suggest, as Dickie would, I think, that they are artists and that their paintings are artworks (albeit, generally poor ones). Such people remain at a distance from the more structured aspects of the Artworld and probably would not identify with those aspects, but, then, the conventions for art making which they use are widely recognized and accepted. Their attempts at status conferral involve the traditional method of manufacture, rather than the more exotic act of mere titling.

Even if we accept the truth of these claims, they do not mitigate the force of the objection. If they seem to do so, it can only be because of the common tendency to equate a person with the role she fills, so that all of her actions are carelessly viewed as actions performed in her capacity as the occupant of that role. That is, the mistake consists in a failure to recognize the institutional limits of the role. Henry Moore was an artist, but it does not follow that the eggs he selected for his morning omelet were artworks, even if he chose them for their aesthetically pleasing shape, because he was not, in cooking his breakfast, acting in his role as artist. A failure to recognize the institutional limits of the role leads in turn to a failure to recognize that not everyone is subject to the same limits. Even if the urinal salesman could create some works of art, it does not follow that he could have succeeded in an attempt to use in a novel way just any of the conventions by which art status might then be achieved. Dickie's avoidance of an elitist conception of the Artworld presents the obvious difficulty of explaining how such a democratic arrangement is consistent with a view of the artist as occupying a special place within an informally structured institution, for, as I have observed, roles occupied by everyone are not, generally speaking, roles of the type by which an institution might be structured, whether formally or informally.

(Note, in passing, that an intentionalist on the definition of art might attempt to distinguish Duchamp's and the salesman's acts, or Moore's acts of sculpting and his acts of breakfast making, in terms of the different intentions involved. In Chapter 7 I indicate why I think such an approach to the problem may lead toward an account that refers, as I have done here, to social roles. Where the *content* of the intentions might be so similar, what distinguishes the acts is the force that the intentions derive from their context within a social practice or informal institution.)

Dickie's account would have to be modified were it to meet the objections raised. I think that there are ways of changing it which would preserve the viability of an institutional theory and outline below the types of modifications which seem to be required.

The Artworld is an informal institution. That is to say, the procedures by which roles within the institution come to be occupied are informal, and the limits of the authority which define those roles are not strictly codified, although there are such limits. As an institution the Artworld is structured in terms of its various roles—artist, impressario, public, performer, curator, critic, and so on—and the relationships among them. Within the wider institution are to be found some formally structured elements—theaters, art galleries, ministries of the arts, and so forth.

An artist is someone who has acquired (in some appropriate but informal fashion) the authority to confer art status. By "authority" I do not mean "a right to others' obedience"; I mean an "entitlement successfully to employ the conventions by which art status is conferred on objects/events." This authority is acquired through the artist's participation in the activities of the Artworld. It is not (usually) formally bestowed upon the artist by other members of the Artworld, and neither does it rely directly on their consent. In exercising this authority the artist acts "on behalf of" the Artworld in the sense that she employs the powers vested in the role of the artist and not in the further sense of "speaking for" other members of the Artworld.

There are institutional limits to the procedures, occasions, and contexts by and in which art status may be conferred, on who can do the conferring, and on the character of the objects/events on which the status may be conferred. (The parallel with christening has been drawn by Dickie. The analogy resides in the way in which christening is similarly constrained. The analogy has been challenged in Mitias 1975, Silvers 1976, and Binkley 1976. Michael Mitias wrongly believes that Dickie thinks that no rules or procedures are involved in conferring art status, whereas they are involved in christening or knighting. Anita Silvers rightly notes that the two activities have different points but does not observe that the parallel does not depend upon their having the same point. Timothy Binkley does not acknowledge the way in which his specifying/indexing is similar both to Dickie's conferring and to christening.) The conventions employed in conferring art status change through time, as does the possible membership of the roles in which there is authority to confer art status through the activation of these conventions. Not even Duchamp could have created readymade artworks had he lived two hundred years ago. Now that Duchamp has established a new use of the conventions by which art status may be conferred, that use of the conventions has become available to lesser lights in the Artworld. There are conventions for the conferral of art status that almost everybody is authorized to employ successfully (such as those used by the hobby-painter), but there are (or have been) other conventions that only a limited number of people would have been authorized to employ.

The emphasis is to be placed on authority rather than skill. The display of artistic skills might be one of the informal ways in which a person qualifies for the special authority that goes with his being a recognized artist. But, allowing this, what matters is the authority and not the way in which it is acquired. When Duchamp created *Fountain,* many people were authorized to use some of the conventions by which art status could then be conferred, but only a few people were authorized to use all of them, or to modify them, as Duchamp did. Duchamp had the authority to do what the salesman could not have done (at that time). That Duchamp had acquired this authority as a result of achieving recognition as an avant-garde artist is crucial, whether or not he needed to display special skills to merit that recognition (Binkley 1977, Fletcher 1982, Donnell-Kotrozo 1982, Goldsmith 1983). When it came to conferring art status on a urinal, Duchamp displayed no artistic skills that the salesman lacked. Perhaps a urinal salesman now might be as capable of turning urinals into artworks as was Duchamp, but to accept this is not to be forced also to accept that the salesman is thereby an artist (or as much of an artist) as was Duchamp when he adopted what was, at the time, a novel use of the conventions for the conferral of art status.

These remarks bear on a number of related issues that have been seen as presenting problems for the institutional theory. Dickie has a tendency to write as if anyone who succeeds (or might succeed) in conferring art status thereby is an artist. Thus he implies that a gallery director who confers art status on a chimpanzee's painting by displaying it in the appropriate institutional context is an artist in being responsible for the conferral of that status. Similarly anyone who confers art status on artifacts made by people acting outside of the Artworld context thereby is an artist, as is the person who confers art status on a piece of driftwood (without altering its physical properties in any way). Such views are counterintuitive—a person who claimed to be an artist *solely* on the strength of such exploits would stretch the meaning of the term so far, I think, as to strike us as being a poseur (Cohen 1973, Blizek 1974, Lyas 1976, Fletcher 1982). Suppose that a person taped the dawn chorus and presented it as a musical work—would we be inclined to accept that the person thereby established herself as a composer? In practice the absurdity is lost because the people who confer art status on such pieces often have established their credentials as artists in the orthodox fashion. This disguises the fact that they are not acting in their capacity as artists in conferring art status on occasions such as I have described above. In the ordinary use of the term, we take artists to be people who *create* objects/events, or specifications for their creation, as well as, and thereby as conferrers of, art status. If this is accepted, the people who, in making an artwork, do no more than confer art status on physically unmodified natural objects, on the products of animals' "typing" or "painting," or on objects manufactured outside the Artworld context, do not act as artists in doing so.

A proponent of the institutional theory of artistic creation need not be embarrassed that not all artworks are created by artists. Artists are authorized within the institution to confer art status, but the role of artist need not be the only role within the institution in which this authority resides. The counterintuitive appearance of such cases as are described above is removed once this is conceded. What follows, of course, is that some artworks, such as random computer drawings, are not the responsibility of any artist (or, at least, not of anyone who was acting *as an artist* in conferring upon them art status). That notion is not difficult to accept, I think, once it is recognized that someone with suitable authority within the Artworld is responsible for their acquiring art status, even if that person did not act as an artist in conferring that status.

With this argument in mind, we might easily justify a reluctance in following Dickie in his claim that anyone is (or might be) an artist. If Dickie means that anyone might have artistic skills, or that anyone might come to qualify for the role of artist, he is perhaps right. If he means, as he seems to, that just anyone might have the authority to employ successfully all of the conventions by which art status might be conferred, then he is mistaken. Equally he is mistaken in implying that everyone who is an art maker is thereby an artist. Once it is accepted that the authority to confer art status accompanies roles other than that of artist, there is no problem in resisting Dickie's unusual extension of the meaning of the term "artist" to cover the activities of curators and the like who confer art status upon chimpanzees' "drawings."

The Relation between the History and the Structure of the Artworld

Danto (1973) states that there are conditions that can defeat a piece's claim to art status. (For a similar account, see Wollheim 1983.) Danto holds the view that artworks necessarily are about something and, accordingly, that each must (be used to) make a "statement." (By this he seems to mean that, like linguistic utterances, artworks must be interpretable—see 1973, 1981, 1986b.) Where there is only the appearance of a piece's making a "statement," the piece's claim to art status is defeated. First, a piece can be an artwork only if it is not a fake. A fake pretends to be a statement but is not one because the speech act involved is of quotation rather than assertion. Picasso could make an artwork by painting his tie, but when a forger paints his tie, he "employed the necktie to copy what Picasso made a statement with, but made *no* statement by means of his" (1973, 10). Second, a piece can be an artwork only if it comes from an artistic provenance. Pieces cannot be made to be art by children, chimpanzees, or customs inspectors. Third, there must be "room" within the Artworld for the piece—"not everything can be an artwork at every time: the Artworld must be ready for it" (1973, 9). Fourth, the piece must find a natural place within the corpus of the artist. Picasso could create an artwork by painting his tie, but Cézanne could not. Cézanne, like the child artist (or a parrot saying "Polly wants a cracker"), is "making noise" rather than making a statement in painting his tie. And (in 1974) Danto added a further, fifth condition: a piece can be an artwork only if it has the appropriate causal history. That is, it must be the product of an intentional action, not the result of an explosion in an artist's studio, for example, because it is only as the product of an action that the artwork could make a statement, could require interpretation.

Compare Danto's views with Beardsley's. Beardsley (1983) claims as a virtue in his definition that it shows that children might make artworks, since they can produce things with the intention that those things be aesthetically gratifying. Once (1970) he thought that a thing's being a forgery is irrelevant to its being art; later (1983) he said that forgeries can be artworks so long as they are produced with an aesthetic intention (even if it is subordinate to other concerns) and are not produced by a mechanically thoughtless process from which such an intention is altogether absent. For Beardsley what defeats a claim to art status is the absence of an intention to produce an object that, when viewed from the aesthetic point of view, is aesthetically gratifying, or the failure to make something in conjunction with the intention, or the failure to make a thing with aesthetically gratifying properties. The difference between Danto and Beardsley, both of whom stress the importance of artists' intentions, concerns two issues: (1) Danto, unlike Beardsley, believes that an artist can make an artwork of an existing object without modifying the material properties of that object; (2) Danto stresses much more than does Beardsley the extent to which artworks are bound to their art-historical and institutional context, although, like Beardsley, he believes that they stand out against their context in a way that, in his terms, prevents them from collapsing back onto reality as "mere real things."

I am not here interested in evaluating the conditions specified by Danto as necessary for something's attaining art status. Instead, my aim is to emphasize that an account of the patterns of authority which structure the roles occupied within the Artworld would lead to a consideration of Danto's second, third, and fourth conditions. Those conditions are concerned with the interaction between the development of the Artworld as an institution, on the one hand, and the history of art and its works (that is, the history of the products of that institution), on the other. The second condition indicates that only someone with the appropriate authority can make an artwork. The third condition indicates that, at any given time, that authority can be used effectively only in relation to some items, or kinds of items, and not with respect to others. The fourth condition points to the way in which the authority of the artist and the history of art are so related that what the Artworld is prepared to accept as art at a given time depends in part on who it is that proposes an item as art and on the direction in which that person hitherto has led the Artworld. Michelangelo, artistic genius though he might have been, could not have turned a urinal into an artwork; nor could Rodin. (Though one might imagine an artist for all the world like Cézanne, who created artworks within an Artworld with a history not entirely dissimilar to that of our own, and who was able to create an artwork by painting his tie.) A van Winkle who awoke in 1991 after 190 years of sleep could not expect to be able to recognize the artworks of the day, and even if he could do so, he could not appreciate them without his acquiring some knowledge of the developments and movements in the arts over the intervening years. What is possible within art depends on what has been art, and what will become possible depends on what becomes the art of the present. This is true not merely because the development of styles of art parallels technological developments and the like, but also because artworks cannot help but to refer, indirectly if not directly, to their predecessors, and through them to *their* predecessors, and so on. Perhaps this historical process stops only when anything might become an artwork, and talk of development in, or of a direction to, the history of art becomes inappropriate. According to Danto (1986a, 1986b, 1987), at that time, which happens to be now, art enters its posthistorical phase and the third and fourth conditions no longer serve as restrictions upon what might become art. (For criticisms of Danto, see Silvers 1984, 1989; Kuhns 1984; Brown 1989; Ross 1989; and Cebik 1990. Shusterman, in 1987, and Bourdieu, in 1987, attack Danto for treating the history of art as if art is autonomous, and they criticize Dickie for being uninterested in the history of the institution about which he writes.)

It is not necessary to follow Danto in his Hegelian/developmental speculations about the history of art to take the point. Art making takes art making as one of its most common subjects. New artworks are made sense of in the light of past artworks and artistic techniques. (Moreover, artworks often refer directly to other artworks by means of quotation, representation, or allusion.) New artworks become part of the history of art and as such alter that history, so that what is possible in the way of new artworks constantly changes. Meanwhile, as artworks are added to the history of art and alter that history, the status and interest of past works change. A work, unacclaimed at the time of its creation, can take on an importance that acknowledges its effects on the art that followed. (Consider, for example, the way in which Anton Webern's music became important not only because it was championed by the avant-garde of the 1950s and 1960s, but because it was such a major influence on their own works. Note the way in which the interest in Webern's music casts new light on the use of melodic fragmentation and pointillistic scoring in works, such as Claude Debussy's *Jeux*, which anticipate Webern's use of those techniques.) Also recall the way in which a work thought to mark a new direction is down-valued (or stands as an isolated masterpiece) as it becomes apparent that the "new direction" was one never to be followed. (Observe, for example, the fate of Charles Ives's music.)

In allowing that artifactuality may not be the only necessary condition for something's acquiring art status, Dickie (1974, 1977) refers with approval to Danto's 1973 paper. He agrees that a chimpanzee's paintings could become art only if a person conferred that status upon them, and he agrees that fakes are not artworks because they lack originality—the artwork uses up the patent, so to speak. (For criticism of Dickie on this point, see Jamieson 1979.) Nevertheless, Dickie does not show much interest in Danto's second, third, and fourth conditions. In allowing that a chimpanzee's paintings are not artworks when displayed in a museum of natural history but that they can become artworks when displayed by a gallery director in an art gallery, he accepts part of what Danto means his second condition to cover. But Dickie does not recognize the second condition as implying any restriction on the kinds of personnel who can create art, since he allows that everyone is or might be an artist within the Artworld. Neither does Dickie recognize the second condition as inviting an account of the history of the informal institution that is the Artworld. In fact, Dickie's theory is ahistorical, and his lack of concern with the history of the Artworld reflects, I believe, the seriousness of his failure to characterize the roles that generate the structure of that institution—their boundaries, their limitations, the circumstances under which they change, the conditions for their occupancy, and so on.

Dickie need not concern himself with the way in which the achievement of art status affects a thing's aesthetically relevant properties (in a way that depends upon its historical location within the Artworld), since his aim is to explain what art status consists in and not to catalog its effects. Dickie need not concern himself with the history of the institution insofar as the details of that history leave unaffected the core of his analysis, since his aim is neither that of a social anthropologist nor that of a historian. Nevertheless, I have suggested that he does need to say more about the structure of the institution in order to explain how it is that at any given time some people in some places in the face of some items have authority to confer art status on those items, whereas other people, or those same people in other places, or those same people faced with different items, could not confer art status on the items in question. To provide this explanation—unless the account is simply to take as given the condition of the Artworld of late-twentieth-century Western culture and then is to proceed as if no other Artworlds in other places and times are possible—will be to say something about the way in which the authority that goes with the roles of the Artworld and the conditions for occupancy of those roles is a function of the prior structure of the Artworld, which in turn is a function of the structure it had before that, and so on. Dickie needs to say something about the history of art not in order to explain why artworks are as they are now, but rather, to explain why the Artworld is as it is, and hence to explain why the process by which art status can be achieved and the restrictions on who might effectively use this process are as they are. Because the Artworld operates like an organic creature—serving as the most important thing in its own environment, constantly responding to changes within itself, being both self-regulating and self-motivating—to explain how it operates is to explain how it persists through time. (Because the explanation must be abstract, the detail of the actual history of the Artworld of late-twentieth-century Western culture is important only as an example.) To explain how the Artworld persists through time is to describe the way in which its history and the wider social context determine its present structure and identity. (For an example of such an approach as applied to the distinction between "high" and "low" art, see Novitz 1989b.)

Dickie adopts a "time-slice" approach to his account of the Artworld, and perhaps some of the more bizarre claims in his theory arise from that fact. If Danto is right in his Hegelian speculations about the condition of our post-Duchampian Artworld, anything might now be made into art, and most if not all of the conventions for conferring art status are employable by most if not all people. Given that, Dickie would not be wrong in holding that all or most people now are members of the Artworld and that all or most people familiar in some general way with the art of the Western world now could use all or most of the conventions by which art status is achieved. Dickie is wrong, however, not to make clear how the present situation became possible only because the institution of the Artworld has had a history in which those things were not always true. Only then could he explain how the authority to confer art status came to devolve to its present, uniformly widespread condition, and how the role of artist came to be democratized as skill became less important in art making, and so on. That is, Dickie can defend his democratic account of the Artworld, in which hobby-painters are artists, only in terms of an account of the history of the Artworld in which hobby-painters of the fifteenth century were not artists. To explain why best we should see the hobby-painter of the present as exercising a role within the informally structured institution of the Artworld, he needs an account of the way in which the present situation in the Artworld arose from the democratization of the roles that marked the more tightly structured Artworld of, say, the fifteenth century.

Dickie cannot insist that the Artworld has always been like this, or could always have been like this, although his ahistorical mode of description is misleading in creating just such an impression. Even if Dickie's description of the $\text{Artworld}_{\text{now}}$ is correct, that description is not true of the $\text{Artworld}_{\text{past}}$; it is not true of the time at which Duchamp made *Fountain* that a urinal salesman might have done the same thing were it not for the want of the courage to do so. A convincing account of the nature of the Artworld must pay heed, in a way Dickie's does not, to the historical dynamism of that institution. (Donnell-Kotrozo, 1982, claims that it is a virtue of Dickie's theory that it does just this. I accept that the theory has the potential to offer such an account, but I doubt that Dickie has realized this potential as fully as is necessary.)

Many critics have objected that Dickie has failed to describe in detail the nature and limits of the roles that constitute the social structure of the Artworld (Cohen 1973; Sclafani 1976; Kjörup 1976;

Silvers 1976; Bartel 1979; Wollheim 1980; Sankowski 1980; Wieand 1980, 1981b, 1983; Sparshott 1987). I have argued that that objection, rather than being a weak complaint to the effect that Dickie's statement of the theory is incomplete, touches on a central flaw in Dickie's account (cf. Davies 1988a). Dickie should describe the structure of the Artworld, showing how different roles within the institution attract to themselves different amounts or kinds of authority. To that story he should add an account of the organic, historical nature of the institution in order to explain how it might come to have its present "democratic" structure. Without those strands to his theory, his version of the institutional theory is bound to look as if it is determined (illegitimately) by the contingent form of our present Artworld (which differs not only from the form of other Artworlds, but also markedly from its own form of eighty years ago). How could just anyone have been an artist in the fourteenth century, when a high level of technical skill then was required in a person aspiring to the role and authority of an artist? How could art status have been conferred then upon just any artifact, such as a paint pot, when the conventions of the time allowed art status to be conferred only upon items manufactured (and not merely appropriated) by the artist? How could Duchamp create as art something that neither a urinal salesman nor Rodin was capable of creating as art at the time?

Roles and Rules

The institutional theory of the definition of art must hold that the Artworld is a structured institution (and not an "institution" merely to the extent that it is social). Ultimately, I have suggested, it must describe that structure in terms of the rules and conventions that define the roles that make up the institution, that govern the membership of those roles, and that govern the limits of the authority of those roles. It is important, then, that it describe the actions of artists as rule governed. Moreover, it must show those actions to be rule governed not merely in the sense of being regular but in the stricter sense according to which rule following is a self-conscious, deliberate action. It is not necessary that a person who acts in accordance with a rule always be able to formulate the rule, but it is essential that that person have a conception of the rule and of what it is to act in accordance with that rule (see Dickie 1989a). Yet further, the institutional theory must show that the rules followed by members of the Artworld necessarily are such as to define the roles that structure an institution. These arguments are required in order to demonstrate both that art making is institutionalized (and not merely a social practice) and that art making is essentially (and not merely contingently) institutional.

One objection denies that the institutional theory could make good the most minimal of these claims. It argues that there must be an incompatibility between the free creativity displayed by artists in the production of novel works and the restrictions imposed by rules on their followers (see Lord 1980; for a reply to Lord, see Brand 1982; and for a more general discussion, see Baxter 1983). A first reply to the objection might note that there need be no incompatibility between the strict application of rules and the creation of the new. There are rules governing the manner in which laws may be passed within parliaments, but their existence does not prevent parliaments' passing new laws. To the contrary, the rules provide the mechanisms by which new laws may be created. As I have already mentioned in Chapter 1, rules do not determine their own applications.

This first reply might be thought not to do justice to the objection on the grounds that new artworks often seem to set out to alter, or even to subvert, the rules and conventions that governed their predecessors. A further reply is needed, and it might go as follows. The fact that the rules of art creation are challenged by the practices of artists need not show that art creation is unconstrained by rules. Rather, there might be a hierarchy of rules, with metarules controlling the way in which first-order rules may be modified. In other words, that the first-order rules for art creation can be changed by artists does not show that, ultimately, art creation is not subject to rules, because the process of change might itself be governed by metarules. Indeed, unless the introduction of novelty is rule governed to some extent, it is hard to see how we could distinguish between something that is novel as a new work of art or art form, and something that is novel as a new form of nonart, such as house demolition, hole digging, or the like. For a new form of art to be a form of art, some continuity with past art must be retained. That art creation is rule governed in certain essential respects need imply neither the stifling of creativity nor conservatism, either in the creation of new artworks or in the modification of the conventions of art creation.

Yet other critics have argued that, while the actions of artists are rule governed, the rules followed constitute no more than a social practice and are, at best, only contingently institutionalized (see Beardsley 1976, 1983; Iseminger 1976; Bachrach 1977; McGregor 1977; Carroll 1988). To some extent this objection has been invited, I think, by Dickie's tendency to characterize the creation of art more as a type of activity than as an exercise of authority vested in a type of social role. Wieand (1981b), more than most, appreciates that social practices, such as waving good-bye, need not entail the existence of structured institutions "on behalf of" which one might act, and that, therefore, the institutional theory must show more than that the actions of those who confer art status are social practices. He doubts that this has been, or could be, demonstrated. Amazingly Dickie agrees with this verdict (1984, 67) and, in doing so, seems to throw his theory away, but his later discussion (72–75) suggests that he means to deny no more than that the structure of the Artworld is formalized. In denying now that artists act "on behalf of" the Artworld in conferring art status, Dickie means only that they are not *formally* authorized so to act by the Artworld. But I believe that Dickie is mistaken in accepting that one cannot act on behalf of an informal institution, provided that the institution in question is one structured (such as the Artworld must be) in terms of distinct roles carrying with them different authorities. In acting on behalf of the institution, the person acts by virtue of his position in the institution (but not by the consent of its other members).

What is at issue here is this: are the actions and practices of artists, art makers, art entrepreneurs, art audiences, and so forth intentional and rule governed in a way that justifies the claim that the Artworld is an institution socially structured in terms of roles such that some role occupiers might be said to act on behalf of the institution in presenting to other members of the institution objects for aesthetic appreciation? If so, is this fact essential to those objects' having the status of artworks? Obviously these are not easy questions to answer, given that the alleged institution is not formally structured (at least, not in all of its elements) and is both extremely complex and diverse. The final acceptability of the institutional theory rests on the plausibility of an affirmative answer to such questions.

The Isolated Artist

There is yet another potential problem for the institutional theory which it might meet by characterizing the institution of the Artworld as generated out of the structure and interrelation of informally established roles. The problem is that of a socially isolated artist. It is counterintuitive to deny that art might be produced by a socially isolated artist. Now if institutions presuppose a social context, the possibility of an artwork's being created outside of any social context cuts the ground from under an institutional definition of art. Some art is created within an informal institutional context—some art perhaps could not be created at all were it not for that context. But, also, some art is produced in a context of social isolation. If social isolation precludes the presence of social institutions, it cannot be essential to something's being an artwork that it is created in accordance with institutional procedures.

The example envisaged in this objection must be distinguished from outwardly similar cases that can be accommodated by the institutional view—for example, that in which an artist creates a work though the full institutional context of the Artworld does not come into play. If both artist and artwork are destroyed by a bolt of lightning on the completion of the piece, an artwork may have been created despite its never being presented to an audience within the fuller institutional context. According to the institutional view, it is *candidacy* for appreciation/understanding, and not the actual occurrence of appreciation/understanding, which is necessary for the conferral of art status. (Terry Diffey, in 1969, surely is wrong in insisting that something becomes art only when it is appreciated by an audience. Jay Bachrach, in 1977, seems to follow Diffey, but a closer reading indicates that his concern is to stress that candidature must be merited by the piece's possessing properties that are appreciable as good or bad, whether or not anyone does appreciate them in fact.) Because it does not require an appreciative public as a condition for the production of art, the institutional theory can allow that a person with an awareness of the Artworld might create art at a time when he was socially isolated. Robinson Crusoe was as capable of creating art before he was joined by Friday as was anyone living in London.

Equally, an institutional account might deal with the case in which the religious artifacts of one culture are taken as art in another culture (cf. Cormier 1977). An institutionalist might here take one of three lines, depending on the facts of the case. (1) The pieces have been art from the outset, having been created within the context of an Artworld, though as artworks they were intended to serve a purpose within a religious institution. This might be the proper view to take, for example, of the church frescoes of Masaccio and of illuminated Bibles. (2) The pieces were not art, having been created within a religious world rather than an Artworld, and neither are they art now. An example could be the tile floors of many churches. (3) As in (2), except that now they are artworks, having had art status conferred upon them by someone acting on behalf of the (our) current Artworld. This may be the view to take of ornately decorated, jeweled crucifixes.

Similar considerations will be involved in the categorization of the objects that result from many other skillful activities, such as needlepoint work, scrimshaw, basket weaving, rug weaving, the making of musical instruments, of pottery, of fly-fishing lures, of decorated quilts, and so on. Where the skill is directed toward practical ends, and the craftspeople do not think of themselves as artists despite their obvious intention to produce an aesthetically pleasing product, then the cases are most appropriately to be classed as falling under equivalents of (2) and (3) above, depending on the extent to which the Artworld has recognized the skills involved as meriting photograph collections and displays in which the products are presented as artworks. In the absence of such recognition—that is, where (2) applies—the products of such crafts might be treated by some as if they are artworks and might be appreciated as "works of art" (that is, as works of skill), without thereby becoming artworks. Which of the crafts might become art kinds depends in part on historical accident—on the authority of the person who finds their products aesthetically pleasing. So rapacious is the pursuit of the aesthetically interesting by the present Artworld (a symptom, perhaps, that much contemporary art has lost touch with the point of art?) that many craftspeople are likely to discover, to their surprise, that they are artists. If they are not artworks already, the musicals of Rogers and Hammerstein (not to mention the songs of Lennon and McCartney) are bound to become artworks in the future (as has happened in the past to the operettas of Lehár and of Gilbert and Sullivan).

Rather than examples of the types described above, the objection to the institutional view conceives of a case in which a person who has no contact with an Artworld (or with society in general) intentionally and self-consciously produces artworks. (Versions of the objection are given in Beardsley 1976 and Levinson 1979.) The person in question might be a Stone Age cave dweller or a feral child raised by wolves. The claim is that such a person might, despite his exclusion from all Artworlds, produce works of art.

How might the institutional account of the definition of art deal with such a claim? It might do so in three ways. First, a proponent of the institutional view might accept that such a person could produce artworks and then defend her view by arguing that a socially isolated individual might create art just because such a person might also constitute an Artworld. That is, the institutional view might be defended by arguing that the informal institution of an Artworld might be constituted by a single individual. Alternatively, the institutionalist might reply by denying that such a person could produce art. That is, it could be alleged that the "paintings" (for example) of such a person should be classed along with those of a chimpanzee or (more charitably) along with the aesthetically pleasing religious artifacts of another culture. It could be denied that such a person could produce art on the grounds that such a person could have no conception of his products as artworks (even if the person's primary intention was to produce something aesthetically pleasing). That is, the institutionalist might deny the possibility of one's coherently describing a counterexample such as has been envisaged. (Dickie favors this second line of defense—see 1984, 52–56.) Finally, it might be suggested that we cannot but view such works as art because we cannot help but see them from the location of the Artworld in which we operate. In other words, it might be said that what matters for their art status is that the pieces be viewed from the perspective of an Artworld, whether their creator could have adopted that perspective or not.

Of these lines of reply, the first is the strongest in that it concedes without qualification the intuition that a socially isolated individual might create artworks. I argue below that this first line of defense is not so implausible as it might at first appear to be. The second line of defense is counterintuitive in denying that a socially isolated individual, such as has been described, could create art. Nevertheless, I contend that, if the first reply fails (which I doubt), it does so in a way that makes the second defense viable. To complete the picture, I develop the third line of response, which clearly reveals the problems that arise in describing the counterexample.

An (informal) institution could exist only where individuals might occupy different roles and act in accordance with rules that define those roles and the authority that goes with them. Commonly we think of different individuals as occupying different roles within a given institution. But we also recognize that a single individual might occupy different roles in different institutions—mortgagee, union member, lawyer, church elder. There is no reason to believe that a single person might not occupy more than one role within a given institution. Thus a lawyer might execute a will in which she is named as a beneficiary (though it might not be regarded as proper for her to do so). So there is no reason why an isolated individual might not occupy all or most of the roles we associate with the Artworld—artist, critic, audience, impressario, curator. (I describe the case as one in which roles are occupied, rather than as one in which points of view are adopted, because the individual may act on her judgments with authority. In this minimal case the authority is solely her own, and where there are no other members, this is sufficient.) On this account the creation of an informal institution need not presuppose multimembership, so there is no problem in accepting that an isolated individual might operate in an Artworld-of-one in which that person could produce artworks. Clearly, when the institution is as minimal as this, it will be virtually impossible that it lose contact with the point of art—but that is a fact an institutionalist might be happy to allow for this unusual case. Admittedly, this story attenuates the notion of an institution near to the point of vanishing, but so too, it might be countered, is the notion of art to which appeal is being made stretched almost beyond recognition.

This reply seems to invite a powerful objection: according to Saul Kripke's account (1982) of Wittgenstein's characterization of the conditions that permit the creation of rules and, subsequently, of rule-governed behavior, no socially isolated individual such as I have been discussing could establish any rules. If this argument is convincing, then it destroys the reply just offered, because an institution could be generated only by a person capable of deliberate rule following, and the individual described above is not such a person according to Kripke's argument.

It is far beyond the remit of this work to review the adequacy of Kripke's arguments and of the discussion that has been provoked. (For my own discussion of Kripke's view, see Davies 1988c.) Fortunately I need not pursue the matter here. If Kripke is mistaken, then the defense of the institutional view I have offered (that is, the "first line") may be adequate. Alternatively, if Kripke is correct, then the second line of defense of the institutional view will be possible (but still counterintuitive).

The second line of defense is as follows: Whether or not one is an institutionalist, it is hard to see how one could avoid accepting that the creation of art involves rule following. The intentions that artists execute in the creation of artworks are such that artists must be rule followers and aware of themselves as such (which is not to say that they must be aware that the rules they follow are rules for art production). For example, they must be capable of formulating the intention to go on in the same way, to create another instance of the same type of thing, and so on. To accept this (while accepting also Kripke's characterization of the conditions for rule-governed behavior) is to concede that a socially isolated individual could not be a rule follower and, hence, could not create artworks. Not only would such an individual be incapable of formulating the rules that might create an institutional context for his actions, but also he would be incapable of formulating any of the rules on which art creation depends. (For an interesting discussion of the musical case, see Wolterstorff 1987.)

The third line of defense was foreshadowed in Chapters 1 and 3. Any question about the prehistory of art, or about the practices of those who stand outside the Artworld, will be on shaky ground in asking about the status of pieces that were produced with the intention of fulfilling the function met for us by artworks, and that were produced in the absence of any full-blown institutional environment. In the same way, any question about the banking practices of some Amazonian tribe presents an obvious difficulty. Even if there is a description such that the members of the tribe do what we do when we deposit money in a bank, the absence of the institutional context calls into doubt the description of their action as banking. That such a description is in doubt is not in any way retrieved if it is a fact that our complex, formal banking institutions arose historically out of practices exactly like theirs.

The problem can be stated more abstractly. The concept of an artwork has a functional point in that we have a need to distinguish artworks from other types of items, since they meet (or are intended to meet) for us a need not met by other items. Whether or not, prior to the creation of an institutional context, something that is designed to meet that need is an artwork is a moot point. There is no reason to assume that anything that meets the point of art thereby is an artwork.

To put the general point another way: if the creation of artworks soon becomes institutionalized and operates for us in that way (so that when the institution and the function part company, the basis for the classification can be seen to be institutional rather than functional), the question about whether *Ur* art (such as prehistoric cave paintings), or the creations of those who do not belong to the Artworld, are artworks becomes for us a question about their place within our *current* institution. Then to ask, But was it art at the time it was made? or, Would it be art if the Artworld disappeared? is to ask a philosophical (and not a straightforwardly empirical) question, which calls for a definition of art by way of answer. (A similar point is made, I think, in McFee 1980.) Certainly such questions are not to be settled by discovering whether or not the *Ur* artworks are regarded (now) as artworks, because, as has been observed already, it would be quite natural for us to reach back to pre-institutional days and, retrospectively, to incorporate within the institution those pre-institutional practices and objects which had led to its formation. In this way one might accept that art was created prior to the formation of the institutional context in the sense that that which was created prior to the formation of the institutional context later could be accorded from within that context the status of art. In the same way, the creations of the isolated individual might be accorded art status by our Artworld. So the philosophically interesting question is not whether pre–art-historic pieces might be artworks, or whether isolated individuals might produce artworks, but is, instead, whether such works could have been art had the course of history been such that the institution of the Artworld never arose. The institutionalist will deny that this would have been the case. If this reply seems to be question begging, so too is the alternative reply.

Dickie's Definition and Aesthetic Properties

Several writers have noted that Dickie needs a notion of the aesthetic so that he can distinguish aesthetic appreciation from other forms of appreciation (McGregor 1974; Blizek 1974; Richardson 1976; Alexander 1976; Iseminger 1976; Beardsley 1976, 1982a; Korsmeyer 1977; Schultz 1978). The point is this: Dickie defines artworks as candidates for appreciation (or, in the later definition, for understanding), and this definition plainly is too broad unless a *type* of appreciation is to be specified. In this case the obvious qualification to introduce is that the appreciation be aesthetic.

The notion of "the aesthetic" is characterized and approached in different ways in the literature (see Zangwill 1986). (Recent books on the nature of the aesthetic are Hermerén 1988 and Mitias 1986, 1988a, 1988b.) According to the first, traditional view, aesthetic properties, such as beauty, have a natural import (which artists intentionally employ), and the aesthetic appreciation of art, like the aesthetic appreciation of nature, involves a concern with, and delight in, such properties. (Such a view has been presented in recent times in Sibley 1959, and retains a qualified importance in Beardsley's account—see 1979, 1982a, 1983.) A second view accepts the characterization of aesthetic properties offered in the first but argues that the appreciation of artworks involves an appreciation of many non-aesthetic properties—semantic properties, for example—which might be called "artistic" properties. (Such a view has been presented in Carroll 1986; see also McGregor 1974, Goldman 1990.) Proponents of this account may go so far as to deny that the appreciation of aesthetic properties has anything at all to do with the proper appreciation of artworks as artworks (see Binkley 1977, and for some interesting criticisms, see Savedoff 1989). The third view argues that all properties relevant to the appreciation of artworks as artworks are aesthetic properties. In other words, the third view extends the notion of the aesthetic to cover the properties recognized in the second view both as important to art's appreciation and as not covered by "aesthetic" as used in its traditional sense. To justify this move, it is argued that there are no "naked" aesthetic properties as conceived by the traditional view, and that all of the properties relevant to art's appreciation—ranging from complex semantic properties to simple, sensuous ones—take their significance entirely from their use in accordance with conventions that are mutable and are both culturally and historically relative. (I take Danto to be a representative of such a view—see 1986b.)

Dickie seems to hold the second of these three views. Although he allows (1977) that most artworks might have appreciable properties of the type traditionally called "aesthetic," it is clear that he believes there is much more to the appreciation of artworks than the appreciation of such aesthetic properties as they possess. This fact might explain Dickie's reluctance to describe the form of appreciation mentioned in his definition as aesthetic.

This reply does not meet the thrust of the objection. Dickie must still qualify the notion of appreciation to which he appeals in his definition, even if he will not choose to qualify it with the adjective "aesthetic" on the grounds that that qualification is too narrow. Presumably Dickie intends that the type of appreciation mentioned in his definition is the type of appreciation recognized as appropriate within the institution of the Artworld. In other words, the type of appreciation to which Dickie refers indirectly in his definition is the type of appreciation appropriate to artworks. For something to be an artwork, it must be appreciable (within the conventions in terms of which the products of the Artworld are to be approached) as an artwork.

This view of the matter raises another issue: artworks cannot be defined in terms of the distinctive mode of appreciation which is appropriate to them if, in its turn, that mode of appreciation only is identifiable as the form of appreciation appropriate to artworks. Accordingly, then, to the extent that Dickie's definition appears to be circular, he cannot break free of the circle by the way in which he analyzes the term "appreciation" (or, in the later version of the definition, the word "understanding"), because that analysis cannot be developed adequately without mention of the fact that that form of appreciation standardly takes artworks as its objects. If he is to break free of the circle, Dickie must focus on what it is about the institutional context which makes possible that form of appreciation.

The Circularity of Dickie's Definition

If we think of artists as persons, rather than as occupants in some of their actions of informally defined roles, then the institutional account of the definition of art cannot avoid appearing to be painfully circular. Art is that which is presented as a candidate for appreciation/understanding within the context of the Artworld; and to present something as a candidate for appreciation/understanding is to act as an artist does. But how can "acting as an artist does" be characterized, with the emphasis on the action instead of on the authority of the role, without invoking the *explanandum?* Or again, if we reject, as Dickie does, any psychological or phenomenological account of the appreciation standardly invited by artworks, how can we characterize the type of appreciation/understanding mentioned in Dickie's definition without presupposing what is supposed to be defined—what an artwork is?

Dickie acknowledges the circularity involved. Indeed, he flaunts it as mirroring the inflected nature of the concept of art. What matters, he suggests, is the distance traveled, rather than the circularity of the route (1984, 77–82). Surely he ought not to be so sanguine. Circularity will be a fault in any definition that purports to have explanatory power (Beardsley 1976, Welsh 1981, Todd 1983, Walhout 1986, McFee 1986, Stecker 1986, Levinson 1987a, Chambers 1989). Moreover, Dickie's attitude cannot but give force to the major worry about the institutional definition of art—namely, that the Artworld is identifiable only because art exists independently of it, and not vice versa (Crowther 1981).

If the circle can be broken, as I believe it might be, then the theory is the better for this fact. There are three ways in which the circle might be breached. Neither the first nor the second approach produces desirable results. The third is satisfactory from the point of view of an institutional definition of art.

The first possibility for breaking the circle already has been rejected as not being available to Dickie. One might argue that aesthetic appreciation is distinctively different from other forms of appreciation. An artwork, then, will be a candidate for this special type of appreciation. Those who have argued that Dickie needs an account of the aesthetic may, in making this point, perhaps (wrongly) see this as the way to avoid circularity in the definition.

But this approach could not appeal to Dickie, who has been a fervent critic of attempts to describe a distinctive aesthetic attitude. (For one exchange on Dickie's views, see Saxena 1978 and 1979, Coleman 1979, Snoeyenbos 1979.) This is not to say that Dickie would wish to dispense altogether with a notion of the aesthetic. He has accepted (1977) that appreciability is a necessary, but easily satisfied, condition for something's qualifying for art status, and to allow this is perhaps also to concede that the piece in question must have some aesthetic properties (here construing "aesthetic" in the traditional sense outlined above). (For criticism of this point see Welsh 1981 and Mendenhall 1982.) It is to say, though, that Dickie does not think that art can be defined in terms of aesthetic properties, or in terms of a distinctive aesthetic attitude. Even were one to succeed in characterizing such an attitude as distinctive, it is difficult to see how that characterization could serve in the attempt to distinguish art from nonart, since it seems obvious that such an attitude could be adopted as easily (if not as profitably) to nonart as to art. Appreciability is mentioned in Dickie's definition, but not because a piece achieves art status in virtue of its appreciability. That a piece is judged to be likely to provide aesthetic appreciation can be a reason for the artist to decide to confer art status upon it, but what makes it art is that it has the status conferred, and not the reasons for the conferral of that status. In which case the appeal here to an aesthetic attitude breaks the circularity of the definition only at the cost of falsifying it, in that that attitude may be exercised just as readily toward nonart as toward art. (Dickie makes clear that this is his argument—see chap. 6

of 1984. Cohen 1973, McGregor 1977, and Mitias 1977 recognize the possibility of such an argument and wrongly think that resort to it would reveal an inadequacy in the institutional account.)

Second, one might follow Lord (1987) in arguing that Dickie's recent definition is indexical in that it "passes the buck" from artifactuality to the artist and thence to the Artworld, which it characterizes as *this* (our) institution. Since the Artworld is a hodgepodge of Artworld systems that have no essential, common property, and since there are non-Artworld systems, such as dog shows, which share the features of Artworld systems as these are described by Dickie, "Artworld" is a term with a reference but without a sense. "Artworld," by this account, is the name of our present system.

This argument breaks the circularity in Dickie's definition in that the definition is stopped short by an act of ostension which does not take us back to arthood. In this view "Artworld" is a proper noun, rather than the name of a kind of thing, and hence is a particular lacking an essence of the type being sought by traditional aesthetics. So it is that ostension, rather than the description of an essence, is appropriate. The cost of breaking the circularity in this way is, however, unacceptably high: nothing created outside of our current Artworld could be a work of art, and no other system, however much it resembled our Artworld, could really be an Artworld.

Dickie has indicated his unwillingness to embrace such consequences (1987). He accepts that his definition is indexical, in that the Artworld is a cultural practice that must be understood within the context of its own time and place. But he also accepts that cultures other than ours might have their own Artworlds (and, within them, create their own artworks). Thus, contrary to the view above, he holds that the Artworld is a kind of thing rather than a unique individual. Further, he accepts that his definition is circular, in that "the buck is passed" all the way round, whatever element of indexicality is inherent in the definition he has offered. Of course, this leaves Dickie with the problem that Lord's suggestion hopes to avoid—that of distinguishing non-Artworld systems from Artworld systems without appeal to the nature of the objects/events generated within them.

Undoubtedly Dickie's insistence on the acceptability of the circularity of his definition dodges, rather than meets, this difficulty.

The third way of avoiding circularity in the definition does so by characterizing the role of art maker not in terms of some type of action that anyone might perform but rather in terms of the limits of authority that define that role. (Anyone might say, "I declare you man and wife," but not just anybody can marry a couple in uttering those words—the person may lack the authority to marry people or may have the authority only in contexts other than the one in question.) Such a story must be available if the institutional theory is to be a plausible one. If an account can be given of the nature and limits of that role (or any role that carries with it the authority to confer art status), and of the social conditions that determine those limits, then the circularity can be broken. Provided that one can describe the limits of the role without appealing to the content of artworks (except indirectly, by reference to the history of the conventions employed in conferring art status), then the circularity is avoided in that the account of the Artworld need presuppose no particular identification of objects/events as artworks.

To put the point in more general terms: the circle will be broken if the institutional version of the definition of art provides an account of both the structure and historical basis of the Artworld as distinct from those of other (formally structured or informally structured) institutions and does so without reference to the character of any particular artworks. The product of the institution, artworks, then is distinguished from the product of other institutions as that which is generated within the institution of the Artworld.

Once again, the institutional theory can meet a difficulty faced by Dickie's formulation of the theory only if it concentrates more than Dickie does both on an account of the way in which the institution of the Artworld is structured in terms of roles differentiated with respect to their membership, authority, and limits, and on an account of the distinctive historical context out of which such an institution could have arisen.

The Point of Art and the Institutional Definition

In Chapter 2 I explained that procedural definitions of art have been attacked on the grounds that those definitions offer no account of the point of art, that is, offer no explanation of the importance of our distinguishing art from nonart. In this connection I cited both Dickie and his critics and rejected the criticism as question begging. An adequate general theory of art could not ignore a consideration of such matters, but an adequate definition of art perhaps could do so. (For an indication of the direction such a theory might take and of the difference between the enterprise of definition and that of theorizing, see Julius Moravcsik 1988.) Indeed, if the Artworld is essentially institutional, as the institutional theory maintains, then we might predict that a definition of art would refer to procedures and roles rather than to that which gives (or gave) them their point.

A different formulation of what is essentially the same criticism might be stated as follows. The institutional theory does not explain why someone who has the authority to confer art status would choose to exercise that authority with respect to one object/event rather than another. So it explains how something becomes an artwork without explaining why it is an artwork. There is an ambiguity in the question, What makes something a work of art? which is exploited by the institutional theory (see Wollheim 1983). It answers one interpretation of that question but, in doing so, ignores the interpretation that asks for the definition of art.

Again, the objection begs the question against the institutional theory's insistence that what is essential to something's being art is the procedure by which it becomes an artwork and is not the reasons the conferrer of art status might have for conferring that status. Art makers might, in any given case, have many different reasons for conferring art status. One good reason for conferring art status on a piece is that the piece would serve the point (or one of the points) of art—for example, that it be highly enjoyable when approached for its own sake as a piece of Driftwood art. An institutionalist on the definition of art might happily allow that the practice of art creation, as well as the evaluation of artworks, will inevitably pay heed to the function served by art in our lives. (Wollheim, in 1980, seems to doubt this; see McFee's 1985 reply to Wollheim.) But, as I have argued, it is far from apparent that the institutionalist must also concede that which would invalidate her theory—that art is to be defined in terms of its point, or in terms of an intention that it serve that point. What makes something an artwork is a matter of the way in which it acquires that status—not of whether, and how, it might merit that status.

The line taken by Dickie in *The Art Circle* (1984, 84–86) to criticisms of this type appears to be different from that which I have recommended. He seems to equate the importance of a thing with its essence and, consequently, denies that the institutional definition leaves out anything of importance. He also denies that art has any particular point, by which he may mean that there is no single purpose served by each and every work of art. (That this should be so is not surprising, given that procedure and point have diverged, so that not all artworks serve the point [or points] of art. But there is no inconsistency in holding both that our having the concept of art is to be explained by reference to art's having an important and distinctive place in the life of the community and that not all artworks serve the same [or any] purpose.) Given his consistent emphasis on the separation of classificatory and evaluative issues, and given also that his latest book (1988) is devoted to the latter and not at all to the former, it is proper, however, not to be misled by the passage to which I have referred. Dickie would agree, I think, that what makes something an artwork need pay no special regard to that which gives art its importance to us, and hence, that by no means all the important issues in the philosophy of art can be settled in a consideration of the definition of art.

PART II

Introduction to Part II

In the first chapter in this section of the book I consider the truth of the claim that it a necessary condition for something's being an artwork that it be an artifact. This artifactuality condition is emphasized by Dickie, who takes up the gauntlet thrown down by Weitz in his claim that the art status of Driftwood art shows that the concept of art is not governed by necessary conditions. In the discussion I focus on this debate, but the chapter is placed apart from the discussion of the institutional theory for the reason that most theorists appear to share Dickie's belief in the truth of the artifactuality condition. Beardsley, for example, regards the artifactuality condition as basically sound. Nevertheless, I argue that artworks are not necessarily artifacts as that word standardly is defined. Artworks often are associated with artifacts and may be embodied in artifacts, but many artworks, especially those which have or might have multiple instances, are not artifacts as such.

The conclusion for which I argue has several corollaries. (1) An artist might work upon a physical object with the result that it becomes indistinguishable in its appearance from a piece of driftwood on a beach. The product of that work might be both an artwork and an artifact. The material worked upon by the artist might originally have been an artifact (a chair, for instance), or it might not have been an artifact (a hunk of wood that could not even be classed as timber, for example), but in either case a new artifact was created. (2) The same person could remove from the beach the piece of driftwood mentioned in (1) and not only use it as an artwork might be used, but also confer art status upon it. The piece of driftwood then is an artwork, although neither a sculpture nor an artifact. That this artwork is not a sculpture does not, of course, prevent its commenting upon the tradition of hewn sculpture. (3) Similarly, a chimpanzee's daubs might have the status of art conferred upon them but would not thereby become a painting, although, as art, it would be paintings to which the piece would refer its audience. (4) As a urinal Duchamp's *Fountain* is an artifact. Duchamp's acts resulted in the urinal's acquiring the status of art but did not affect its artifactuality. *Fountain* is an artifact, but it is an artifact as a urinal, not as an artwork.

In a brief, following chapter I take up a similar issue—whether or not it is true that art and its objects come "indissolubly linked"—and, once again, my conclusion is negative. I approach the issue through a consideration of two different arguments. The first, presented by David Carrier, attempts to establish that people who live without artworks could not appreciate nature as we do. The second argument, offered by Richard Sclafani, holds that the concept of art, like that of a person, irreducibly contains both physical and interpretational or intensional elements.

My rejection of both the artifactuality and indissolubility conditions does not in any way represent a return to idealism. Rather, my point is that those who propose such conditions mistake a fact about the determinants of our concept of art *in general* for a fact about the conditions that determine the ontology of *each and every* artwork. Our concept of art would not be what it is were it not for a history of production in which artworks are physically embodied, usually in artifacts, but from this it does not follow that it is a necessary condition for something's being an artwork that it be embodied in an artifact or in any physical object.

Although these two chapters consider theses about the ontological nature of artworks, theses cited or implicit in many definitions of art, at first sight it might appear that they lead away from the theme of Part I, with its concentration on different approaches to the definition of art. That impression is misleading, for what emerges from the views discussed in Chapters 5 and 6 is a widespread commitment to the idea that artworks are distinct from natural objects in being the products of intentional human actions. The indissolubility condition, if it were true, would guarantee that artworks cannot be divorced from human "forms of life." The artifactuality condition, if it were true, would guarantee that artworks must be the products of intentional human actions. The artifactuality and indissolubility conditions together would guarantee that artworks must be different in kind, and not merely in degree, from natural objects.

As the importance of the intensionality of artworks emerges from a consideration of the artifactuality and indissolubility conditions, it becomes obvious that on this issue definitional and ontological questions intersect. This intersection is most clearly seen in approaches to the definition of art taken up in Chapter 7. As a definitional analog the version of the indissolubility condition which emphasizes the social character of art are the historicist definitions of Lucian Krukowski and Noël Carroll. As a definitional analog to the version of the indissolubility condition which emphasizes that the characteristics of art depend upon its intentional production is the intentionalist definition of Jerrold Levinson. The discussion of these views is preceded by a quick survey of influential theories that set the scene for the historical/intentional approaches. I am critical of the historicist's approach to the definition of art to the extent that it tends toward nominalism. Although the history of art is the history of a unified concept, the unity of the concept is not secured solely by its historical continuity, I believe. Such an approach is best to be conjoined with the type of intentionalism found in Levinson's definition, according to which what makes something an artwork is an intention that it be viewed as art has properly been viewed in the past.

At first glance historicial/intentional definitions fall outside the framework in terms of which I described the debate about the definition of art in Part I. I argue that this impression may be misleading because I believe that, when push comes to shove, such theories are inclined to lean either toward the functional approach or toward the procedural approach. Still, even if I am right in perceiving historicist/intentionalist theories as intermediate between the functional and procedural approaches, it need not follow, of course, that such theories can be assimilated to these approaches.

Does an emphasis on artists' intentions lead toward, or does it finally oppose, a functional or procedural account of the nature of art? If artists' intentions stand autonomously above the functionally or procedurally based conventions of art in that, although they might be influenced by such considerations, they control and give shape to them, then the intentionalist's definition not only will be distinct from but will be preferable to the two approaches to the definition of art on which I concentrated in Part I. On the other hand, if artists' intentions ultimately are subservient to such conventions, so that an appreciation of artworks and their properties is governed by impersonal conventions (and by artists' intentions only insofar as they sustain such conventions), then the intentionalist approach to the definition of art should be reducible to a form of functionalism or proceduralism. Much of the argument in Chapter 8 is devoted to a consideration of these alternatives and, contrary to what appears to be the prevailing position on the issue, I prefer the second view.

Although the argument in Chapter 8 offers a defense of both functionalism and proceduralism against the rival intentionalist account, I turn in the final chapter to a consideration of the comparative merits of functionalism and proceduralism in accounting for the relation between artists' intentions and the artistic conventions to which those intentions so often give expression. The issue is an important one because it has been argued by Susan Feagin that the institutional theory, in particular, has difficulty in according a proper place to the role of artists' intentions in allowing, as it does in Dickie's version, that it is a necessary condition for something's being art that it be produced with the appropriate intentions. I argue that, in this, Feagin is mistaken and that, in fact, the procedural approach to the definition of art fares better than does the functional approach in explaining why we regard artists' intentions as critically relevant without, at the same time, treating them as autonomous determinants of the conventions in terms of which critical practice structures its interpretations of artworks.

It should not be surprising that, finally, a concern with the definition of art leads for its completion to a discussion of artists' intentions. Both Dickie and Beardsley include among the necessary conditions for something's being an artwork that it be intentionally produced with certain aims in mind. Moreover, intentionalist definitions, such as Levinson's, treat the appropriate intentions not only as necessary but also as sufficient for a piece's being an artwork. Obviously the elaboration of all these theories invites a close consideration of the place of artists' intentions in securing those qualities of their products which audiences attempt to understand and appreciate.

In brief: Part II begins with a consideration of ontological issues that arise alongside the definitional question and soon leads to a consideration of a major rival to the approaches to the definition of art on which I concentrated in Part I. Through a discussion of the status of artists' intentions, I attempt to show not only that the rival theories are not as autonomous as at first appears but also that it is the proceduralist, rather than the functionalist, approach which better explains the nature of our critical practice with respect to artworks.

CHAPTER 5

The Artifactuality Condition

So far one of Dickie's more important claims has remained unexamined—that a thing's being an artifact is a necessary condition for its being an artwork. Dickie is by no means alone in holding to the artifactuality condition. Indeed, the artifactuality condition is regarded as perhaps the least controversial part of his theory. To cite just a few examples: John Hospers says that "the quality of being man-made constitutes one necessary condition for an object's being called a work of art" (1967, 39). Marcia M. Eaton claims: "It is not possible that a thing count as a work of art unless it is also an artifact" (1969, 165). Richard J. Sclafani maintains that "artifactuality [in the primary sense of the term] is a necessary condition for applying the term 'sculpture' (and the terms 'art' and 'work of art' as well)" (1970, 109). Denis Dutton writes: "Every work is an artifact, the product of human skills and techniques" (1979, 305). For George Schlesinger "a work of art is an artifact which under standard conditions provides its percipients with aesthetic experience" (1979, 175). According to Thomas Carson Mark, "one may easily suspect that the alleged connection between art and work amounts to no more than the familiar (through important) observation that artworks must be made or done; that is, they must be artifacts and not just naturally occurring things in the world" (1980, 31). Edward Sankowski asserts "that Dickie is right in making artifacthood a necessary condition of artwor[l]dhood" (1980, 69). Harold Osborne holds the view that "whatever among natural objects is capable of arousing and sustaining aesthetic experience . . . we call beautiful; and whatever among artifacts is capable of arousing and sustaining aesthetic experience . . . we call a work of art" (1981, 10). Beardsley notes: "Dickie's stipulation that artworks must be 'artifacts', the product of human intentional activity, is to my mind sound" (1982a, 311). For George Todd (1983), "all works of art are artifacts, so long as 'artifact' is construed liberally to mean something like 'product of an intentional constructive act' " (1983, 262–63).

Randall Dipert goes so far as to suggest that the artifactuality condition renders unnecessary the rest of Dickie's institutional account. He writes, "If one can ever safely say that there is a consensus building, it is that art works must indeed be artifacts" (1986, 401). To which he later adds: "When we turn our attention whole-heartedly to the artifactuality of art works . . . it is not difficult to see that here is where the 'social' element enters the picture, and that it need not be introduced as a second, clumsy condition. The recognition of artifactuality, and of the particular intentions with which an object was made, is certain to require numerous social institutions and conventions" (1986, 404). Here Dipert rightly recognizes that artifactuality entails intentionality, and that the relevant intentions will be interpretable only when seen as operating within the appropriate institutional context. But he moves too hastily in dismissing the larger part of Dickie's theory, because that "second, clumsy condition" is what is needed to give content to the conditions of *relevance* and *appropriateness* which Dipert stresses elsewhere in his account.

Dickie has insisted on the artifactuality condition from his theory's first formulation. He now admits (1984, 44) that he once thought (1974, 45) that the act of conferring art status upon a piece, even were that act not to involve a change in any of the piece's properties other than its status, would automatically amount to the artifactualization of the piece. (Margolis 1975, 1979 rightly questions the acceptability of such a notion of artifactuality, as do Stalker 1979 and Fletcher 1982.) Usually the act by which art status is conferred involves the artist's working on a medium out of which a piece is created or thinking in terms of a medium and producing a specification to be followed by others in creating a work. Dickie's view was quite plausible for these standard cases. But Dickie also allowed that art status might be conferred on a piece of driftwood without its being altered beyond its being moved to an art gallery. In this non-standard case he thought that the piece achieved artifactuality just as, and through the same acts by which, it acquired art status. The artifactuality condition was a trivial condition in that its satisfaction was guaranteed by the success of the attempt to confer art status. The satisfaction of the artifactuality condition required of the art maker no thought or effort beyond that involved merely in conferring a title.

Dickie came to a new understanding of the notion of artifactuality, however, with the result that now he places yet more emphasis on the artifactuality condition. First, in 1975a he realizes that art makers might use (and have used) the machinery of the Artworld without giving that machinery a job to do and so might create (and have created) antiart. (Also see Sclafani 1975b.) It is not clear to me whether Dickie, at the time of writing his attack on anti-art, takes it to be an impoverished type of art or not to be art at all. Whatever he thought then, in 1979 and 1984 he plainly believes that art makers might use the machinery of the Artworld without their succeeding in producing artworks. He now recognizes that no *mere* attempt at status conferral could be successful without its involving work. He wishes to deny that a person could confer art status on a mountain range, for example, merely by an act of titling (cf. Binkley 1976, 1977). To acknowledge that the creation of art involves work, Dickie abandons talk of the artist's *conferring* art status in favor of talk of the artist's *achieving* art status. It is the work involved in this achievement which artifactualizes what is made into the artwork.

We need to recall here the polemical place of the artifactuality condition in the early formulations of Dickie's theory. Dickie insisted on the artifactuality condition in direct reaction to Weitz's statement (1956) that the existence of Driftwood art shows that not even artifactuality is a necessary condition for a thing's being an artwork (see Chapter 1). Weitz reasons as follows: (1) a piece of driftwood can become an artwork without its being modified in any way beyond its removal to an art gallery; (2) the piece of driftwood is not artifactualized in the course of its achieving art status (because it is not worked on); so (3) the artifactuality condition fails to hold. Now in the earlier days Dickie rejected the truth of the argument's second premise, so he took himself to be able to reject the conclusion although he agreed with Weitz on the truth of the first premise. Moreover, and quite unreasonably, he took Weitz to be conflating the descriptive and evaluative uses of the word "art" (1969, 1971) since he believed that Weitz thought that the driftwood might become art without being removed from the beach. Weitz's discussion clearly suggests otherwise, which may be why Dickie has not repeated the charge in his more recent writings. (Dickie's confusion misled one commentator, who took Dickie to be saying that a piece of driftwood never could become an artwork—see Lyas 1973.)

Where, given his changed view of artifactuality, does Dickie stand now in his debate with Weitz? How can he now reject the second premise as false and continue to stand by the artifactuality condition? He does so by insisting that the driftwood, as well as achieving art status, is transformed into an artifact by the artist's work. In effect, then, the disagreement between Dickie and Weitz is (or has become) a dispute about whether or not the treatment as a result of which a piece of driftwood can acquire art status amounts to work of a kind that generates artifactuality.

Two Kinds of Artifactuality

I analyze below the notion of artifactuality to determine whether it is Dickie or Weitz who has the better of the argument. But before I turn to that analysis, I wish to elucidate a certain ambiguity in the word "artifact" as used by aestheticians and others.

In its primary (*a*) sense "artifact" means that which is modified by work, by contrast with that which occurs in its natural state. Many aestheticians and a very few dictionaries recognize the following as an alternative (*b*) meaning: that which has significance for the members of a culture; that which invites interpretation as opposed to mere explication. The ways in which these meanings differ is obvious. Implicit in the primary sense is the idea that an artifact is manufactured via the direct manipulation of a material item, the existence of which predates the creation of the artifact. This idea suggests in turn that the artifact must share at least some material properties with its progenitor, and hence, that artifacts are items of substance (and so to be distinguished from events, relations, attitudes, and so forth). By contrast, in acquiring social significance an item need not be altered in its physical properties. (For instance, a mountain might be invested with a religious significance for the members of a community as the home of the gods, or a saint's finger might be preserved as a relic.) More than that, there need be no physical, manipulable item out of which the item with cultural significance is created. (An item with cultural significance might be produced from nothing, as meaningful utterances are, for example.) Finally, things that between them realize the full gamut of ontological possibilities might acquire cultural significance. Socially significant items are as likely to be events, relations, fictional objects such as unicorns, abstract objects such as classes, and so on, as they are to be material objects subject to manipulation.

The point about the materiality of (*a*)-type items deserves amplification. The meaning just given implies that there is something that precedes and is worked on in the manufacture of an (*a*)-type item. That idea makes sense, I think, only if the progenitor of the (*a*)-type item is a locatable, modifiable individual. For example, a particular lump of wood is artifactualized in having a stool carved from it, even if the carver was interested in it only as a lump of wood and not as the individual that it was. If these observations are correct, linguistic utterances—for example, "This is a good theory"—cannot be viewed correctly as (*a*)-type items "manufactured" from the stock of words and combinative rules that constitute the language, for it is not as if there are lots of instances of the words of the language—for example, "good"—lying around for speakers to take up and use in the creation of sentences. In the sense relevant here, linguistic utterances are conjured out of thin air, rather than being manufactured out of locatable individuals with a prior existence, and so are not (*a*)-type items.

The claim that the meaning given in (*b*) characterizes a legitimate secondary meaning of the word "artifact" is debatable. Few dictionaries recognize such a use. I do not intend to enter into that controversy here. My aim is to mark the distinction, which I shall do by discussing (*a*)-type artifacts, on the one hand, and items of (*b*)-type cultural significance, on the other. The distinction is important for my purposes because it is clearly (*a*)-type artifactuality that is at issue in the debate between Dickie and Weitz.

Many writers in aesthetics invoke (*b*)-type cultural significance in discussing the artifactuality of artworks. Insofar as their usage is consistent, I have no argument with them. Yet others set out to analyze (*a*)-type artifactuality but quickly slide to a discussion of (*b*)-type cultural significance. No one makes this move more explicitly than does Joseph Margolis, who says: "We need not deny what is fairly to be taken by Weitz's opponent to be a necessary condition for an object's being a work of art, 'namely, that of being an artifact' " (1980, 84); "the work of art is of the genus 'artifact' " (88); "to say that an artwork is an artifact is (for the central cases) to say that some human being deliberately made it" (90); "we can liberalize the concept of an artifact . . . by conceding found art, readymades, anti-art, machine art, and animal art. The clue to doing so . . . simply construe as an artifact any object that may be said to have a culturally specified function" (91). I take Margolis's intention to be to preserve the artifactuality condition and to acknowledge the price of doing so: even if most artworks are (*a*)-type artifacts, not all are. (Francis Sparshott, in 1980, develops an account of art not unlike Margolis's, but he is less inclined to preserve the necessity of the artifactuality condition through the move from [*a*]-type artifactuality to [*b*]-type cultural significance.) One writer who does not make explicit his slide between the two uses of the term is Dipert (1986). With no suggestion that he is departing from ordinary, primary usage, Dipert soon is writing as if "artifact" means no more than that which is regarded as the outcome of an intentional action—and, according to his account of "regarding," one might regard something as the outcome of an intentional action without also believing it to be one (1986, 402–404).

Such a slide may be dangerous for this reason: while all (*a*)-type artifacts are (or have been) items with (*b*)-type cultural significance, not all items with (*b*)-type cultural significance are (or have been) (*a*)-type artifacts. There is nothing controversial about one's insisting that artworks necessarily are items with (*b*)-type cultural significance, whereas it is debatable that they necessarily are (*a*)-type artifacts. The dispute between Weitz and Dickie is a disagreement about whether or not the treatment as a result of which a piece of driftwood acquires art status amounts to work of a kind that generates (*a*)-type artifactuality. (Glickman, in 1976, takes the line that the debate between Dickie and Weitz concerns [*b*]-type cultural significance rather than [*a*]-type artifactuality, but he is rightly attacked on this score in Mitias 1978.) That disagreement cannot be resolved if what starts as an account of (*a*)-type artifactuality comes quickly to focus on the wider notion of (*b*)-type cultural significance.

Eaton, Sclafani, and Dickie on Artifactuality

Before discussing Dickie's views on artifactuality, I present and criticize the views of both Marcia Eaton and Richard Sclafani, since their accounts set the basis for Dickie's own.

According to Eaton (1969), workmanship or modification is at least a necessary condition of a thing's being an artifact. By "workmanship" she seems to mean intentional use. She describes this case: My friend is walking along a beach and wishes to warn me of an impending tidal wave. He comes across pieces of driftwood arranged by the wind and tide in the configuration TIDAL WAVE IN ONE HOUR. Without touching the driftwood, he uses it to warn me of the danger that threatens and then hastens down the beach to warn others. By his use of it, Eaton says, he turns the configuration of driftwood into a warning and an artifact, whereas formerly it was neither. So, on Eaton's account, it is a sufficient condition for something's becoming an artifact that it be used as such. She continues: a monkey cannot type a poem, but a person can make the product of a monkey's typing into a poem through her use of it—for instance, by submitting it to a journal that publishes poetry.

One might assume that Eaton here is discussing (*b*)-type cultural significance rather than (*a*)-type artifactuality. This presumption is strengthened by her choice of example—something that (in her view) becomes a sentence via its use as such. Linguistic utterances are not (*a*)-type artifacts. Nevertheless, her insistence on workmanship suggests, after all, that it is (*a*)-type artifactuality that is the target of her analysis. Her point, perhaps, is that the kind of work that generates (*a*)-type artifactuality is a matter of someone's using a thing as some (corresponding) (*a*)-type artifact standardly is used.

Sclafani (1975a) writes on a different issue while using Eaton's example. He considers a further case, suggesting that something with the form of an ax becomes an ax in being used as an ax might be used—in his discussion, as a decoration. In his view, mere recognition of the *possibility* of a use *as of an ax* would not make a thing with the form of an ax into one. The thing is transformed into an ax by being used intentionally as an ax could be used. (His discussion indicates that what matters is not that the thing be used in the standard manner, but that it be used knowingly in some way in which an ax might be used. What makes it an ax is its form, as well as its being used deliberately as an ax might be used.) On the matter of the typing monkeys, Sclafani agrees with Eaton—a thing might become a work of art through its being used intentionally as such.

Now an ax is an instance of an (*a*)-type artifact if anything is, so Sclafani's position develops Eaton's in suggesting that a thing might become an (*a*)-type artifact as a result of its being recognized to share the form of an (*a*)-type artifact and its being used intentionally as that (*a*)-type artifact might be used. If (*a*)-type artifactuality is a consequence of workmanship, then, Sclafani intimates, the intentional use of a thing (as a result of an acknowledgment of its form's adaption to that use) involves workmanship that results in the creation of an (*a*)-type artifact.

Dickie (1984) develops an analysis along the same lines as those followed by Eaton and Sclafani. In his case there is no doubt that now it is (*a*)-type artifactuality and not (*b*)-type cultural significance which is being discussed (see 1984, 43–44). In Dickie's current view (*a*)-type artifactuality can be achieved through a thing's use as a work of art. Just as a piece of driftwood used to dig a hole is made into a tool by its use, so a piece of driftwood uses as an artistic medium thereby becomes an artifact of the Artworld system by virtue of its use. The driftwood in either case becomes a "complex object"—*driftwood-used-as-a-tool* or *driftwood-used-as-an-artistic-medium*—and the (*a*)-type artifactuality acquired by the driftwood results from its intentional use. The piece of driftwood (which is not an artifact of any kind prior to its use) becomes an (*a*)-type artifact as the "complex object"—*driftwood-used-as-an-artistic-medium*—as a result of its use as an artwork. By comparison the urinal on which Duchamp conferred art status was already an (*a*)-type artifact as a urinal, but it became a "double artifact," a newly complex object, as a result of Duchamp's use of it as an artistic medium. Necessarily, Dickie insists, all artworks are artifacts.

As a characterization of (*a*)-type artifactuality, Dickie's account fails. It is not the case that one makes a thing into an (*a*)-type artifact merely by using it as an (*a*)-type artifact might be used. That a thing may be used as an ax or a spade commonly is used does not show, I believe, that it is an ax or a spade. (If a salesman tries to sell me a piece of driftwood when I have asked for a spade, I would object that it is not one, even if I appreciate that it might be used effectively as a spade.) To make a thing into an (*a*)-type artifact is to work on it. Not just any change wrought on a thing through its use amounts to work upon it. Eaton, Sclafani, and Dickie talk about the work that may be performed *with* a thing, through its use, rather than the work performed *on* it. That a piece of driftwood might perform the function of a spade does not show that it is a spade. That a thing is given the standard (or a possible) use as of an (*a*)-type artifact does not show that it has been made into an (*a*)-type artifact. Dickie has not demonstrated that the type of work which results in (*a*)-type artifactuality has been performed on the piece of driftwood through its use as an artwork commonly is used. (For a different critique of Dickie's views on artifactuality, see Ryckman 1989; and for Dickie's reply see 1989b.)

Iseminger's Analysis of Artifactuality

I turn to Gary Iseminger's account (1973) of artifactuality, since it accords more closely with the view I support than do the positions already considered in that he holds that (*a*)-type artifactuality requires the modification of the thing artifactualized and not just that thing's use in modifying other things (also see Devereux 1977, Crowther 1981). In his view "artifact" is not the name of a type of thing but, rather, a way of indicating how a thing has acquired some of its properties. That is, things may have properties artifactually but not the property of being an artifact. The artifactuality of a thing is a matter of the causal history of (some of) its properties and of their intentional production. If a thing is an (*a*)-type artifact, someone has responsibility (as a consequence of his intentions) for the thing's having (at least one) "nonintentional" property, where nonintentional properties are properties not dependent upon any particular person's current mental state. (To use Iseminger's examples: "Being enjoyed by me" is an instance of an intentional property; "being enjoyable" is not—a thing is enjoyable or not, irrespective of its being currently observed and irrespective of its being enjoyed by any individual observer.) He continues: when a person creates an (*a*)-type artifact in creating a work of art, that person must be responsible for the generation of (at least some of) the artwork's aesthetic properties. By "aesthetic properties" Iseminger means properties of the kind characterized by Frank Sibley (1959). Iseminger is reluctant to specify just how many, or what proportion, of such properties must be generated before the (*a*)-type artifact one has created becomes an artwork, but he certainly believes that the generation of some aesthetic properties is a necessary condition for something's being made into an artwork.

If a person's creation of an (*a*)-type artifact does not alter its progenitor's aesthetic properties, and the progenitor was not already an artwork, then the artifact produced is not an artwork in his view.

Iseminger focuses on Duchamp's readymades. According to his account, Duchamp drew the attention of the Artworld to the aesthetic properties of a urinal when he presented *Fountain* as a work of art. These properties were properties *Fountain* possessed prior to Duchamp's act. Had Duchamp's act resulted in his intentionally generating new aesthetic properties in *Fountain,* Duchamp would have created an artifact that was an artwork. Duchamp's act has no such consequences, and, accordingly, either *Fountain* is not an artwork or it is not Duchamp's artwork. Duchamp is responsible for the readymades' acquiring some nonaesthetic, nonintentional properties, such as that of *being in a museum.* To that extent Duchamp "surely is responsible for their being artifacts" (1973, 12). These Duchamp-conferred properties do not quality the readymades as artworks, or, if they are artworks, as *his* artworks.

It seems to me that Iseminger is wrong here on four counts.

First, he is wrong in thinking that Duchamp did not alter the aesthetic properties of *Fountain.* I accept Danto's view that, as a result of Duchamp's actions, *Fountain* has properties lacked by other, indiscriminably similar urinals. For example, *Fountain* is about the whiteness it exemplifies, whereas other urinals do not refer to their properties, and, more important, *Fountain* refers to the antecedent tradition of sculpture. (Admittedly, the notion of an aesthetic property as used here is wider than that envisaged by Sibley, but so much the worse for the narrowness of Sibley's views on what sorts of properties can be aesthetically relevant—see the discussion of the notion of the "aesthetic" in Chapter 4.)

Second, Iseminger is wrong in holding that, had Duchamp altered the urinal's aesthetic properties (as I claim he did), he would thereby have produced a new (*a*)-type artifact. Not just any change in a thing's properties will result in the creation of an (*a*)-type artifact. If I paint my car a different color, I do not produce a new (*a*)-type artifact. If I paint a bit of driftwood, I do not create an (*a*)-type artifact (or if I do, much more needs to be said). In holding that "artifact" designates how a thing got at least some of its properties, Iseminger seems to commit himself to the unacceptably strong position that any deliberately produced change in a thing's "nonintentional" properties results in some degree of artifactuality. In Iseminger's view a person produces an (*a*)-type artifact in intentionally changing a thing's nonintentional properties, and the more properties altered by the person, the more that thing is artifactualized. It seems to follow (unacceptably) from his view that if I deliberately chop off your arm, then I have artifactualized both it and you to some extent. (Perhaps, though, it is part of Iseminger's view that the work not only be intentional, but also that the intention pay regard to the functional importance of a change in the thing's nonintentional properties.)

By contrast with Iseminger, I do not think that (*a*)-type artifactuality admits of degree. The (*a*)-type artifact may be more or less simple or may involve more or less alteration of its progenitor, but that does not mean that it is more or less artifactual. Unlike Iseminger I believe that, in the sense that is at issue, we use the term "artifact" to designate a type of thing and not just a type of property. For Iseminger it is both a necessary and a sufficient condition for a thing's being artifactual to some degree that some of its properties result from work performed on its progenitor. By contrast, in my account this is merely a necessary condition for something's becoming an (*a*)-type artifact.

Third, and similarly, Iseminger is wrong in holding that Duchamp is responsible for *Fountain*'s artifactuality in his causing it to have nonaesthetic properties, such as the property of being in an art gallery. Just as an (*a*)-type artifact is not necessarily produced merely as a result of one's altering a thing's aesthetic properties, neither is an (*a*)-type artifact produced merely as a result of one's altering a thing's relational properties—for example, by moving it to an art gallery. One does not turn something into an (*a*)-type artifact where it was not one before (or into a new [*a*]-type artifact where it was already one before) merely by changing its relational properties. I do not create a new (*a*)-type artifact merely by moving my car from the street to its garage; neither do I create an (*a*)-type artifact by moving a piece of driftwood nearer the north pole. (It has been suggested to me that natural gas becomes an [*a*]-type artifact as a result of being transported to a refinery prior to being treated. Obviously I do not accept that this is the case.)

Fourth, Iseminger is wrong in holding that *Fountain* is not created as an artwork by Duchamp. That is, I think that *Fountain* is an artwork and that *Fountain* is Duchamp's artwork, but that in creating *Fountain* Duchamp did not create a new (*a*)-type artifact. (Like Dickie and Weitz, I accept not only the truth of the first premise of Weitz's argument but also that the artwork is Duchamp's.)

To summarize: Dickie, Sclafani, and Eaton apparently accept that workmanship is at least a necessary condition of the creation of (*a*)-type artifactuality but think that workmanship of the type required might be exercised through the use of a thing, instead of on it. Iseminger recognizes that the work must be performed on (and not merely with) the artifact's progenitor, with the result that the progenitor's properties are modified. In my opinion Iseminger's is a step in the right direction for a perspicuous analysis of (*a*)-type artifactuality. But the kinds of modification which he countenances as generating (*a*)-type artifactuality seem to me not all to be of the right sort.

An Alternative Account of Artifactuality

So far I have been attacking the analyses of (*a*)-type artifactuality offered by Eaton, Sclafani, Dickie, and Iseminger. Those analyses strike me as very much at odds with the commonsense notion that they are trying to capture. Central to that notion, I have suggested, is the idea that, in artifactualizing a thing, work is done on it rather than with it. At this stage I should offer my own account of the character of that work. Instead of an analysis, however, I have no more to offer than a series of observations about what I take to be our standard use of the term "artifact." These observations will suffice, I hope, to set a context in which I can return to the main question addressed in this chapter: Can a piece of driftwood attain art status without also or thereby becoming artifactualized?

(1) An (*a*)-type artifact is a kind of thing derived from the alteration or combination of some locatable, manipulable (although not necessarily nameable) individual or individuals from which the artifact differs. (2) The progenitor of an artifact must be a material object or objects (in order to be capable of being selected for alteration and to be manipulable in the appropriate way). (3) An (*a*)-type artifact might be created by physical modification (for example, fiberglass is molded to shape a boat's hull), or by combination (for example, pistons and other parts are assembled together to form an engine). (4) Artifacts are material in the way in which their progenitors are. (5) The progenitor of an artifact can be another artifact. For example, plowshares can be made from swords. (6) Often the progenitor of an artifact, in being artifactualized, ceases to exist as the thing it was. For example, a hunk of wood ceases to exist as a hunk of wood in being made into a chair; ingots cease to be ingots in being cast as cutlery. This is not always the case. A piston remains a piston in being included in an engine. (7) Neither is it a sufficient condition for the generation of an artifact that the original item be transformed out of existence. For example, a car could be reduced to junk without thereby being artifactualized. (8) Usually the difference between an artifact and its progenitor is perceptible (since changes in material properties usually are perceptible). (9) And conversely, if something is altered in imperceptible ways, usually that thing has not been artifactualized. (10) The alteration of the progenitor must involve work of the "hands on," rather than the "minds on," variety. (If magicians really did change rabbits into handkerchiefs simply by waving a wand over a hat, those handkerchiefs would not be artifacts.)

Wieand, Silvers, and Wollheim on Artifactuality

The previous discussion has not exhausted all the possibilities. I mention here three other writers, all of whom recognize that work must be performed upon a thing if that thing is to become an (*a*)-type artifact (as well as a work of art), and each of whom gives a different characterization of the nature of that work.

Jeffrey Wieand (1980) allows that an artifact is something made by a human being, and he also allows that no person makes the piece of driftwood. He also notes that the piece of driftwood is featured as an element in a display that someone creates. In his view the artwork is the display in which the piece of driftwood is used. And this artwork is an artifact by virtue of its being manufactured by a human being.

Ingenious though this ploy is, it strikes me as no more than a ploy. Someone is responsible for the display in which *Mona Lisa* is the centerpiece—that is, is responsible for the wall color, the lighting, the height and angle at which the painting hangs, and so on—but we would not normally say that that person has created an artifact, and neither would we say that she has created an artwork. (Admittedly the analogy is not exact. Wieand's presenter of the driftwood must decide its orientation, and that is not a choice left to the discretion of the hanger of the *Mona Lisa.* Such considerations lend plausibility to his analysis—but not sufficient plausibility, I think.) Wieand's proposed solution to the problem of the alleged artifactuality of Driftwood art strikes me as ad hoc. The piece of driftwood (and not the display in which it features) is the artwork if anything is—though this is not to say that its institutional setting is unimportant, and neither is it to say that the piece of driftwood would have been an artwork if it had been left on the beach after having been admired (but no more than that) by an artist or gallery director. Driftwood art is unusual as art, but its peculiarity does not consist in the fact that, whereas the display of the piece is incidental to the identity of the artwork ordinarily, in the case of this art form the display of the piece constitutes the artwork.

Anita Silvers (1976) takes a line not unlike Wieand's in arguing that such pieces as Duchamp's readymades involve in their creation (as art) work that goes beyond mere status conferral. She notes that they have signatures, titles, and the like—that Walter de Maria's *High Energy Bar* includes, as well as the iron bar, a certificate made by the artist testifying to *High Energy Bar*'s authenticity as a work of art.

Again I find the line unconvincing. I agree with Dickie that *mere* titling does not amount to the kind of work which gives rise to artifactuality. But I do not accept that every artwork has been marked in some way that distinguishes it perceptually from its (putative) real counterparts, and neither do I accept, therefore, that every artwork has been worked on in a way that artifactualizes its progenitor. It might be hard work to carry a urinal to an art gallery, but that is not the kind of work, I have argued, which results in artifactuality. For many artworks, no artifactualizing work—no marking, certifying, or whatever—is performed in their achieving art status.

Richard Wollheim (1973) presents a different view. He notes that the work done by artists in making works of art might take three forms: (1) work *tout court* (for example, applying the paint to the canvas); (2) the decision that the work has gone far enough; (3) destruction—that is, the fragmentation, differentiation, or disintegration, perhaps to the point of nothingness, of some image that prefigures the artwork. Minimal art celebrates the second form of work, Wollheim suggests. According to his view, when Duchamp says of a urinal, "That's how I want it," his gesture is continuous with an art-making tradition in which the artist, qua master, tells the audience what they are going to get.

Thomas Carson Mark (1980) has objected that, at best, Wollheim's argument establishes that Minimal (so-called) artworks are artifactual, not that they are art. In fact, careful as ever, Wollheim claims to establish neither thesis. Clearly he takes artifactuality to be important (see 1980, sections 43, 44, and 54), but he seems to stop short of endorsing the artifactuality condition. Wollheim is wise to be circumspect because, even if the second form, when coupled with the first or third, is a recognizable phase in the production of artifacts and artworks, it is not clear that the second form, on its own, amounts to work, or to work of a kind that results in the creation of an artifact. When it is not preceded by work of the first form, "That's how I want it" is indistinguishable from "I'll take it just as it comes." And "I'll take it just as it comes" reports a decision not to work on the thing, and not some special form of work.

The Views of Beardsley and Sankowski

Where does the discussion of artifactuality leave us in the dispute between Dickie and Weitz? The disagreement was about the soundness of Weitz's argument, which I characterized thus: (1) a piece of driftwood can become an artwork without its being modified in any way beyond its removal to an art gallery; (2) the piece of driftwood is not artifactualized in the course of its achieving art status (because it is not worked on); so, (3) the artifactuality condition fails to hold.

One might agree with Weitz that (2) is true and also agree with Dickie that the argument is unsound, provided that one disagreed with both Dickie and Weitz on the truth of (1). In effect this is the position taken by Daniel Devereux (1977), Edward Sankowski (1980), James Fletcher (1982), and Monroe Beardsley (1983).

Although he does not analyze the notion closely, Sankowski comes close to my own view in insisting that artifactuality involves the modification of something's perceptible, intrinsic (by contrast with relational) properties. But because he insists that the artifactuality condition holds for art, he argues that both Weitz and Dickie are mistaken in believing that the piece of driftwood could be an artwork, since it is not artifactualized in being treated as Weitz describes. Sankowski's reason for believing that the artifactuality conditions holds is this: artifacts, as the products of intentional actions, have properties associated with artworks which could not be possessed by items that are not intentionally produced. Wieand (1980) has attacked this enthymeme, as well he might. All that follows from Sankowski's claim, according to Wieand, is that, as an artwork, the driftwood could not have the same properties as an intentionally produced artwork. Whereas, to make good his insistence on the artifactuality condition, Sankowski would have to argue that we can recognize as art only those items whose aesthetically relevant properties depend upon their intentional production.

Beardsley holds that artworks must be the products of intentional human activity and continues: "I think it is a mistake to confer artistic status on found objects untouched by human hands, or arrangements, however aesthetically interesting, in the genesis of which no intentions at all played a part" (1982a, 312). This seems to imply that one could confer art status on a found object, although one ought not to do so. But elsewhere in the same paper, Beardsley makes quite clear that, while such things might be called "art," he does not regard them as artworks in the fullest sense of the word, so the "mistake" to which he refers must be the mistake of trying to do something that, anyway, is impossible. (There is another possible ambiguity in the quoted passage which should be clarified: Beardsley does not mean that a piece of driftwood might attain full art status in being transferred to an art gallery, but that it could not be art so long as it is left on the beach. His view is that, to become *real* art, a piece of driftwood would have to be worked on and not merely relocated. Note that Beardsley may not be against regarding so-called Driftwood art as art in something less than the full sense of the word, given that it was presented with the appropriate intention and that the piece rewarded the effort of aesthetic appreciation. That is, he seems to imply that Driftwood art is not so far beyond the pale as is so-called Conceptual art, which amounts to no more than "indexing one's own anxieties.")

I have already discussed the claim to art status of Driftwood art in Chapter 3 and look more closely at the importance of artists' intentions in Chapter 8, so here I only state that, unlike Devereux, Sankowski, Fletcher, and Beardsley, I see no major problem in our accepting that a piece of driftwood might become an artwork (in the classificatory sense of the term), as might a urinal, though I also maintain that it is possible for a piece of driftwood or a urinal to become artworks only within an established tradition within which most artworks are not of these types.

Back to Dickie versus Weitz

My acceptance of the truth of the first part, (1), of Weitz's argument, when coupled with my views on artifactuality, leads me to side with Weitz in his dispute with Dickie about Driftwood art. I agree that a piece of driftwood can become a work of art without its being turned into an (*a*)-type artifact and, hence, that artifactuality is not a necessary condition for art status. The piece of driftwood is not worked on and, therefore, not turned into an (*a*)-type artifact when its treatment consists in no more than its removal to an art gallery. The driftwood is used as an artwork standardly is used without thereby becoming an (*a*)-type artifact, even if most artworks are (*a*)-type artifacts and were designed as artifacts specifically for that use. Similarly, I maintain that Duchamp's use of his readymades did not amount to his working on them in such a way as to turn them into new kinds of (*a*)-type artifacts. Their status as (*a*)-type artifacts was determined by the actions of those who made them originally and was not altered by Duchamp's acts.

How, if not by being artifactualized, does the driftwood become an artwork? Is it simply a matter of the driftwood's being used as if it were an artwork?—not according to the account I have defended above. Just as a thing might be used as an (*a*)-type artifact is to be used without its becoming an (*a*)-type artifact, so a thing might be used as an artwork standardly is to be used without thereby becoming an artwork. I believe, in short, that the use of a thing as of an artwork is not a sufficient condition for its becoming an artwork. A piece of driftwood, or a bottlerack, might have been used as artworks commonly are to be used without their having had art status conferred upon them.

How, if not by being artifactualized and if not by being used as artworks standardly are to be used, does the driftwood become an artwork? Dickie is right to think that, merely to utter the words "I dub thee an artwork called 'Fred' " in front of a mountain or whatever, is not, usually, a way of creating an artwork. To that extent Dickie is right to be skeptical of attempts to create art merely by acts of titling. By no means everybody is entitled to employ the procedures of the Artworld in that fashion. But an institutionalist might allow that titling can create an artwork as long as the person involved is authorized so to create them. "Mere titling" is mere word mouthing. What makes the attempt at titling successful is the agent's authority and the use of that authority within the appropriate context. This is not to say that what brings off the trick, when it succeeds, is the tactic of not pronouncing the words until the item in question has been dragged inside the portals of an art gallery. The authority exercised in art making resides in the role, rather than in the mortar of a building, though it might be harder to exercise the role successfully out in the fresh air than within the hallowed walls.

The Connection with Ontology

My denial of the necessity of (*a*)-type artifactuality for art status should not be surprising, for by now it should be obvious that, according to my analysis, many artworks of the most familiar kind are not (*a*)-type artifacts as such. A book or a manuscript is an (*a*)-type artifact. But *Anna Karenina* is not an (*a*)-type artifact, since its creation (as a story, rather than as an inscription of the story) does not involve a physical alteration in the properties of some preexistent thing. Literature might be created and perpetuated within a purely oral tradition. In fact, any art form the artworks of which might have multiple instances—performances, copies, prints, casts—involves the creation of artworks that are not (*a*)-type artifacts as such. Typically, however, such artworks are recorded and transmitted via the creation of (*a*)-type artifacts—books, manuscripts, musical scores, woodblocks, molds, silkscreens, film—though this incarnation is by no means necessary for their survival, as ballet testifies.

Compare this with the view of Margolis in 1977. Margolis insists, and I agree, that all types of art are instantiated by either a token-instance or a notation by reference to which admissible instances of the particular type-work may be generated. I note, however, that his concentration on the embodiment of artworks in objects (see 1974) leads him to ignore such cases as an oral tradition of literature. I also agree that Duchamp made a token-of-the-type of *Bottlerack,* even though he did not make the bottlerack that is *Bottlerack*'s raw material. But I do not accept the inference Margolis draws from this without further argument (1977)—that these facts show that artifactuality is never superfluous. I have denied that the work involved in conferring art status in such cases is work of a kind that results in (*a*)-type artifactuality.

By contrast with "novel," "symphony," and the like, "sculpture" and "painting" often designate (*a*)-type artifacts, I believe. (Casts, lithographs, and the like will not result in artworks that are [*a*]-type artifacts, as previously indicated, but a hewn sculpture and an oil painting are such artworks.) The sculptor may produce no more than a specification executed by the workers at a foundry, but the sculpture is what is produced by the cooperative effort. The sculptor might not dirty his hands but, in producing a specification executed by others, cannot be indifferent when acting as a sculptor to what is involved in working with and within the physical medium involved. The point, of course, is that a singular sculpture is the product of work upon a preexistent (collection of) material that is altered in its physical properties in being transformed into a sculpture.

If, as I claim, (*a*)-type artifactuality is not a necessary condition for a thing's acquiring art status, what then is the connection between art status and (*a*)-type artifactuality? Most artworks are either (*a*)-type artifacts (oil paintings, hewn statues) or are embodied in or specified by (*a*)-type artifacts (musical scores, scripts, books, manuscripts, prints, cast sculptures). It is highly improbable that a people might share our concept of art were their aesthetic experience confined exclusively to objects that are natural in their occurrence. It is similarly odd to suggest that a people whose aesthetic experience was confined only to an equivalent of our Conceptual art would share our concept of art. Our concept of art would not be what it is were it not for the fact that artworks typically are, or have been betokened by, (*a*)-type artifacts.

To explain the central importance of a connection between artworks and (*a*)-type artifacts, we need not hold that only (*a*)-type artifacts can be works of art. Rather, we need allow no more than that Conceptual art could be art only because art in the past was neither solely conceptual nor solely natural in its occurrence. The importance of (*a*)-type artifactuality in the specification or embodiment of artworks is historical rather than ontological. The Minimalist artist works against the background of the prevailing conventions and, hence, the history of art. As a result her works must be seen as referring to all the aesthetic techniques and properties that she has eschewed. The same is true of the "beach artist." Similarly, the Conceptual artist cannot but refer to the physical properties that are absent for their relevance in his work.

Necessarily an artwork possesses at the time of its creation (*b*)-type cultural significance. Typically, investing something with (*b*)-type cultural significance as an artwork involves more than conferring upon it mere status. Usually art creation goes hand in hand with the production of (*a*)-type artifacts, some of which are artworks and others of which are specifications for, or instances of, artworks. No artwork, however, need be an (*a*)-type artifact; neither need it be embodied in an (*a*)-type artifact in order that it refer to the tradition of artistic creation as involving the manipulation of a physical medium. The appropriate reference is guaranteed by the location of the piece within the art-historical context. Just as no artist can succeed in casting aside what Danto has called "the atmosphere of theory" which surrounds art because its objects are items with (*b*)-type cultural significance, so no artist can succeed in casting aside an *atmosphere of practice* which acknowledges that the work of art creation commonly results in the production of (*a*)-type artifacts.

This then is the connection between (*a*)-type artifactuality and art status: our concept of art presupposes a history of artists' working to produce artworks. Typically, though not necessarily, that work manifests itself in the creation of (*a*)-type artifacts (some of which are artworks and some of which embody or specify artworks). This does not mean that every artwork must be, or must depend for its existence on, an (*a*)-type artifact. Neither does it entail that any of the artworks of the future need involve the creation of (*a*)-type artifacts. Those who hold to the artifactuality condition mistake a historical for an ontological necessity. The artifactuality condition is false.

CHAPTER 6

The Indissolubility Condition

At the end of Chapter 5, I denied that instances of artworks need be embodied in material objects. It might be thought that this claim goes too far. Even if it has been established that artworks are not necessarily artifacts, it is not thereby established that artworks are not necessarily embodied in physical objects. This second condition is weaker than the artifactuality condition in being more general. If I am to dismiss the necessity of this further condition for something's being an artwork, additional discussion is needed.

Wollheim and the Indissolubility of Art and Its Objects

In *Art and Its Objects,* Richard Wollheim says that art and its objects come indissolubly linked (1980, preface). Divorced from the context of his discussion, the remark is enigmatic. Is it an empirical claim, that these two things happen always to occur in constant conjunction? Or, instead, is a conceptual point being made, that objectivity is a necessary condition for art status? And if it is a necessary claim, does it state that, necessarily, two things, irreducible with respect to each other, are inseparable? Or is it, instead, a way of stating their identity? More than this, is "art" to be understood here as referring to no more than its instances, artworks, or to be understood as referring, instead, to some wider notion, paying heed to the skills and circumstances of production? And is "object" to be understood as referring to mere physicality, or to artifactuality, or even to artworks (that is, the objects of art)?

The detail of Wollheim's discussion provides a grip on these questions. His concern is to oppose two theses: that artworks merely are physical objects and that artworks are "ideal" objects. One way of glossing the indissolubility thesis is this: necessarily, to be recognized as art, the objects of art (that is, artworks) must be interpretable as such, and the possibility of such interpretation presupposes both that the production of art takes place within a form of life and that this production results in a public object (typically, an object with physical existence) which then, and as such, is available for interpretation.

Suppose now that this is a correct account of Wollheim's position and also that his position is correct. Still some issues remain to be resolved. For instance, does the position rule out the possibility of Conceptual art, as pseudo-art the objects of which are "ideal?" And does it rule out the possibility of Minimal art, as pseudo-art the objects of which are merely physical? Does it rule out the possibility of a world in which there are no artworks but in which the inhabitants view nature as if it were art? And does it rule out the possibility of artworks retaining their art status when the form of life from which art derives its point for us is lost? These are not questions Wollheim answers explicitly, although he has written about Minimal art as if it is art (1973); so, in pursuing such questions, I investigate arguments offered by Carrier and Sclafani and not those presented by Wollheim himself.

Carrier on the World without Artworks

David Carrier (1979) aims to reach what he takes to be Wollheim's conclusion by a different route. According to his approach, we look at nature as we look at art. That is to say, in viewing nature we do not solely concern ourselves with the kind of beauty that might be exhibited by an attractive person or a sunset. Rather, we view aspects of nature in terms of the conventions against which we understand artworks, seeing them (counterfactually) as representational, expressive, as rococo rather than classical, and so forth. In adopting an aesthetic attitude to nature, we consider it as if it were the product of an artist who works within the conventions that characterize an artistic style or period.

This fact raises for Carrier the following question: Is our aesthetic concern with nature merely influenced by our attitude to art or, rather, is it dependent upon our attitude to art? Carrier believes that the latter is the case and attempts to demonstrate this view by arguing that, in a world like ours in all respects except for the absence of artworks, people could not experience nature aesthetically as we do. In such a world the people might adopt an aesthetic attitude to nature, concerning themselves with natural beauty, for example, but our aesthetic experience of nature goes far beyond this concern. So, Carrier argues, the inhabitants of this other world could not share with us our different and richer aesthetic experience of nature.

I agree with Carrier that we experience nature aesthetically through the prism of art, and, further, I agree that the artistically relevant properties of artworks are different in kind, and not merely in degree, from the aesthetic properties exhibited in nature when it is not regarded as art is regarded. Nevertheless, I am unconvinced by his argument to the conclusion that people in a world without art could not experience nature aesthetically, as we experience both art and nature. That is, I reject his conclusion that people without art could not experience nature aesthetically as if it were art.

Carrier's argument has two parts, the second being "an analogous point." He does not explicitly connect the two parts of his argument, but there is a way in which they might be seen as connected.

Part 1: Carrier (rightly) points out that the way in which we view art presupposes its intentionality. "In scrutinizing an art work we assume that every feature is intentionally planned, and hence meant to be interpreted" (1979, 60). The people in the world without art, if they are to experience nature as we do, must experience it in a similar way.

He believes that it is "incoherent" to claim that they might do so: "The society of 'art without its objects' looks at the world as if it were an art work. They behave, that is, as if they had our concept of an art work, and thus our concept of an artist who intentionally creates every feature of his work. But what is incoherent, finally, about that fantasy is to imagine the society behaving in such a way without having the 'objects of art,' art works" (1979, 60).

Carrier's point here cannot be that, for the people in the world without art, any such aesthetic experience of nature must rest on thoughts entertained without belief. If that were his point, it would count equally against us, since our experience of nature as representational and so on is just as counterfactual as is theirs. Rather, his point must be this: whereas it is "coherent" for us to imagine that nature has been created by artists, since we have already the idea of art as the product of artists' efforts, it is not "coherent" to think that the people in the world without art would or could make an equivalent imaginative leap.

I find this claim implausible. Perhaps it is unlikely that the people in the world without art would make the imaginative leap, given that they are not familiar with worldly artists. But that which is unlikely is not thereby "incoherent." (If one invents fantasy worlds for the sake of argument, one ought to be prepared to allow their denizens to perform possible but unlikely feats!) They might need to be more adventurous than we need to be in imagining that nature is the work of an "agent" who acts as an artist does (that is, as our artists do), but it is by no means "incoherent" to accept that they might display this type of imaginative adventurousness.

Another point is relevant: if the people in the world without art believe their world to be created by a god or gods with aesthetic sensibilities, they would not need to assume counterfactually that nature exhibits the kind of intentionality also displayed by our artworks. It is not "incoherent" to think that the inhabitants of such a world might believe that their gods act as our artists do, even if none of their members act as our artists do. (See, for example, the Socratic dialogue *Timaeus*.)

Part 2: Carrier (rightly) notes that, for us, art has a history that affects the aesthetic properties presented by artworks. Following Danto (1973), he notes that Duchamp could turn a urinal into an artwork only because the history of art had made such a development possible, and that, as an artwork, Duchamp's *Fountain* possesses aesthetic properties not displayed by its perceptually indiscriminable, nonart counterparts. And he (rightly) notes that *Fountain* would not be seen as art by the members of a world without artworks, who would be blind to its aesthetic properties as an artwork.

Carrier's point cannot simply be that the people in the world without artworks could not recognize *Fountain* as an artwork; neither can his point simply be that they could not appreciate the artistically relevant properties that *Fountain* displays. Those cannot be his objections because those objections apply equally to other people on our planet who have artworks but, because they live in cultures that differ from ours, operate within an Artworld, a cultural history, which is not shared with us. His point cannot simply be that the people in the world without artworks cannot appreciate *Fountain* aesthetically because they do not share *our* tradition of art history and appreciation. Rather, his point must be this: a people could appreciate nature aesthetically as we do only if, like us, they have a developing, historical tradition of appreciation; such a tradition could arise only in a world, like ours, in which there is a continuing history of the production of artworks recognized as such.

If this is his claim, I find it unconvincing. The issue is whether or not the people in the world without artworks might have (as we have) a history of appreciation which leads (as does ours) to altered experiences of what they view aesthetically. Carrier himself explains how, in his fictional world, a historical tradition of aesthetic appreciation might develop: "Before a certain date, nobody thought the aesthetic qualities of fogs worth appreciating. Then, once 'their Turner' discovered fogs, snow storms and heavy rains were also 'discovered.' All these scenes, previously disliked for not being clear, were now found to possess a beauty all their own, the beauty of indistinctness" (1979, 57). Following the advent of a Turner-like way of experiencing fogs, the aesthetic appreciation of the people in the world without artworks takes on a new character. They now notice, as they did not before, the absence of vague forms in aspects of nature which they have previously appreciated aesthetically, and so their appreciation of those aspects is altered. Just as we have a continuing tradition of artistic appreciation which, as it changes, affects the way in which we experience the art of the past, so, too, they have a continuing tradition of aesthetic appreciation which, as it changes, affects the way in which they experience natural events, such as sunsets, which duplicate the sunsets of the past.

So much for Carrier's arguments designed to show that the people in the world without artworks could not experience nature as we do (through the prism of art and art history). Such people might have a developing and continuing history of the aesthetic appreciation of nature (as we have for artworks and nature). And such people might (counterfactually if necessary) appreciate nature aesthetically as intentional, just as we (counterfactually if necessary) appreciate art and nature aesthetically as intentional.

As I noted, Carrier does not connect the two aspects of his argument. How could they be joined? One might argue as follows: even if the people in the world without artworks might have a history of aesthetic appreciation, they could not have a history of aesthetic appreciation such as ours, because there are intentions that artists have which could not "coherently" be imagined by the inhabitants of the world without artworks. Artists deliberately work with and within media—paint, marble, the twelve-tone scale, and so forth. These media are recalcitrant, in the sense that, for example, marble does not lend itself to the representation of the warm softness of skin, or the translucent lightness of lace. As Peter Kivy has observed (1984), the sculptor's success consists in her overcoming the intransigence of the medium in representing such things in her statuary. (Kivy's claim is too strong, but the sculptor must, at least, show an awareness of what it is to take account in her work of the properties of the work's medium—see Mitias 1978 and cf. Glickman 1976.) An appreciation of art is, inevitably, an appreciation not only of what is represented but also of its representation *through* a medium (Danto 1981). The medium of an artwork appreciated as an artwork is never transparent to its content. Accordingly, the appreciation of an artwork as such involves an appreciation of the artist's working with and through a medium that differs from, and is in some way recalcitrant to, its subject. Moreover, the choice of medium affects the artistically relevant properties of the resultant artwork, so that a correct awareness of the work's properties requires a recognition not only of the medium's recalcitrant character but, more generally, of the artistic possibilities offered by the medium. If we were to discover that a statue we had wrongly taken to have been worked in marble had really been worked in soap, we would not only revise our assessment of the skills displayed by the artist, we would revise our assessment of the work's artistically relevant properties. To appreciate art as art (or nature as if it were art) is to appreciate the (actual or imagined) artist's working with the medium, and to appreciate this use of the medium as generating the piece's aesthetic character. As I said previously, art is as much surrounded by an atmosphere of practice as it is surrounded by Danto's "atmosphere of theory."

By contrast with us, the people in the world that lacks artworks would not recognize the natural world as a medium. Even were they to believe that their world was created by an omnipotent god, the idea that the world's creator had to accommodate herself to the available materials would be foreign to them. Such a god would create what would become media for the lesser beings who come after and who must work within the terms set by the properties of the media as determined by their world's creator. Accordingly, in appreciating nature aesthetically as they do, they could not appreciate nature aesthetically as we do, for they would find in nature no evidence of artistic skill. They could not experience in nature many of the properties that we experience and appreciate in art as depending on the artist's mastery of his or her craft. They might have a historical tradition of aesthetic appreciation, but their history of aesthetic appreciation would differ from ours, which is a history acknowledging, at least in part, the solution of technical problems posed by recalcitrant media as generating (some of) the artistically relevant properties of artworks.

Once again the argument is underwhelming. If the people of the world without art practice crafts, such as bonsai, origami, and flower arranging, they will appreciate nature as presenting recalcitrant materials and so might imagine their world's creator as working within constraints inherent to the materials to achieve her effects. Indeed, if they believe their world to be created by superhuman, but not omnipotent, gods, this would be a matter of belief rather than imagination. (Again, see *Timaeus,* in which it is indicated that air, fire, water, and earth each have properties that constrain what can be done with them by the gods who work with them.) Even if the imagination of the inhabitants of this world does not take them so far, part of their aesthetic appreciation of nature might be an appreciation of its sublimity. Kant and Schopenhauer discussed nature as sublime—as inspiring awe in the face of its grandeur and immensity. Such an experience could involve, say, an awareness of the eons taken by the wind and water gradually to erode the sea cliffs, mountain ranges, and Grand Canyon (in the world in which they live) to their present, aesthetically pleasing shapes. Here indeed is appreciation of nature as a recalcitrant medium! Their aesthetic appreciation of the sublimity of nature would parallel our appreciation of artistic craft.

The debate might be taken a step further. It might be said that the preceding reply does not succeed entirely in meeting the objection. It shows that the people of the world without artworks might have a developing history of aesthetic appreciation, but it does not (of course) show that they have a developing tradition of art making as we do. Nature comes readymade, as it were. Today's sunset does not draw on and develop a genre established by the sunsets of the past, whereas artworks, through their constant creation, comment on their predecessors. (Elsewhere, and in another connection, Carrier implies that he might wish to develop his position in this way—see 1982.)

Two replies might be made to this point. It could be conceded that the tradition of aesthetic appreciation in the world without artworks differs from our tradition of artistic appreciation in the way indicated, but then claimed that the difference is one of degree rather than of kind. (After all, the aim is not to show that the occupants of such a world have exactly the same tradition of aesthetic appreciation as we do but, rather, to show that they might have a similar tradition.) Alternatively, it might be argued that the people in the world without artworks might indeed see each sunset as commenting on its predecessors—counterfactually, in imagining the sunset to be the work of an agent, or actually, in believing the sunset to be the work of a god with aesthetic intentions (and not necessarily the same god as the one who created yesterday's sunset, or stormy sunsets, or dawns, or whatever).

I think that Carrier argues against the possibility of a world in which nature is appreciated as we appreciate art, despite the absence in that world of artworks, because he believes that the possibility of such a world would show that art might exist in the absence of artworks. In fact, I doubt that the failure of Carrier's argument does carry with it the consequence he fears—that the inhabitants of such a world have art without the objects of art. What it shows (instead) is that there could be a world in which nature performs for its inhabitants the same function as is performed for us in this (our) world by art. It is not obvious that what performs the function of art thereby is art. The point is not that art is what we have and the inhabitants of Carrier's fictional world do not have what we have. Rather, the point is that there is no reason given here to believe that what settles whether or not something is an artwork is its performing the function or functions served by art. (Not even a thoroughgoing functionalist committed to the view that a minimal degree of functional efficacy is necessary for something's being an artwork need accept that functional efficacy is a sufficient condition for something's being art.)

An objection to my characterization of Carrier's argument is this: I have taken Carrier to be arguing about whether or not the world without makers of art is a world in which art exists, but his concern is not with the existence of art as such but, rather, with the possibility of anyone's adopting an aesthetic attitude in a world without ordinary, human art-makers. He talks about *art* as a way of avoiding the controversy that surrounds talk of an *aesthetic attitude*—and he wishes to avoid the controversy only because he does not wish to enter into that debate in making the points he has in the paper of 1979.

Even if it is true that Carrier means to show that the people in his fictional world could not adopt an aesthetic attitude to nature (as we do), it is not clear that he could (or would wish to) treat that argument as devoid of ontological implications. The story about the alleged impossibility of their adopting an aesthetic attitude to nature relies on the claim that the skill of anyone's adopting an aesthetic attitude must first be acquired with respect to artworks before that attitude can be taken with respect to nature (or to other kinds of person-made things). Just as I have rejected the claim that people without art could not view nature as we do, so I would reject the claim that people without artists could not adopt an aesthetic attitude to nature as we do.

Carrier's argument fails to show that the people in the world without art cannot approach nature aesthetically as we do. That failure however, does not entail that art and its works are not indissolubly linked. It would entail that only if their capacity to adopt the same aesthetic attitude as we adopt to nature depends upon their having art in their world, and I have argued that it does not. It depends, instead, on the possibility that something in their world fulfills for them the function fulfilled for us in our world by art. It is possible that this occurs without its also being the case that their world contains artworks.

Sclafani on the Indissolubility Condition

I have a related objection to a paper by Richard Sclafani (1975a), in which he claims that the existence of artworks presupposes their physical embodiment. He argues that artworks are no more dualistic in nature than are people and that, like the concept of a person, the idea of an artwork is a "conceptual primitive" with both physical and mental (or interpretational) aspects. Both aspects, he says, are necessary for something's being an artwork. Note that Joseph Margolis argues for very much the same position in 1968, 1974, 1977, and 1979. He too insists that artworks, or their specifications, must be materially embodied, that artworks have intensional, culturally emergent properties that cannot be analyzed reductively in terms of the properties of the material items in which they are embodied or in terms of which they are specified (see also Harrison 1968). In these and other respects, artworks are said to be more like people than they are like ordinary things. Many of the criticisms I offer below might also be applied to Margolis's view.

Sclafani illustrates his argument with two examples. The first is Eaton's driftwood naturally configured as TIDAL WAVE IN ONE HOUR, which then is used, without modification, as a warning. The second is that of something with the form of an ax which is taken and used as an ax might be—specifically, as an ornament hung above the mantel. Sclafani claims that these two cases are analogous in that the objects did not become a sentence and an ax until they were recognized as such and used. Sclafani thinks that mere recognition of the potential use would not make the objects into a sentence and an ax. They must also *be* used. He emphasizes that the recognition must be a "possible" one and that which recognitions are possible "must be given factual content by reference to detailed information about the histories, conventions, and social practices of communities of speakers as they relate to a particular issue at hand" (1975a, 21). The point of his argument is to show that, in these cases and by analogy in the case of art, what makes an *X* an *X* is as much its interpretation as its physical properties, that it is not an *X* solely on the strength of its having some particular set of physical properties.

I share Sclafani's intuition that these cases are analogous, but I disagree with his analysis. I do not think that the configuration of driftwood becomes a sentence in being used as one. There is, instead, something that is used *as if* it were a sentence, and it can so be used just because of its form. (Suppose, though, that the person found bits of driftwood shaped like letters and arranged them in the configuration TIDAL WAVE IN ONE HOUR. In that case a sentence would have been created. It would be a sentence composed not of letters but of things used as if they were letters. There is no reason why a sentence, to be a real sentence, must be composed of things that are real letters. After all, sentences can be spoken as well as written.)

Why deny that the configuration of driftwood becomes a sentence when its potential for use is recognized? I do so because I believe that, on Sclafani's beach, the driftwood is used as if it were a sentence in only one trivial respect. The person recognizes that others will wrongly assume that the driftwood has been deliberately arranged as a sentence. The person takes advantage of the likelihood of this understandable error, and the use of the driftwood amounts to no more than that. In particular, it does not consist in using the driftwood as if it were a sentence in the much more important sense of investing it with meaning. If the driftwood is not used as if it were a sentence in such a way that it becomes meaningful, are we to say that it is meaningless? If so, how can we make sense of the idea that those who follow have understood something about the weather which the first person wished them to understand? In general, users' intentions determine meaning on particular occasions of use, provided that there are conventions by which the audience can read off the utterers' intentions. Once in place the conventions take on a life of their own, carrying forward the job of conferring what H. P. Grice has called (1957, 1968) "timeless word-meaning" in the absence of an intentional use. So it is that dictionaries of the meanings of words can be compiled. Thus meaning and use are not always directly linked. My utterance might mean something other than what I mean by it, or "Polly wants a cracker" might be meaningful when enunciated by a parrot, or TIDAL WAVE IN ONE HOUR might be meaningful prior to its being seen by anyone. So it is that the first person who comes across the configuration of driftwood appropriates a meaning without thereby creating one. It is not improper to talk of the meaning of TIDAL WAVE IN ONE HOUR as not depending on anyone's using it in the standard manner as a sentence. It is not improper to speak of the meaningfulness of TIDAL WAVE IN ONE HOUR, although no one, not even the first person who expects others to take its meaning as something intentionally created, means anything by it. (For an application and adaption to aesthetics of the Gricean view, see Tolhurst 1979.)

Analogously, I do not believe that the piece of wood and slate naturally combined with the form of an ax become an ax in being used as one. There are, instead, two things that are used as if they were an ax, and they can be so used just because of their form. Axes (now) are like the vacuum cleaners described in Chapter 2.

Whether or not the analogy holds in the way that I have suggested perhaps is not important. What is important to Sclafani's argument is that there be an analogy between arthood and axhood according to which, just as something's being an ax is not merely a matter of its having a certain form, but necessarily is also a matter of its being understood/interpreted as having a potential for use and being used as such, so something's being an artwork is not merely a matter of its form, but is also a matter of its being understood/interpreted as having a potential for use and being used as such. That analogy is one I accept for the sake of the argument.

Even if we accept the analogy Sclafani aims to establish, clearly it fails to entail the conclusion he would have us draw, which is that artworks necessarily are indissolubly a mix of the material and the significant. Instead, the conclusion that follows is that artworks must be interpreted as artworks if they are to be recognized for what they are. This truth leaves open the question of the necessity of artwork's being materially or physically embodied.

Does Physicality Matter?

Where does all this leave the claim that art and its objects come indissolubly linked? That claim is presented by Carrier as a conceptual one with ontological implications. The ontological point is this: artworks necessarily have both a physical and an interpretational aspect. Minimal art is not art at all, since it denies the interpretational aspect; Conceptual art is not art at all, since it denies the physical aspect.

Sclafani seemingly shares this view and draws a further moral from the indissolubility thesis. He claims that when artworks become uninterpretable as such, they cease to be art. In his view a Martian archaeologist who comes across the miraculously undamaged *Mona Lisa* in sifting through the ashes of our long-dead civilization has not discovered an artwork, because no one could interpret it as such (see also Cox 1986). This strikes me as an overdramatic way of insisting that art be seen, as Wollheim would have it, as finding its place within the context of a form of life. That might be true without our also having to say that artworks cease to exist as artworks when later they are removed from that context. We say of Egyptian hieroglyphics that their meaning was lost to us until the discovery of the Rosetta Stone. By this we indicate that they had a meaning that we could not read until the discovery of the Rosetta Stone, and not that they were meaningless for the period during which they were untranslatable, only to become meaningful again with the discovery of the key to their translation. So, contra Sclafani, it would be quite reasonable to say that *Mona Lisa* remains an artwork although the Martian cannot recognize it as such. Just as I (for any "I") do not make something an artwork solely on the strength of my interpreting it as such, so something that has once become an artwork remains one in the absence of any or all *I*s.

This is not to say that artworks are indestructible. It is to say only that they are not destroyed solely by making their interpretation as artworks impossible. The *Mona Lisa* would be destroyed if the canvas on which it is painted were vaporized—though so many copies exist that the destruction of the *Mona Lisa* would not result in our losing a knowledge of all its properties. Artworks that exist in multiple copies are harder to destroy. Not only must all the existing copies be removed, all the means for reconstructing specifications from which copies could be made must also be destroyed. To rid the world of Tchaikovsky's *1812 Overture*, it would be necessary to obliterate all the recordings and films of the work's performances, all the scores and copies of orchestral parts, all the partial memories that might be pooled in the reconstruction of a copy of the score, all the tapes and computer disks on which digitalized versions of the work might be stored; to switch off all the computers that had such digitalized versions in their "memories"; and so on.

By now it should be clear that the indissolubility thesis, as Carrier and Sclafani understand it, is a stronger thesis than is warranted by their arguments. According to the indissolubility thesis as propounded by Wollheim (and Danto), the concept of art involves a marriage of artistic theory and practice. The concept of art would not be what it is had there been no history of art theory realized through an art practice that involves the manipulation of physical media. But, accepting this claim, it does not entail the untenably strong ontological thesis adopted by Carrier and Sclafani: that (at least one instance or specification of) each and every artwork must be both physically embodied and understood as an artwork. Rather, all that is entailed is the weaker historical thesis that our concept of art would not be what it is were it not for the fact that most art making in the past has involved the physical embodiment of artworks and/or their instances.

Compare these views with Margolis's in 1974, 1977. As indicated in Chapter 5, I agree with Margolis that either one instance of any artwork is physically (but not necessarily materially) embodied, or a specification from which a work's instances may be generated is physically embodied. I do not accept, however, that the truth of this disjunction allows one validly to deduce anything about the ontology of artworks. For example, from a requirement that the specification for an artwork be physically embodied, one cannot deduce that the artwork must possess a physical aspect.

Minimal art can cast aside the use of certain techniques without its being able to deprive those techniques of their importance within art in general and to deprive them of their importance in being absent within a Minimalist work. In the same way, Conceptual art can cast aside physicality without its thereby breaking the conceptual link between artworks and the practices by which they are embodied and hence also without its being able to deprive those practices of their aesthetic relevance within Conceptual art, from which they are absent. Equally, if Duchamp tries to eliminate the difference between artworks and what Danto calls "mere real things" in conferring art status on urinals, combs, and the like, he does not thereby succeed in removing the difference between art in general and mere real things in general. Neither does he close the gap between his readymades as artistic creations and the mere real things from which they are perceptually indistinguishable, for the historical/social/art-theoretical context that makes his attempt at art status conferral successful in such cases guarantees also that the readymades will differ in their significance, if not in their materiality, from the mere real things they resemble so closely in appearance.

CHAPTER 7

Historical and Intentional Definitions

For those who hold to them, both the artifactuality condition and the indissolubility thesis have their place within a wider project. Just why these conditions attract as much attention as they do would be mysterious, I think, were it not for their contribution to the broader picture. This wider project being to show that artworks necessarily are the products of intentional actions (by contrast with items that occur in nature or that are an accidental consequence of human action). The artifactuality condition takes its importance from its providing a guarantee that art is intentionally produced. If artworks necessarily are artifacts, then necessarily they are the products of intentional actions and, as such, are to be located within historically rooted social practices. The indissolubility thesis derives its importance from its locating art within a "form of life."

Let me illustrate these claims with quotations from Beardsley and Dipert. Beardsley writes:

> Dickie's stipulation that artworks must be "artifacts," the product of intentional human activity, is to my mind sound. If I have suggested the broader term "arrangement", it is to include activities, earthworks, smoke rings, ideas not carried out but recorded on paper, and other items that may be artworks but don't fit easily under the rubric of "artifact". . . . I don't know that we need to draw sharp lines here, and I am personally inclined to be quite generous. But I think it is a mistake

> to confer artistic status on found objects untouched by human hands, or arrangements, however aesthetically interesting, in the genesis of which no intentions at all played a part. . . . To be a genuine work of art, an object or arrangement must be something for which some person or group of persons takes responsibility, stands behind. Without that we are back to nature. (1982a, 311–312)

For Dipert:

> the reason for the desirability of [the] . . . artifactuality condition lies in the common attribution of numerous of the more important proposed functions of art—representation, expression, suggestion, and assertion, to name a few that seem to presuppose an attribution of prior intentional activity. The attribution of some intentions to a creator of the object firmly separates regarding an object as an art work from regarding it as a non-artistic aesthetic object. (1986, 402)

These views, as well as those quoted from Carrier in Chapter 6, make clear that the insistence on the intentional production of art is itself just one step in the dance. That step is there to guarantee that artworks are distinct from natural objects. The importance of this distinction lies in the fact that the modern analytic approach to the philosophy of art wishes to distance itself from the more traditional approach to aesthetics conceived as the analysis of natural beauty. It is widely accepted among the philosophers I have been discussing that artworks have aesthetically relevant properties (by which I mean properties that we must grasp to understand and appreciate the artwork as an artwork) which natural objects could not have. (For example, if Danto is right, artworks always are "about" something, even if sometimes what they are about is merely the fact of their being artworks locatable within a historical tradition of art appreciation and art making.) The aim then, finally, is to articulate a distinction between the kinds of properties which are aesthetically relevant in artworks and the kinds of properties relevant to an aesthetic experience of nature, and to characterize that distinction as following from the conditions under which and contexts within which artworks are created. As I have indicated already in Chapter 4, sometimes that distinction is expressed by our saying that aesthetics has nothing to do with art, and sometimes by our saying that a much wider range of aesthetic properties occur within artworks than occur within nature viewed as such.

Of course, the story is completed in this way: the traditional approach in aesthetics involves describing the aesthetic response to nature and then as treating the response to artworks as derivative. Now, though, the traditional view has been turned on its head by the argument that nature is viewed through the prism of art, and not vice versa (see Forge 1971/72 and Hepburn 1971/72; also see Crawford 1983). In the most radical version of the argument, the view expressed is not simply that there is a distinction to be made between "purely aesthetic" properties and the artistically relevant properties of artworks. Instead, it is suggested that there may be no such things as "purely aesthetic" properties, or that such aesthetic properties as there are are both unexpectedly thin and scarce. The claim, then, is not solely that we look at nature as if it were the product of artists' actions but, further, that we cannot view it otherwise. In other words, the claim is not simply that it is difficult for us to put aside the knowledge that we bring to our understanding and appreciation of artworks when we interest ourselves aesthetically in nature, but rather that, were we to put our understanding and appreciation of art aside, we would find nothing (or only a little) of aesthetic interest remaining (Danto 1986b). This view has led, in recent aesthetics, to theories emphasizing the intensional character of art, and from them have sprung new accounts of the definition of art. Before discussing such definitions I quickly sketch the background of theorizing that they draw on and develop.

Function, Symbolism, and Interpretability

Nelson Goodman (1968) argues that art forms are symbol systems. More recently (1978) he approaches the issue of the definition of art by suggesting that "just by functioning as a symbol in a certain way does an object become, while so functioning, a work of art" (67). It is because symbols are not types of things but, rather, a use of things that Goodman thinks we should ask, When is art? in preference to, What is art? According to Goodman, as symbols artworks possess some properties that distinguish them from other types of symbols. These features tend to have the effect of making the work, rather than what it symbolizes, of primary importance. The "non-transparency" of artworks, far from involving a disregard or denial of its symbolic functions, derives from certain characteristics of the work as a symbol (69).

In 1968 Goodman claimed to be characterizing the necessary and sufficient conditions for something's being a work of art. By 1978 he is more careful, noting that to regard his characterization of the symbolic function of art as stating the necessary and sufficient conditions for something's being an artwork would "call for some redrawing of the vague and vagrant borderlines of the aesthetic" (68–69). He also allows that to say what art *does* is not to say what art *is*, and that a Rembrandt remains an artwork (and a painting) while functioning as a blanket, say, and not as a symbol. (But see 1984, 145, where he inclines more toward the functionalist's view.)

Beardsley (1979) has criticized Goodman on two counts (see also Dickie 1988, Chap. 6). First, he thinks that Goodman is presupposing a notion of the aesthetic in distinguishing a particular use of art from all other possible symbolic uses of art, and Goodman should not presuppose what he claims to be analyzing. Second, Beardsley objects that much "abstract art," such as most symphonic music, is not *about* anything at all. The same objection is raised by Margolis (1974), Dickie (1984), and Tilghman (1984) against Danto's claim that artworks always are about something (see Sparshott 1976 and Danto's reply, 1976). The objection misreads what I take to be the point of Danto's talk of the semantic character of art. The point (in his theory, if not in Goodman's) is not that the artwork necessarily *refers* or *denotes*, but that the artwork necessarily is *interpretable;* that it must be understood not just as if it is a naturally occurring item, but as a bearer of import (also see Margolis 1979 and Levinson 1987a).

The importance of the interpretability of art is stressed concurrently in the writings of others. Margolis (1974; see also 1977, 1979, 1980) argues that artworks are physically embodied and culturally emergent entities. To identify an artwork as such (and not merely as the physical object in which it is embodied) is to understand the work in terms of intensional properties that it possesses only in the light of its cultural and historical context. The word "is" in "The artwork is a material object"—that is, the "is" of embodiment—is different from both the "is" of identity and the "is" of composition.

The most extravagant statement of an equivalent position can be found in the works of Danto. At first (1964) Danto introduced a difficult-to-understand notion, the "is" of artistic identification. (William Kennick, in 1964b, found this idea more confusing than helpful. For a critical discussion of Danto's use of the "is" of artistic identification, see Tilghman 1984; Margolis 1979, 1988; and Sartwell 1988b.) Although he reverted to the notion (1981, 126–129; 1986b, 41–45), Danto sought other ways of expressing his main thesis. He insisted (1973, 1974) that artworks are unlike "mere real things" in that artworks make statements, whereas mere real things just are. Even an artwork that seeks to impersonate a mere real thing preserves a distance between itself and reality in that it says that it is "no more than a mere real thing." By contrast, no mere real thing asserts the nature of its own existence. Artworks are linguistic (only) to the extent that they admit of semantic assessment; to the extent that they are bearers of meaning and, to be appreciated, must be approached as such and interpreted. Later still, Danto (1981, 1986b) says that artworks are about their subjects (rather than that they make statements). Like Goodman and Margolis, Danto emphasizes that in art the medium (the way in which a subject is presented) is never indifferent to the message (what the subject is presented as) and that this fact guarantees that artworks cannot collapse back onto reality. Artworks are to be interpreted as representations, and not incarnations, of their subjects.

In the crude form in which I have presented the preceding views, it is doubtful that a functional definition is being proposed. It may be true that artworks function *as* symbols, but it is not plainly true that their function is *to be* symbols. If art has a function, then that function is met, presumably, by what it is that art symbolizes, or by the way in which art performs its symbolic function. The point of art (in terms of which a functional definition is to be established) is not simply that art be a symbol of some peculiar sort but is some end to which the symbolic character of art might be the means.

Moreover, in the crude form in which I have presented these views, it is doubtful that a definition of any kind is being proposed. The suggestion that artworks are "symbols" (construing that notion widely) seems to give no more than a necessary condition for something's being an artwork, however distinctive a kind of symbol it is. The suggestion is that art is a distinctive type of "discourse," but it is far from clear that the same type of discourse does not occur outside of art. (Danto, for one, has been fascinated by the parallels between modern art and modern philosophy: see 1973; 1981, chap. 3; 1984a; 1984b; 1986a; 1986b, preface and chap 8; see also Charlton 1974, and Alperson 1987a). Neither is it clear that the arena of the discourse of art could be mapped without one's appealing to an independent, prior notion of art. In either event, important and interesting though the thesis is, there is no basis here for a definition of art.

Nevertheless, the account of art as symbol opens the door to any number of functional definitions of art—art is a symbol designed as such to do a certain job (which could not be achieved in any other way). An example of such a theory, I suppose, would be Susanne Langer's account of artworks as presentational (that is, nondiscursive) symbols of the forms of feelings (see especially 1953 and 1957). Although such accounts sometimes contain powerful insights, they are not now much in vogue (though see von Morstein 1986), and I do not consider them here. Instead I examine a view that fits more closely with the emphasis in Goodman's and Danto's writings on the opacity of art as a symbol: rather than serving as a mere vehicle that directs attention through and beyond itself, artworks turn their symbolic function inwards, as it were, upon themselves and their kind.

Krukowski's Definition

Lucian Krukowski (1980) is one who accepts that, necessarily, an artwork is a Goodmanian symbol. He has argued that what an artwork is about is past and future art, and that something qualifies as an artwork if it provides a valuable link between past and future art. Accordingly, classification necessarily involves evaluation. Krukowski's idea is that a piece establishes its candidature for the status of art by virtue of its similarity with past artworks and its prediction that the characteristics on which its own candidacy are based are those which will later be recognized as constituting artistic value. The art of the past is reconstituted by the candidature of the present work; that is, past art is redescribed in terms of the qualities of the present candidate. Krukowski controversially holds that a work succeeding as a candidate, in that its qualities are taken up in the art of its immediate successors, might later have its art status revoked as the far future of art takes an unexpected course. He takes this line because he follows Margolis in seeing artworks as physically embodied and culturally emergent entities (see Kuspit 1988 and Krukowski 1981, 1987, 1988)—although he regards the embodiment relation more freely than does Margolis. He holds, for example, that an artwork ceases to be an artwork when it can no longer be appreciated as such—for example, where ethical considerations make it impossible that it be approached in the appropriate manner. He also believes that an artwork might exist prior to the time of its embodiment and might survive the destruction of all its embodied instances.

Krukowski's argument is stimulating (and more subtle in its detail than my brief exposition indicates). He is right to emphasize (as have many before him) the way in which the aesthetic possibilities for any given artwork depend upon what has been achieved within artworks prior to that moment, and the way in which developments in art lead us to reconsider and reappraise the art of the past, looking there for the pointers to the future, which had not been appreciated at the time. Danto (1964) and Wollheim (1973, 1987) have stressed how the artistic processes and aesthetic qualities that sometimes are absent in contemporary art retain their importance within that art just for the very fact of their having been put aside. Artists work within an ongoing, historical heritage, either by developing or by reacting against its conventions, and their efforts reshape that heritage and so alter the context within which their followers work.

Despite its importance, Krukowski surely is wrong to see the achievement of art status as relying exclusively upon this transaction between the past, present, and future of art. In his view one can know that a piece might become an artwork by virtue of its similarity with other artworks, but one cannot know whether or not it succeeds in becoming an artwork until one is in a position to examine whether it establishes a consistent link between the art of the past and future candidates for art status. Even then, one cannot be sure that the candidature of those future pieces might not eventually fail, with the result that the present piece is demoted from the status of art. A thing's claim to art status might be controversial and fragile, and such a claim might be rendered invalid by future discoveries (for example, perhaps, that the piece had been forged), but the scenario described by Krukowski is yet more radically insecure, and unacceptably so, I believe. The claim to art status of many works appears to be uncontestable and irrevocable. That claim would seem to be authenticated *now* at least in this sense—if our paradigms of art cease to be art, our concept of art would have been revised out of existence and not merely modified. It is not that we accept the claim with confidence simply because it is unlikely that the future path of art would break contact with such works. Rather, if the future path breaks contact with such works, then the new path, whatever it might be, would no longer be the path of art. Moreover, art status, once acquired, does not seem to be reversible in the way Krukowski suggests. Generally speaking, once an artwork, always an artwork. Not that an object might not acquire art status in midlife, as it were, as did the urinal that Duchamp turned into the artwork *Fountain* (cf. Beardsley 1983). I agree that the claim to art status of some, even many, works might not come to be revoked. My dispute with Krukowski here concerns the proper description of the demotion of a piece from art status (see the related discussion in Chapter 6). The defeat of a work's claim to art status at some future date does not show that it was art for a time but is art no longer; rather, it shows that the piece never was an artwork. "Once an artwork, always an artwork" does not mean that we can never be proved mistaken in our judgments about what is or is not an artwork. It means this: artworks do not come into and go out of existence as cultural contexts alter and/or the focus of our interest in artworks changes through time, although beliefs about what is art may alter under such circumstances, and, if the changes were sufficiently radical, the notion of art might disappear altogether.

I have other objections to Krukowski's position. He seems to treat resemblance as a primitive, rather than technical, notion and hence as a possible basis for classification. The discussion of family resemblance in Chapter 1 will have exposed, I hope, the dangers inherent in such an approach. Moreover, the argument derived from Danto to the effect that a thing's acquiring art status affects its aesthetic properties is bound to render problematic any theory, such as Krukowski's, according to which art status is warranted or not insofar as a thing shares its aesthetic properties with established artworks. (Krukowski is aware of this difficulty and stresses, by way of reply, that the transaction between the present candidate and the art of the past and the future is based on those properties which will be acquired if the candidature is successful—see 1987.) Krukowski is committed to the view that the history of art is continuous, but he seems not to give due weight to the fact that the past history of art making has been shaped and directed by the point of the activity. As I understand his view, he does not believe that there is a continuing point to our classifying art as such. Although he regards evaluation as central, artworks are evaluated in terms of their success or otherwise in forging links through shared properties with past and future art, and not by reference to a notion of functionality or by reference to the procedures of the Artworld. His account appears to be a nominalist rather than a functionalist or proceduralist one, in that what is art is what is consistent with what has been called art in the past and will be called art in the future. Since any activity might in one sense or another be consistent with the past history of art, his account can explain the course of art history as no more than accidental. While such a view might explain the present condition of art, because now there seems to be no limit to what might become an artwork, it provides no way of accounting for the fact that this state of affairs marks a change from the past. The notion of historical continuity is too weak to show how the former history of art making might have made the present, seemingly directionless, situation possible.

Carroll's Narrational Theory

Recently, Noël Carroll (1988) has developed a less controversial version of a similar theory. Carroll views art as a cluster of cultural practices (that is, as a complex body of interrelated human activities governed by reasons internal to the activity and to their coordination) which is perpetuated and modified through time by the repetition, amplification, and repudiation of the established practices of the moment. (Repudiation does not involve a break with the past, since it self-consciously sets itself against elements in the prevailing practice and, in doing so, often aligns itself with practices formerly prominent within the tradition.) The coherence and unity of the practice can be established by "narration"; by a story that establishes how the strategies of repetition, amplification, and repudiation forge a continuous path from the state of affairs within the practice at any given moment to previous states of affairs within the practice and also to later ones. This approach accounts for the unity of the concept of art in terms of a model of historical evolution, so that the past practices of art affect, without predetermining, the course of art's present toward its future. (A narrational account of art is recommended also by Novitz in 1989a; for a commentary, see Silvers 1990.)

In this view the *Ur* artworks and the origins of art practice are identified retrospectively as that from which the more or less well-established practice first emerged. Because at its origin art practice was not clearly demarcated from other practices (especially religious ones) and the *Ur* artworks were not necessarily created with any clear view of their artistic purpose, Carroll's theory explains how the origins of the practice can be recognized and invested with significance retrospectively. Near the historical boundary of the tradition, he allows, the core activities and objects are located by reference to their functional significance. Once the core works and activities are established, the practices grow up around them and "the process of identifying the new objects to be included in the series is pursued by means of narratives whose elaboration, in turn, explains the historical unity of the practice to us" (1988, 153).

With his stress on the way in which art is an ongoing social practice, Carroll aims to steer a path between a purely functionalist definition of art and the nihilism of nominalism. He implies that art can survive as a coherent and unified practice, even where that practice no longer is controlled directly by its subservience to the point of art making and art appreciation, because its unity is preserved in the strategies that structure the narration and its historical continuity. As I have indicated previously in discussing both Weitz's and Krukowski's views, however, I am doubtful that the notion of resemblance/repetition (whether or not supplemented by notions such as amplification and repudiation) can sustain the burden placed on it within such a theory. Repetition is not an atheoretical mechanism generating "naturally" unified groupings. Activities characteristic of art making and art appreciation might be described as historically consistent with many other activities. What unifies the narrational account of art, if it is not the recognition of a common function of the practice, is, according to Carroll, the discovery of repetition, amplification, and repudiation. But if these are not themselves structured, rule-governed practices with a unity that derives from the context of their use—that is, if we have no basis for sorting artistically significant repetitions from incidental resemblances—the appearance of narrational unity will be no more than illusory.

Carroll rejects the institutional account of the definition of art on the grounds that the practices structuring institutions must be formal and explicit in order to do that job, and he (quite sensibly) doubts that art practices are formally structured. Institutionalists have argued that informal practices might give rise to informal institutions, so they disagree with Carroll's view of the conditions for institutionality. Their disagreement, though, might go deeper. Unless Carroll's narrational strategies are themselves structured by the Artworld context, appeal to them cannot easily explain the unity of the concept of art in view of the long and varied history of art practices and the many nonart practices repeated, amplified, or repudiated within art practice. Carroll's narrational strategies must reveal the organizing principles that underlie art practice if they are to account for the concept's unity. It is not clear to me how talk of cultural practices founded on repetition and the like can reveal such principles without themselves presupposing a framework for such practices. To presuppose such a framework is to move in the direction of an institutional account.

Short of adopting an institutional account, how might one provide a skeleton that could hold together in a single body the diverse practices making up the history of art? One might hope to do so by reference to a common intentional stance adopted by the practitioners of art with respect to the history of art production and art appreciation. Such a view might complement and strengthen the historicist approach to art, avoiding the difficulties to which I have drawn attention in this and the previous sections. One such definition of art has been developed by Jerrold Levinson, and to it I now turn. (For recent comments on Carroll's and Levinson's views, see Stecker 1990; on Levinson, see Sartwell 1990, Kolak 1990, and Haines 1990. Levinson 1990 replies to Sartwell and Kolak.)

Levinson's Definition

Levinson (1979) offers a historicist definition that relates the artwork to an independent individual who makes reference via his intentions to the history of art. Levinson, like Carroll, contrasts his view with the institutional account that sees the artist as conferring art status within the context of an institutional setting. He insists that an adequate definition must mention what the artist conceives his product as intended for, and how it is to be regarded, and he provides a historical account of the latter: how art_{now} is to be regarded depends upon how art_{past} was correctly or standardly regarded. The connection between art_{now} and art_{past} does not depend (simply of solely) upon similarities between the two kinds of art, or upon their being the sole source of a kind of response ("aesthetic experience"). Rather, it depends, according to Levinson, upon the intention that they be regarded or approached in a certain manner. Levinson comes up with the following rational reconstruction of the process of accretion, which yields the history of art: *Ur* artworks are stipulated to be art; their immediate successors become art by relating themselves to the purpose of one (or possibly more than one) of the *Ur* arts (243); yet later, artworks are defined recursively with respect to their predecessors and so, ultimately, with respect to the *Ur* arts. The recursive step in the definition requires that some person or persons with the appropriate proprietary right over the piece in question nonpassingly intends the piece for regard in any way (or ways) in which previous artworks are (or were) correctly regarded. By way of clarification Levinson emphasizes that the agent need not realize that past art is correctly to be regarded as he intends the new work to be regarded; that "intending for" allows the kind of making or appropriating that goes into readymades and Conceptual art; that the "correct regard" is not necessarily reducible to the most common or rewarding way of regarding a kind of art; that "proprietary right" amounts to ownership and that one cannot "artify" what one does not own; and that "nonpassingly intends" aims at ruling out intentions that are merely transient.

Lately (1989) Levinson has restated his position and replied to objections raised to it by Beardsley (1982a). While he accepts that there is no one "correct regard," he is happy to allow that the artist's intention be (whether transparently or opaquely) that the object be regarded in any one of the ways in which past art has been regarded correctly. He also appreciates that the intended regard must be a relatively complete or total regard of the item in question. There are respects in which traffic lights might be viewed as Impressionist paintings are but they are not thereby artworks, because such a regard would not be the total or complete approach intended by their makers. Moreover, now he emphasizes that, while his is an intentional rather than a functional definition, implicit in the notion of intending artistically is the idea that the intender believes it to be worthwhile doing so. He allows that the definition might be amended to read that "the person intends that the regard be adopted *so as to derive certain rewards therefrom*" (22–23).

This account avoids some of the problems I raised in connection with Krukowski's. It allows that a piece can prove its credentials as art now. It gives due place to the interaction between the aesthetic character of a piece and its place within the artistic heritage. It links the art of the past, present, and future, but rather than doing so in terms of the notion of similarity, it relies on artists' intentions to forge the connection. It allows a place for the *Ur* works. It is not nominalist, but it retains the advantage of allowing that the point of creating art now might not be what it was initially. In these and other respects the theory is appealing. But I believe that it faces some serious objections.

(1) First, Levinson has abandoned talk of arthood as a status, and to leave this out is to make mysterious the way in which artworks take on aesthetic properties lacked by indiscriminably similar items (or perhaps by their former, humble selves—as urinals, bottleracks, and the like) when they become artworks. Without some such notion it becomes difficult to see how Levinson can distinguish the following cases: that in which an artist creates an artwork in the manner in which Levinson suggests; that in which an artist intends something to be viewed as a work of art (and thereby to make it one) when in fact, unbeknown to the artist, it is one already; that in which the artist wants us to regard something as an artwork just because she believes it to be one already; that in which the artist wants us to regard something he believes not to be an artwork as if it is an artwork, without believing that he thereby could transform it into an artwork; that in which the artist wants us to regard something that she believes

not to be an artwork as if it is an artwork, while believing that she could transform it into an artwork but not in fact wishing to do so.

(2) I think that anyone who defines art with reference to the artist's intentions must believe also that artists' intentions determine the interpretations, or the range of interpretations, proper to understanding and appreciating their works of art. The intention that an audience view a piece in one of the ways in which the art of the past has been appropriately regarded lacks interest and relevance unless it is the case that the piece in question possesses properties relevant to such a regard. That intention becomes interesting and relevant only if the artist is responsible for conferring such properties on the work, thereby determining to some degree that which must be understood if the work is appreciated aesthetically. That is, the art-regarding intention takes its force from the fact that artists' intentions are relevant, either directly or indirectly, to the appreciation of their works' aesthetic/artistic properties.

Levinson agrees, declaring that his view shows that the "intentional fallacy" is no fallacy at all. Beardsley disagrees (1982a, 1982b), suggesting that there is no inconsistency in holding both that the ontological status of an item as art might be determined in part by the artist's intentions and that it is fallacious to treat artists' private, or personal, intentions as relevant to their works' interpretations. (This disagreement may be more apparent than real. It is possible that the two writers mean different things by the "intentional fallacy." Levinson appeals to a broad notion of intentions which takes in a consideration of historical and social contexts presupposed by the artist and against which he works, whereas Beardsley perhaps has in mind a narrower notion of the artist's intention.)

I believe that the place and importance of artists' intentions as regards the interpretation of their works is misunderstood and overrated. So I am suspicious of an attempt, such as Levinson's, to accord definitional primacy to an art-regarding intention that derives its importance by transference from artists' art-interpreting intentions. So complex are the issues regarding an account of artists' art-interpreting intentions that the development of my objection is postponed until the next chapter, where such matters are considered in detail.

(3) I think that anyone who includes in a definition of art a specification of how the audience must approach or must experience an artwork is bound to insist that some approaches or experiences are more correct than others. Both Beardsley and Levinson appeal to a standard of correctness in their definitions—and how, given the variety of ways in which art might be approached and the variety of ways in which the experience of art might be affected, could they do otherwise? If we wish to rule as artistically irrelevant the enjoyment taken by a person in the rate at which the financial value of an artwork appreciates, or the enjoyment of someone affected by a hallucinogenic drug, or the enjoyment of someone warmed by the flames of a burning painting, then we need some standard of correctness for approaches, experiences, and responses to artworks as art. The appeal to such a standard raises problems for Levinson (as it does for Beardsley).

Three approaches to the issue are possible. First, if one allows (as Beardsley does) that the correct approach is one yielding the most enjoyment, then it will be impossible to find a nonarbitrary way of ruling out the effects of drugs, image intensifiers, and the like, while allowing for the use of opera glasses at the ballet, bifocals for those who need them, a morning cup of coffee for those who need it before they can see straight, and so on. The first strategy concentrates on the response of the individual and supposes that, at that level, it will be possible to give content to some notion of "standard conditions." So much do the conditions for individual responses vary, I doubt that any usefully uniform set of conditions could be enumerated on this basis. Second, one might characterize the proper attitude in terms of its object, as that attitude best suited to the understanding and appreciation of any artwork qua artwork. Third, one might accept that the proper attitude is determined socially within the appropriate institutional context. Objects are to be approached aesthetically in terms of socially established conventions for aesthetic understanding and appreciation. (Note that, if art is to be defined institutionally, the second and third views might come to the same thing.)

Levinson rejects the first way of characterizing the aesthetic point of view, and neither is he an aesthetic-attitude theorist who believes that the experience has a distinctive phenomenology. The second view will be unacceptable, however, because it leads to the circularity of his definition. That is to say, the second strategy is unavailable to Levinson since the notions of a correct approach or a correct response can then be analyzed only by reference to their objects' being treated qua art, and so those notions cannot be used in turn to define art. The remaining, third strategy is also one Levinson appears to reject, since his position is dedicated to avoiding the claim that art making or art offering is a matter of social procedures; he denies that his is an institutional account. Nevertheless, Levinson does seem to regard standards for the correctness of approaches to artworks to be socially determined, even if he does not regard them to be thoroughly institutionalized, and in this he allows for a social dimension to art appreciation which he is at pains to exclude from the process of art creation. Whether he can maintain a distinction between art making and art appreciation in this way, and whether he can succeed in steering a path between the question-begging second approach and the institutionality of the third approach, is far from clear.

(4) The fourth objection comes to this: there is nothing to stop an aesthetically minded tour guide showing to the members of her tour party some natural scene, the Grand Canyon say, and intending that they regard it in a way that is the correct manner for regarding some type of art, such as an earthwork sculpture (in an Impressionist style). The guide's intention is no wild hope, because the scene invites just that regard. Yet we would not be inclined to say that the aesthetically minded tour guide turns the Grand Canyon into an artwork.

How might Levinson reply to this objection? (1) He might emphasize that the regard be a total and not a partial one, and that this stipulation is intended to exclude cases in which one takes a passing aesthetic interest in elements in the scene before one's eyes. I doubt that this reply is adequate to the counterexample, for what is intended by the tour guide in the case described is the adoption of a total regard—total in that the regard is intended to cover all the perceptible aspects of its object, and total also in that one is to bring a full and educated interest in Impressionist landscape paintings and sculptures to the scene before one. (2) Levinson might deny that such an intention is "nonpassing." So vague, though, is the stipulation that the artist's intention not be transient that this reply lacks force. (3) Levinson might draw attention to his requirement that the "intender" have a proprietary right over the item intended for regard as art has been regarded. The tour guide does not have a proprietary right over the Grand Canyon and "you cannot 'artify' what you do not own and thus have no right to dispose of. All your intentions will not avail in such a case, because another person's intention, that of the owner, has priority over yours" (1979, 237). He goes on to add that one can make something that one does not own into an artwork so long as one acts with the owner's permission; that one standardly attains the right in question by creating an object (but that this is not a sufficient condition for one's attaining the right); that the ownership condition does not rule out Conceptual art (in which, for example, the Empire State Building is incorporated into an artwork) because in such cases the artwork is not the object/person/event but is instead "a directed complex of the description and the object" (1979, 237). If Levinson's appeal here to proprietary rights is legitimate, the reply clearly meets the objection. But I doubt the legitimacy of the move, as is evident from the following discussion. (4) Or, finally, Levinson might argue that the Conceptual artist and the aesthetically minded tour guide have different intentions in that, whereas the former intends to create an abstract artwork incorporating the Grand Canyon, the latter merely intends that some nonartwork be viewed as if it were an artwork. This is a possibility I discuss further below.

It is, to say the least, unusual to find mention of proprietary rights in connection with the creation of artworks (but see Karlen 1986). That alone does not show Levinson to be mistaken, of course, but it does give pause for thought. In fact, the notion of ownership does seem to be irrelevant since an artist can be commissioned to produce a sculpture and provided with a block of marble from which to do so—and the "right to dispose of" the piece is never his, but lies with the work's commissioner. A composer can write a symphony and can thereby own the score, the rights to the reproduction and use of the score, and so on—but beyond the rights of that sort, in what sense does the composer *own* the materials from which the symphony is composed? A Conceptual artist might (let us suppose) make into an artwork a "complex of the Grand Canyon and the artist's description of it," but in what sense could the artist claim *proprietary* rights over the Grand Canyon which would license her use of it? Or would the Conceptual artist be able to succeed in the attempt to create such a work only if she acted with the permission of the American people? (Levinson does not suggest that the Conceptual artist who makes use of the Empire State Building needs the permission of the people of New York.)

Perhaps to understand the notion of proprietary right in Levinson's definition of art is to understand the use to which he puts it. Clearly he does not mean to use it to exclude the possibility of a Conceptual artist's intending the Grand Canyon to be regarded as some type of art has correctly been regarded, and so creating an artwork. But what would he say about the aesthetically minded tour guide? Would he allow that this person too has the "appropriate proprietary right" and so can create an artwork in intending that the Grand Canyon be regarded as an Impressionist earthwork sculpture is correctly to be viewed? Alternatively, would he distinguish the tour guide from the Conceptual artist precisely on the grounds that the Conceptual artist has here the "proprietary rights" that the tour guide lacks? Either way there are difficulties, I think.

Suppose that he takes the first course: both the artist and the tour guide have the "appropriate proprietary right" with respect to the Grand Canyon and over the idea of its being viewable as large-scale earthwork sculptures are to be viewed. In that case it is hard to see how the "proprietary condition" in the definition serves any useful function in such cases, for all people will be "owners" of all the things from which art might be made. Moreover, the counterexample is then dealt with simply by conceding that the tour guide does create an artwork. This misses the fact that the counterexample is offered as a *reductio.* Any definition that allows that art might be created so easily is too liberal to be plausible. If the "proprietary condition" does not explain how an established Conceptual artist might have an authority to make art which the tour guide lacks, then it is not doing the job it ought to do.

Suppose that he takes the second course: the artist has the "appropriate proprietary rights" but the tour guide does not, and so the former can create an artwork where the latter cannot do so. In that case Levinson is using the notion of "appropriate proprietary rights" to establish who has and who has not the authority to create artworks under given circumstances. For that job the notion of proprietary rights seems to be inappropriate. Perhaps in some cases the appeal should be to a notion of artistic skill as demonstrated in the activity by which the artwork is created. This approach is unconvincing in the present day simply because art making often presupposes no special skills, or any skills the average, aesthetically minded tour guide might lack. So if neither proprietary rights nor skill establishes grounds for differentiating who has what authority when it comes to art making, how might one make the distinction? One way of doing so, of course, is by appeal to the social roles occupied by the people in question, and to the authority attaching to each of those roles. Within the Artworld an established artist holds a position not held by an aesthetically minded tour guide. It may be by virtue of the authority of that position that the artist can employ successfully conventions for art creation which the tour guide cannot use.

A different approach to the problem which might be available to Levinson is to argue that, despite my description, the intentions of the artist and the tour guide have different effects because they are intentions of different types. The artist intends to incorporate the

Grand Canyon within a Conceptual work (and presumably believes herself capable of doing so). The tour guide invites a counterfactual regard of the Grand Canyon as if it were an artwork (and presumably does not believe herself capable of using the Grand Canyon as the Conceptual artist can). The artist intends that the Grand Canyon be viewed as (part of) an artwork; the tour guide merely intends that it be viewed as if it were (part of) an artwork.

But is the only difference between the two the tour guide's lack of self-confidence? Or is it, rather, that the tour guide *must* intend something different from the artist because she is not capable of achieving what the artist might achieve, whatever the tour guide's beliefs and however her intentions are formulated? As I have already intimated in the first of the objections to Levinson's position, I do not see how Levinson can distinguish the different intentions that something be regarded as art, that it be regarded as if it is art, and so on, without relying implicitly on assumptions about the social context that gives such intentions their power and shapes their effects. The characterization of the difference between art-making intentions and the similar, non-art-making intentions of the tour guide presupposes some account of the conditions that place social limits on who can intend what, when, and under what circumstances. That is to say, just as Levinson's appeal to proprietary rights seems to hint at social (and possibly institutional) conditions for art making and art appreciation, so too does some such presupposition provide the basis for his individuating seemingly similar intentions by their different effects.

The institutional account of the definition of art is explicitly rejected by Levinson, who sees his own theory as avoiding difficulties faced by such an approach. Nevertheless, I suspect that a more thorough and detailed development of his theory would reveal its implicit commitment, if not to a full-blown institutional theory, then at least to the view that art creation and art appreciation are activities that depend upon, and must be understood in terms of, a structured social context.

Conclusion

I have argued against the promising theories by Krukowski, Carroll, and Levinson that, if a functionalist account of the definition of art is rejected, something more than intentions or unstructured cultural practices is needed if we are to explain, on the one hand, the extraordinary diversity of art-making activities and of artworks, and, on the other, the continuing unity of the concept of an artwork. I have indicated that, if we are to avoid the nonsolution offered by nominalism, an underlying (procedural) structure should be sought by which it is possible to explain the success and relevance in moving forward the history of art and the kinds of intentions and practices that are highlighted in their theories. A context is needed within which it is possible for artists to articulate and carry through the intentions mentioned by Levinson, and an underlying structure is needed to explain the unity of some patterns of repetition over others, so that those patterns are seen as the cement binding the concept of art, rather than as accidental or incidental similarities between art making and other activities and practices.

Of course, those who propound historicist/intentionalist definitions of art might concede much of what has been said here without, at the same time, accepting that their approach to the definition of art has been invalidated. Art, as we know it, might come to presuppose and rely on the (informal) institutionalization of its practices, but its doing so does not settle the issue of whether art is to be defined in terms of the history of those practices or in terms of their institutionalized form. Even if certain artistic intentions are not realizable in the absence of underlying conventions and institutions, equally it is true that the existence of the relevant institutions and conventions might presuppose a particular type of historical process or context. My arguments may have stressed the extent to which the historicist/intentionalist account of the definition of art involves a notion of art practice as being (informally) institutional, but those arguments do not determine whether it is the history or the proceduralization of art which is to take definitional precedence. Equally, the historicist/intentionalist account might seek to find a place for the functionality of art, perhaps as a prime consideration in motivating the relevant intentions and directing the artistic practices in which such intentions find their place, but in doing so it is not forced automatically to concede that the functionality of art should take definitional precedence.

CHAPTER 8

Artists' Intentions and the Intentional Approach

At the close of the previous chapter, I did not resolve the question of whether or not definitions of art regarding artists' art-making intentions as sufficient for the conferral of art status might take precedence over functional or procedural definitions. In this chapter I consider that issue, and related matters, in some detail. I do so in terms of a consideration of the relevance accorded to artists' intentions in the interpretations of their works. If the art maker's intention is that her products be approached qua artworks, and if the art maker's intentions also determine, either directly or indirectly, the character of those properties that must be understood and appreciated in approaching her products qua artworks, then not only will intentionalist definitions be autonomous, they will be preferable to the alternatives. Because I argue against the autonomy of the intentionalist approach, it is my aim in this chapter to show that artists' intentions do not have the independence claimed for them and, more particularly, that such intentions are not regarded as determining the appreciation of their products in the manner just claimed to be the case.

It is appropriate to consider this issue in terms of a discussion of the relevance of artists' intentions for the interpretation of their works qua art for this reason: not only did an appreciation of the extent to which artworks are embedded in historically shaped cultural practices lead to a clearer distinction between art and nature and to the development of historicist/intentionalist definitions of art, it led also to the rejection of the so-called intentional fallacy in the interpretation and appreciation of artworks. In doing so it allowed for the possibility Beardsley was keen to reject (1982a, 1982b)—that the art maker's intention to produce an artwork must filter down, as it were, to a level at which that intention also might determine the proper interpretation, or range of interpretations, of the artwork produced. In this view the art maker's intention is that the work be approached as art has been approached in the past, which is an intention that the properties designed into it, qua artwork, are to be understood and appreciated aesthetically, which is an intention that the work be interpreted correctly. Because the nature of the properties that must be appreciated is fixed by the art maker, the first intention determines what is required in an audience's meeting the last intention.

While I accept that a proper appreciation of art depends on an awareness of factors, such as historical context, which lie beyond the boundaries of the work, I contend that among such external factors artists' intentions are not taken in critical practice to have the crucial role on which the preceding argument depends for its plausibility. After considering and rejecting some alternative approaches, I assign this role to (impersonal) artistic conventions. Despite an intimate connection between the conventions in question and artists' intentions as regards the interpretation of their works, I suggest that the conventions are not the servants of such intentions. In this way I hope to demonstrate that the intentionalist approach to the definition of art fails to establish its distinctness from the functional and the procedural approaches.

The Rejection of the Intentional Fallacy

The interest in the extent to which artworks are to be understood in their cultural and historical context—the interest discussed in the previous chapters—correlates with the growing awareness within the philosophy of art of the degree to which the aesthetically relevant properties of any artwork are (partially) determined in their character by matters external to the work, so that the appreciation and understanding of any work necessarily supposes a knowledge and an interest extending beyond the work's boundaries. (Perhaps the first to appreciate this were Ziff 1951, 1953; Danto 1964; Marshall Cohen 1965; and Wollheim 1980. Their attack is directed against the common view, that in appreciating art for its own sake we must forget about external matters and approach artworks as if they are objects isolated from their cultural setting.)

The argument always comes to this: aesthetic properties do not sit in the work like threepences in a Christmas pudding—to be discovered by those with taste. Rather, the nature of those properties is determined at least in part by matters external to the work. Two materially identical works could have different properties were they to be created at different periods, or were they to be created by different people, or were they to be classed as falling within different styles or genres, or were one to be the original and the other to be a copy or a forgery. Moreover, it is not simply that the properties of the work are affected by factors external to the work, but also that the properties so affected are aesthetically important properties, such as the work's expressive properties.

To take just one example from the literature: Kendall Walton (1970) points out that, within any category of art, some properties are standard in being common to all works falling within the category (the two-dimensionality of paintings, for example), some properties are variable within the category (for instance, the representational content of a painting), and some properties are counterstandard in weighing against category membership (such as collage and the consequent tendency toward three-dimensionality in the category of painting). Walton reasons that differences in the aesthetically relevant properties of different works within the same category must depend mainly on differences in their variable properties. Imagine a work that lies at the intersection of two categories. Which of its properties are standard and which variable depends upon which category it is placed in, and, accordingly, whether or not it is expressive, for example, will depend upon its categorization. (For another version of the same argument, see Sagoff 1976, and on Sagoff, see Sartwell 1988a.)

To make the point, Walton considers a hypothetical example. Within our category of paintings, representational content is a variable. Picasso's *Guernica* is highly expressive at least in part because of its subject matter and the style in which that is represented. Now imagine a tribe of people who have an art category of GUERNICAS. Within this category representational content is a standard feature; that is, every work shares the same representational features in the same style. (If it makes the example more plausible, assume that, in terms of the tribe's conventions for representation, this work is non-representational, so that what is standard in their view is an abstract design.) As it happens, what is variable within the category of GUERNICAS is the extent to which the depicted masses are brought out in bas-relief from the canvas, the texture of the reliefs, and so on. Were it to be (wrongly) classified as falling within the category of GUERNICAS, Picasso's *Guernica* would represent a limiting case (since the masses are not built out from the canvas at all) and would be judged, relative to other works within the category, to be inexpressive, restrained, understated, and so on. A work perceptually indiscernible from Picasso's *Guernica,* but differing from it in belonging within a different category of art, would thereby possess quite different, aesthetically relevant properties from those possessed by Picasso's painting. (For a different attack on the claimed separateness of the internal and external properties of artworks, see Goodman 1978.)

Of course this line runs counter to a traditional view, according to which, in approaching artworks "for their own sakes," external consideration must be put aside. One is supposed to put aside all one's knowledge and concerns in order to consider artworks as unique, isolated, unclassifiable objects, since (it is said) to do less is to deny ourselves access to the totality of their aesthetically relevant properties. (For an example of this view, see Ducasse 1929.) But the claim that we adopt to artworks a special aesthetic attitude (a kind of disinterested attention—see Edward Bullough 1912) or a special mode of perception (a variety of "seeing as" or "seeing in"—see Virgil Aldrich 1963, 1977) has attracted criticism from Dickie (1964, 1965, 1966, 1968, 1974), and rightly so in my view.

Nevertheless, I believe that it is possible to preserve the important insight captured by the slogan "art for art's sake" without falling foul of the objections that plague the traditional view. An aesthetic interest in an artwork is an interest in it as the individual that it is, and not an interest in it merely as the means to some independently specifiable end. Whereas the interest in a thing merely as a means to an end is an interest concerned solely with those of the thing's properties relevant to one's achieving the desired end, an interest in an individual for itself focuses on particular properties only because those properties reveal their importance within the experience of the individual viewed as a whole. (These attention-grabbing properties need not be unique to the individual in question. To be interested in something as the individual that it is is not necessarily to be interested only in those of its properties which mark it as unique.) An aesthetic interest is an interest in artworks for themselves, but *for themselves* as what? The object of interest is not an individual *tout court*, it is an individual *something*. Typically the classification most likely to open up the richest aesthetic experience of an artwork will be the classification that places it in the appropriate category, genre, period, school, movement, style. An aesthetic interest in Mozart's *Marriage of Figaro* for its own sake is, typically, an interest in that work as a late-eighteenth-century opera buffa written in the courtly language of Italian, and so forth. (Note, though, that a person with an aesthetic interest in the opera need not be able to bring it under such a description.) To understand and appreciate the work as the individual that it is, to enjoy it for its own sake, is to approach it as such an opera, which is to approach it in terms of the artistic conventions within which the work was created. To approach it as such an opera is to know and understand something of the practices of the theater, of opera, of operas of this type, of singing, and so on. Obviously some people have more knowledge of such matters than do others and so might more richly enjoy the experience of the work, but I do not mean to suggest that the appreciation of art is open only to an elite, few experts. On the whole, so familiar are we with such a wide range of artistic practices and conventions that we spectacularly underestimate how much we know and bring to the experience of art, and so practical is this knowledge that we cannot always articulate it clearly, claiming it as our own. (For a more detailed characterization of the aesthetic attitude in these terms, see Davies 1987a.)

One element commonly found in the received view is the belief that there is an "intentional fallacy." The fallacy is said to consist in one's taking artists' intentions to be determinative of, or even relevant to, their works' interpretations. Interpretations of artworks should be tested only against evidence internal to the work, and external factors, which include artists' intentions, are of no critical importance since the aesthetic import of the internal evidence is apparent without a knowledge of external factors.

Whether Wimsatt and Beardsley (1946) intended that their account of the fallacy should be taken in this way is debatable. It may be that they aimed to rule as illegitimate only a concern with private meanings and intentions not coupled to the use of the artistic conventions relevant to an appreciation of the work in question, and it may be that they did not intend that their attack on one particular critical approach to poetry be generalized to all art forms or to all circumstances in which interpretation occurs. While they distinguish between "internal" and "external" bases for interpretations, they allow for an "intermediate" category of evidence and thereby accept that the artistic import of a work's properties may not be apparent to a person who lacks knowledge of interpretationally relevant factors that lie beyond the work's immediate boundaries. For that reason, perhaps, they would not disagree with the points made in the following two paragraphs.

An attack (such as Walton's) on the neatness of any distinction between internally and externally relevant properties of artworks very obviously becomes an attack on the claim that it is fallacious to regard evidence of artists' intentions as essentially relevant to the understanding and appreciation of their works. The aesthetic character of a piece's properties often is recognizable only in the light of a knowledge of "external" matters. For example, whether or not the style in which a book is written is deliberately archaic will depend upon when it was written. Artists' intentions are one of the more important of the "external" matters that can determine the aesthetic nature of artworks' properties. Representation, symbolism, irony, allusion, allegory, parody, metaphor—to name but a few—all are essentially intentional, and aesthetically important, properties found in artworks. The respect in which intention is essential, to take representation as the example, is this: it is a necessary condition of A's representing B that A be intended to represent B. (Beardsley, in 1982b, argues, unconvincingly in my view, against an intentional account of irony.) If it is also true that one could not fully understand or appreciate an obviously representational painting, for instance, as an artwork if one failed to notice that it is representational, then artists' intentions (sometimes, at least) appear to determine what one must understand or appreciate in understanding or appreciating the painting as an artwork.

Moreover, even if artists' intentions often do not determine the aesthetically relevant properties of their works in quite such a direct fashion as is the case with representation, allusion, and so on, they do appear to determine other "external" factors, such as the work's category, which in their turn restrict the possible range of a work's aesthetically important properties. (For example, the artist's intentions determine whether or not a work is a forgery, and the fact of its being a forgery determines properties of the work relevant to its aesthetic appreciation and understanding, such as whether or not it fits into a pattern of development that led, say, to Expressionism.) That is, where artists' intentions do not directly determine properties relevant to the appreciation and understanding of their works as art, those intentions seem to determine other of the factors that constrain the range of available interpretations of the work.

I maintain that artists' intentions are not determinative of what we must understand if we are to understand their works aesthetically, although I accept that external factors are relevant in determining the character of aesthetically relevant properties. The two cases described above—that in which artists' (first-order) intentions appear to determine directly the artistically relevant properties of their artworks and that in which artists' (second-order) intentions appear to determine factors that in their turn determine the range of artistically relevant properties—require different treatments. My discussion begins with the first case, and the properties in question are those previously described as essentially intentional—representation, irony, allusion, allegory, parody, metaphor, and so forth.

Essentially Intentional Interpretation-Relevant Properties

If it is allowed that artists' intentions directly determine whether or not their works are representational, allusive, and so on, and if it is also held that one could not fully appreciate a representational work if one ignored its representational character, or an allusive work if one were ignorant of its allusive character, and so on, then it seems that there can be only a restricted range of correct interpretations for each work—namely, those consistent with the artist's intentions. Multiple interpretations will be available only when artists' intentions (as regards representation and the like) are confused, or ambiguous, or contradictory. (Danto, for one, seems to believe that there is only one correct interpretation of an artwork, that which was intended by the artist—1986b. This aspect of Danto's view was commented on as early as 1974 by Tormey.)

The idea that a full interpretation of an artwork is narrowly restricted to the reading or readings intended by the work's artist runs counter to three widely held intuitions about our approach to, and interest in, artworks. (1) It challenges the common view that an artwork invites different, even contradictory, interpretations, and does so not because the artwork is confused, but rather because artworks are multi-interpretable. (2) It rejects the legitimacy of readings of artworks that are at odds with the readings intended by their artists, and it does so even in those cases in which the alternative reading is a plausible one and is manifestly superior in its aesthetic rewards to the readings recommended by the works' artists. (3) It sits uncomfortably alongside the fact that the interpretation of artworks seems not to be seriously inhibited or impaired in the great many cases in which the artists' intentions are unknown.

An account that avoids these three difficulties without at the same time denying to artworks their semantic or representational or expressive character would have the advantage over the view that accords interpretational primacy to artists' intentions. The trick, in providing such an account, is to deny the determining importance of artists' intentions without thereby rendering aesthetically irrelevant the fact, for example, that representational paintings present a represented content that must be grasped if the work is to be fully understood and appreciated. In the following I consider two possibilities—that the aesthetically important content of artworks might be secured by audiences' rather than artists' intentions, and that the aesthetically important content of artworks might be sustained by the conventions within which artists work.

Substituting Audiences' for Artists' Intentions

It might be said that (a member of) the audience could supply the intentions that give significance, under the resulting interpretation, to the artwork in question. I, as reader, might intend that a line in a poem be understood as an allusion, an allusion the poet could not have intended, and by so doing I could make available an interpretation of the poem in which that allusion plays a part. The poem is not stripped bare of those aesthetically relevant properties which are essentially intentional when the poet's intentions are ignored, for *I*, the reader, might supply the relevant intentions for myself, and thereby create the possibility of a range of readings that go beyond the limits set by an exclusive concentration on the reading compatible with the poet's intentions as those intentions were realized within the work.

Such an approach faces at least five difficulties.

First, it is not always the case that, where an intention is necessary for some outcome, it is also sufficient for that outcome. Because my intentions are not embedded, as are the artist's, within the context of creative action, it may be that I cannot achieve the results that can be achieved by the artist. For example, representations are *made* to be representations, as well as being intended to be representations. I could not bring it about that an Abstract Expressionist painting by Jackson Pollock represent Napoleon, or that the *Mona Lisa* represent a man, merely by intending that they do so. My intentions would be ineffective unless I acted upon them in making a suitable representation, and that would involve my modifying the paintings in question. Whatever I might intend or hope, I differ from the artist in that, as a member of the audience, I receive, and do not create, the artwork. So the first critical point comes to this: not all of the aesthetic properties likely to be relevant to an artwork's interpretation could be generated by substituting the intentions of (a member of) the audience for the artist's intentions.

A second problem is that far too many and too wide a range of interpretations would be legitimized if the audience might substitute its intentions for the artist's, since the imagination of the audience faced with an artwork might be given unfettered rein. Under those circumstances there would be as many readings of each work as there are bizarre, idiosyncratic intentions that could be applied to it, and there would be no basis for preferring one interpretation over any other.

This objection invites a reply. There is no point in one's departing from the artist's intentions unless one thereby comes up with something more aesthetically rewarding and enjoyable than the reading intended by the artist. There is good reason to suppose that that will not be a common event. Artists set out very often with the general intention of producing works that will reward an aesthetic interest, and the fact that, when we are indulging such an interest, we focus on artworks, rather than on rubbish dumps, suggests that artists must be successful more often than not in doing so. If our own imaginations could produce aesthetically interesting results so easily, then we would use our imaginations in connection not just with artworks but with any natural or manufactured objects/events, and there would be no point to our giving a special place, as in fact we do, to artists and their works.

Third, to encourage the audience to overrule the artist in this way is to license an intolerable disrespect, both for art makers and for their works. If I can "improve" on the artist's work by substituting my own intentions for the artist's, what then is to stop me from altering the very words of the poem, or excising the boring last chapter from the book, or touching up the canvas with my own brush, or re-orchestrating the symphony's last movement to include electric guitars, synthesizers, and other instruments that were not available to the composer?

Again a reply is appropriate. Notice that all the things just listed have been done in fact—usually by another artist—so actions of that sort are not entirely out of the question. If, however, the worry expressed in the objection is a concern that irreplaceable works (painting, statues, or manuscripts and scores existing in only one copy) will be defaced and thereby destroyed, then it might be answered. Of course, there is no guarantee that artworks will not be vandalized, lost, or destroyed, but few people interested enough in art to seek to understand and appreciate it would risk its destruction at their hands. Even if I think *Mona Lisa* would be the better for having blue eyes, rather than brown, I would be peculiarly arrogant, insensitive, and ignorant to take to the canvas with my brush. I would be ignoring the fact that my judgment is as likely to be proved fallible as were the judgments of those who, in the past, dismissed Shakespeare as a mere wordsmith, Beethoven as no more than a bombast, and so on. Moreover, I would be ignoring the way in which a change in *Mona Lisa* would affect all those later works that derive at least a part of their aesthetic importance from reference to da Vinci's painting and to the tradition it exemplifies. I would be ignoring that what artists do today and will do tomorrow affects the way in which we view the art of the past and very often reveals to us unsuspected ways of understanding the most familiar of artworks, schools, and periods.

Fourth, if I read into a poet's poem things that she did not intend (and which no one at the time of the poem's creation could have intended, let us suppose), then the object of my interpretation has properties that differ from and could not belong to the poet's poem. Therefore, the piece that I interpret is not the piece that the poet created. This is not to say that I am a poet (or some other kind of artist) who, by interpreting the piece in the light of intentions that I supply as its reader, thereby create a *new* artwork. But it is to say that the "aesthetic object" that my interpretation aims to characterize cannot be the "aesthetic object" that is the artwork the poet created. (It has been said that there are no artworks except insofar as each critical interpretation amounts to the creation of a new, autonomous artwork. I am not of this view. I believe that critical interpretations might be of interest precisely because they are different interpretations of an artwork that is identifiable independently of any interpretations as the work that is—see Davies 1988b.) In this view, giving the audiences' intentions a status similar to that of the artists' has the effect of proliferating, if not artworks, then aesthetic objects. The attention shifts from the artwork as such, to the aesthetic objects that might be generated from it.

This fourth objection is unlikely to strike someone who prefers to talk more in terms of "aesthetic objects" than in terms of "artworks" (as was Beardsley in 1958) as posing a problem. But to someone (such as I) who holds a commitment to describing an aesthetic interest in nature as parasitic upon the interest typically taken in artworks as such, then the objection raises a serious worry. If allowing audiences' intentions to have the status accorded to artists' intentions has the effect of shifting attention from artworks to "aesthetic objects" (which are only causally connected with the artworks from which they are generated), then the response to artworks cannot be primary in the way supposed. If the focus of attention is an aesthetic object produced by the "intentionalization" of an object of interest, then that object might as easily be a natural object/event/scene, or an item made for some prosaically practical purpose, as be an artwork. In which case there is no basis for our giving priority to the interest in artworks. In this view the aesthetic response is not typically, not characteristically, a response to artworks. Rather, it is a response to "aesthetic objects" that might as easily be natural in occurrence as manufactured, or be manufactured to be a fruit picker or a shopping list as manufactured to be a statue or a poem. So the objection is a powerful one, provided that one shares (as I do) the objector's view that an aesthetic response to artworks is primary and that an aesthetic response to nature is derivative.

A fifth objection to the substitution of audiences' intentions for artists' intentions might be developed as follows. The difficulty in regarding artists' intentions as determinative of how their works must be understood is that this presupposes that only one correct reading (or too narrow a range of readings) of a given work is possible, and the move toward counting as relevant the audiences' intentions is aimed at accommodating a wider range of interpretations. This tactic permits a wider range of interpretations, certainly, but it does so only by allowing that the audiences' intentions determine a wider range of "aesthetic objects." To consider intentions as determinative, be they the intentions of the artist or of the audience, is to suppose that one multiplies the number of possible interpretations only by multiplying the number of things to be interpreted. The point of rejecting artists' intentions as determinative was, however, precisely to allow for the possibility that the same, *single* thing—artwork or, if one prefers, aesthetic object—might be multiply interpretable. In view of that aim, the broadening of the criteria for interpretation to include audiences' intentions, as well as artists' intentions, does not achieve the desired goal in the desired manner. While more interpretations now are possible, the aim of demonstrating the possibility of multiple interpretations of the same, single artwork has not been achieved. The aesthetic significance of artworks remains determined, as it was before, by artists' intentions, even if now there is more scope to seek elsewhere (among aesthetic objects each of which is determined in its nature by the intentions of members of the audiences) for aesthetic rewards.

Artistic Conventions as Determinants of Aesthetic Properties

The fourth and fifth points given above suggest that the shift from artists' intentions to audiences' intentions is misconceived, because the intentions retain their determinative role in either event. If we are to allow for the case in which the same, single artwork permits multiple interpretations, we must not be restricted in the interpretation of artworks by anyone's intentions—neither by artists' intentions, nor by audiences'. But how could intentions be ignored in the interpretation of artworks without one's also ignoring the relevance of those aesthetic properties—representation, irony, and so on—which depend for their existence upon someone's having the appropriate intentions? How could the work be appreciated, and so understood, if such properties are disregarded? An answer to these questions is suggested below.

Audiences do not intuit artists' intentions, they read those intentions off from artists' uses of artistic conventions—conventions for representation, for example. Such conventions are developed and sustained by, as well as convey, the relevant intentions. Once in place, however, such conventions are vehicles for meaning even when not used as such. Instead of concerning ourselves with what an artist means by any particular use of the conventions, we might direct our attention to the interpretations that can be put on the work in the light of the conventions that are applicable to it, whether or not those conventions have been used by the artist. In Tolhurst's terms (1979) we might concern ourselves not with the "utterer's occasion-meaning" of an artwork (= "utterance"), but rather, with the "utterance meaning" of the artwork. (Tolhurst's "utterance meaning" is impersonal in the way that Grice's "timeless word-meaning" is, but unlike the Gricean notion, it allows for historical and social constraints on the meaning of a text. For that reason Tolhurst's would seem to be the more appropriate notion where the concern is with the meaning of a "text" that is irremovably embedded in a historical/social context, as artworks are.) That is, we might concern ourselves not with what the artist meant by his artwork but rather with the meanings that might be put on the artwork (with regard to its historical context but, perhaps, without regard to its intended significance).

To ignore what the poet intended is not to render the poem into gibberish, any more than a painting is to be made abstract by our paying no special heed to that which the artist intended to represent, because in either case the conventions of linguistic meaning and of pictorial representation remain effective in allowing an interpretation (more than one interpretation) of the work's meaning, or allusive character, or representational character, and so on. The conventions, as given within the history of artistic activity, constrain how any artwork is to be interpreted, while allowing for the possibility of a variety of interpretations of the work in question. An interest in the readings that might be put on an artwork, as allowed by the sets of conventions in terms of which its significance might be interpreted appropriately, takes its focus not primarily from the desire to understand the work as its artist intended but rather to understand and appreciate the work aesthetically in a way that makes that experience the more pleasurable. We are interested in discovering the more aesthetically rewarding readings of artworks, and readings that ignore artists' intentions, but that do not ignore the context of the conventions against which artists work, might be more rich and more interesting than the readings intended by the artists.

To reiterate: just as the conventions of language have the purpose of making utterers' intentions transparent to an audience, so too the conventions of art make artists' intentions transparent. The conventions of language allow one to consider the meanings that can be put on a sentence—neither as a matter of discovering what the utterer meant, nor as a matter of one's meaning something oneself by those words, but "simply" as a matter of one's considering the meanings those words might sustain, given the conventions of language use applying at the time of utterance. In the same way, artistic conventions allow one to consider the interpretations that can be put on an artwork—neither as a matter of discovering what the artist intended, nor as a matter of one's meaning something for oneself by the way the artwork is, but "simply" as a matter of one's considering the interpretations the artwork might sustain, given the conventions of art making appropriate to the work in question. While it is true for the most part that the conventions reveal the artists' intentions, equally it is true that those conventions do not cease to do the job of generating interpretable significance when the fact of their use (or nonuse) is ignored. For every aesthetically relevant property (for example, representation, irony, or allusion) for which intentions are necessary, there is an equivalent and no less aesthetically significant property or properties (for example, representational character, ironic character, or allusive character) for the generation of which the mere existence of the relevant artistic conventions is sufficient.

(I wonder if the view I have defended here is far from the one Beardsley might have wished to endorse. It allows that those of an artist's intentions which are not expressed through her use of the artistic conventions will be irrelevant to an appreciation of the work. It accords importance to artist's intentions where those intentions are apparent in the work as a result of the artist's employment of the relevant conventions, but it does not regard those intentions as determinative of all that one might appropriately concern oneself with in appreciating the artwork qua artwork. It places more emphasis on the general artistic context than on the personal circumstances of the artists. One might suspect that Beardsley's account of the "intentional fallacy" is motivated by just such considerations.)

At a single stroke this attractive view solves both of the major problems identified above. It retains properties equivalent to those that depend on artists' (or others') intentions, so that ignoring intentions does not strip artworks of semantic, representational, expressive, and semiotic content. At the same time, in freeing interpretation from the iron rule of artists' or audiences' intentions, it allows for the possibility of more than one interpretation of a single, independently identifiable item, the artwork (Davies 1982).

Suppose that the suggestion for which I have argued above succeeds in showing why we might deny to artists' intentions a power to determine *directly* the aesthetically important properties of their works and thereby to restrict too narrowly the range of legitimate interpretations in terms of which their works might be understood and appreciated. Accept, that is, that artists' intentions are, with respect to properties such as the representational character of their works, subservient to the conventions within which they operate, because an interest in their works qua art is a concern with the rewards of the different readings made available by the context of appropriate conventions. If we are interested in what a painter represented, then it is not because an interest in the painting qua artwork must be confined to a consideration of the work's essentially intentional properties. Rather, it is because what the artist succeeded in representing is likely to correspond with, and to reveal most clearly, the representational character of the piece in question. Where this seems not to be the case, we might look beyond what was represented, even if the attempt at representation was successful, allowing the search for an interesting or rewarding interpretation to be constrained only by the conventions of the practice against which the work was created and in relation to which it retains its identity as the object of interpretation. Artists' intentions are bound to be of special interest to us—but not because such intentions set the acceptable limits to interpretation, rather because they are more than likely to point toward the more rewarding of the interpretations available.

What so far has been established? If it works, the previous argument interposes artistic conventions between the interpretation of the work and its artist's intentions. What might be called direct, or first-order, intentions as regards the immediate contents of artworks have been shown not to determine and narrowly restrict the range of interpretations invited by the attempt to understand and appreciate the work qua art. To establish this, though, is not to establish that artists' intentions never are of determinative importance, for it might be that the conventions on which I have placed so much emphasis are controlled in their turn by artists' second-order intentions.

A consideration of this issue shifts attention to the second of the levels mentioned on pages 187–188. At this second level artists' intentions may be determinative of the categories, styles, schools, movements, or genres to which their works belong, and these in turn may determine both the sets of conventions from which member-works derive their character and the range of interpretations to which member-works are susceptible. This plausible account avoids at least one major difficulty faced by the view that treats artists' first-order intentions as determinative—it allows scope for a wider range of legitimate interpretations. The categorization of a work affects which of its properties are aesthetically relevant—for example, in a passacaglia one would expect to find a clearly stated theme and to concern oneself with its subsequent melodic transformations and harmonic settings—but the work's categorization does not narrowly determine which properties will be important in any particular work, neither, therefore, does it narrowly restrict the scope of available interpretations.

In the following section I outline one powerful argument in favor of the view that the correct categorization of artworks involves, implicitly if not explicitly, reference to their artists' intentions. This argument is taken, once again, from Kendall Walton's "Categories of Art." In a subsequent section I offer a reply to this argument and, in doing so, continue my attempt to undermine the view that artists' intentions are not subordinate to other considerations.

Walton's Objection—Second-Order Intentions

How, if not by appeal to their creators' intentions, are artworks to be categorized correctly? Seemingly a work might be categorized in one or another (or both) of two ways—either (*a*) by placing it within an established category by virtue of its resemblance to works within that category, and/or (*b*) by classifying it in such a way as to maximize its aesthetic interest and value. Walton (1970) challenges these suppositions in pointing out that neither of these criteria for categorization (or their combination) is adequate. He draws attention to artworks that are discontinuous with the previous traditions (such as Schönberg's first twelve-tone compositions) and that cannot be categorized, therefore, on (*a*)-type grounds. Then he argues that (*b*)-type grounds do not provide an acceptable basis for categorization. The instruction that we maximize the aesthetic enjoyment obtainable from any difficult-to-categorize work provides little restraint on the way in which we might categorize it, because, he says, there are many categories within which any given work would be a *masterpiece.* Because neither (*a*) nor (*b*) sets a reasonable standard for the correct categorization of artworks, Walton sees the need to appeal to further criteria for categorizing artworks as such. To (*a*) and (*b*), as determinants of any work's proper category, he adds (*c*), artists' intentions, and (*d*), the fact (if it is one) of the work's falling within an already-established category of art, and so, as not inviting the invention of some new category.

Daniel Nathan (1973) has objected to Walton's move beyond (*a*) and (*b*) to (*c*) and (*d*). He interprets Walton as making an epistemic point—that sometimes it is easy to overlook (*a*)-type factors and to be struck instead by the discontinuities between any given work and its predecessors. Nathan responds by suggesting that, where (*a*) and (*b*) are used in combination, there need be no confusing the correct categorization of any given work. As he reminds us, there were, after all, many features common to both Schönberg's early twelve-tone works and the atonal works that preceded them. Schönberg himself was keen to emphasize the way in which his compositional technique is rooted in practices of composers of tonal music and saw himself as continuing and developing the tradition within which they worked. With an awareness of these continuities coupled with a desire to appreciate Schönberg's music, the correct categorization of the twelve-tone works presents no special difficulty. They belong to a type in which tonality is supplanted by serial procedures that fulfill a structural function analogous to that of tonality.

Walton (1973) has replied to Nathan's criticism and in doing so makes clear that the point he has in mind is a conceptual, rather than an epistemic, one. The claim is not that we might have trouble categorizing a radical work because we lose sight of the continuities between it and the tradition from which it has sprung (or against which it is a reaction). Rather, the point is that *any* work, even one appearing to be of the most familiar kind, might be seen as falling under many categories other than the seemingly obvious one(s), with each of these categories being continuous in some way or another with past artistic practice. Among the categories in which it is a possible member are many categories in which any given work will be revealed as a masterpiece. So the specification that the classification of a work ought to maximize its aesthetic value provides no useful standard for the correct categorization of any work. Therefore, neither (*a*)- nor (*b*)-type factors, nor a combination of the two, sets an acceptable standard for the proper categorization of artworks, since each and every artwork will be categorizable in terms of such factors in a way that reveals each and every artwork to be a masterpiece, and that possibility is an absurd one. Walton concludes: factors other than (*a*) and (*b*) must be involved in categorizing artworks and, in view of the relevance of (*c*), the "intentional fallacy" is no fallacy at all. Artists' intentions determine the category in terms of which their works are correctly to be viewed, and a work's category in turn determines the character of its aesthetically relevant properties.

This reply suggests that the problem, as Walton sees it, does not lie exclusively with radical, difficult-to-categorize works, but lies also with works that meet (*d*) in appearing to fall squarely within established categories—(*d*) is not so innocuous as we might at first have supposed. The appeal to artists' intentions does not come into play only when other considerations are indecisive. It operates, implicitly if not explicitly, in all cases of our determining an artwork's proper categorization and, hence, aesthetically relevant properties, since such properties are category relative.

The Reply to Walton's Argument

First, observe that, while Walton's argument establishes that aesthetically relevant properties of artworks are category determined, it does not establish the further point that he assumes—that aesthetic evaluations are category relative. Within the category of GUERNICAS, Picasso's painting might be condemned as insipid, boring, characterless, and flat (!), but equally, it might be praised as calm, serene, muted, and ethereal. This indeterminacy should not be surprising, because neither is it the case that the categorization of Picasso's *Guernica* as a representational painting determines whether it is to be praised as dramatic and passionate or to be condemned as crude, bathetic, and overstated. That is, although Walton claims in his argument that the categorization of an artwork affects those properties relevant to its aesthetic evaluation as a masterpiece or not, in fact it is not clear that his argument reveals anything at all about the way in which artworks are evaluated as such.

His argument allows for the judgment that some GUERNICA is good of its kind—meaning that it is *typical* of the category in displaying most of the standard features of the category, in not displaying features contrastandard to the category, in employing "the usual" number of variable features to "the usual" effect, and so on. However, to judge a symphony as a good example of its kind—it has four movements paced quick, slow, medium, quick; it emphasizes the development of thematic materials and tonal contrasts; it uses the full range of orchestral textures and colors, and so on—is not thereby to evaluate it as an artistic masterpiece. Many exemplary members of the category "classical symphony" are mediocre in their artistic value, whereas Mozart's *Prague* Symphony, which is a poor instance of a symphony in containing only three movements, is an artistic masterpiece for all that. It is true that Walton's argument allows him to make a point about the evaluation of artworks *as exemplars of the categories to which they belong.* But it is by no means clear that the argument allows him the use that he makes of the claim that the aesthetic evaluation of artworks *as art, and not merely as exemplars of the categories to which they belong* is category relative. Walton's argument derives an appearance of plausibility only by equivocating on the term "masterpiece," by shifting illegitimately between the idea of something's being a masterly paradigm of an artistic type and its being an artistic masterpiece.

In Chapter 2 I suggested that artworks are evaluated as such in terms of the efficiency with which they promote the function(s) of art. With that point in mind, it is not difficult to see why Walton can have nothing useful to say about aesthetic value, since he does not explain how differing categorizations of an artwork would affect its efficiency in promoting the function(s) of art. Because of this lacuna in his account, it is possible to reply to his argument.

Instead of appealing, as Walton does, to artists' intentions, one could appeal instead to the functionality of art as setting the proper standard for how artworks ought to be categorized. An artwork might be characterized in many ways and might, within many such categories, be an exemplary member of the category. Not all pieces, which are "masterpieces" in being the best examples of their kind, necessarily are artistic masterpieces, as Walton supposes. Without that equation, his argument ceases to be compelling. Any piece might be a "masterpiece" within some category (in the sense that it is a paradigmatic member of that category), but not all of the categories in which it might be such a masterpiece are categories in which it could serve the function of art as an artistic masterpiece. Historical continuity alone (that is, [*a*]-type factors) will not always guide one to an appropriate classification of a work, but a combination of (*a*) and (*b*), where (*b*) is concerned not with whether a work is paradigmatic but, instead, with the value of the work as assessed in terms of its serving the function of art, provides a good guide to the appropriate classification of an artwork.

It may be thought that, if the preceding argument demonstrates anything, it demonstrates only that Walton fails in his attempt to show that more than (*a*) and (*b*) are needed to categorize a work correctly and does not show that Walton is wrong, nevertheless, to regard intentions as determining a work's correct categorization. But I hope to have shown more than that. In effect my argument rejects the idea that there is in principle a single, correct categorization for an artwork. Just as I previously rejected the idea that artists' first-order intentions determine a single meaning to their works, a meaning that is grasped if the works are "correctly" understood, so here I am rejecting the claim that artists' second-order intentions determine a single, correct categorization of their works. As the conventions of representation and the like make possible different interpretations of the contents of artworks, so the conventions that serve the functionality of art open the door to a search among possible categories for those which permit an aesthetically interesting and enjoyable reading of the work in question. There is, in principle, no "correct" way to categorize a work, although in practice most works are functionally at their most effective only when they are placed in a definite, established category, the one intended by the artist, just as in practice most works are functionally at their most effective when seen as possessing the content that the artists intended them to have.

As an illustration I discuss Mozart's *Don Giovanni.* Mozart's opera is subtitled a "comedic tragedy." Works of tragedy, Shakespeare's *Macbeth,* for example, regularly contain comic elements to provide relief from the tension of the tragic development and, thereby, to heighten the effect of that development. To see Mozart's opera in such terms, however, is to miss its character. There was an established tradition and genre of tragic operas in Mozart's day, opera seria, to which Mozart contributed such epic examples as *Idomeneo.* But *Don Giovanni* is written in accordance with the (different) conventions of opera buffa, comic opera. The hero in opera buffa usually finds himself in trouble in the finale of the act, which falls in the middle of the opera, only to triumph in happiness at the work's end. Mozart's protagonist is subject to this pattern except that, as an antihero, he dies at the end of the opera. Yet his death *is* a triumph for the principles of evil for which he stands, for he resolutely and courageously holds by those principles in choosing death rather than repentance. *Don Giovanni* stands entirely alone, among opera buffa, in using the conventions associated with comedy to tragic ends. As such, the opera is not easily to be classified. More to the point, it is not obvious that it has one correct categorization.

To develop the claims made above I rely on points made already in the context of the discussion of the relevance of artists' first-order intentions. Conventions are sustained by their intentional use, and they are altered through deliberate attempts to alter them. In that sense artistic conventions depend on artists' having relevant intentions. But this does not show the primacy of artists' intentions over artistic conventions, for the process also works in reverse. It is only through the use of the appropriate conventions that the artists' intentions can be carried through in a public way to the works they produce. "Intentions" divorced from the means by which they can be put into effect are no more than hopes or wishes. The relation between the intentions and conventions is, in this way, symbiotic. But that they stand in such a close relation does not mean that one cannot ask which is to take logical primacy.

If we were interested in artworks as we standardly are interested in other forms of "utterance"—that is, if our concern was to discover the "utterer's" meaning—then, finally, the "utterer's" intentions would be determinative, and the conventions used in conveying them would be their servants. Our interest in artworks, I have suggested, does not seem to be of this kind. Our interpretation of art would seem to be guided by a pursuit for enjoyable aesthetic experience. We would not be interested in art, as opposed to natural or nonart items, were it not the case that artists intend to satisfy such an interest and succeed more often than not in doing so. To admit this, however, is not to concede that the interest in art can be assimilated to an interest controlled solely by a concern with what artists intended. (Of course we are interested in what artists "have to say," but they might have much more to say than can be captured by a concern that focuses too narrowly on their intentions.) Such an interest relies on the fact that the conventions of "utterance," once in place, have a life of their own in conferring "utterance meaning" and thereby permitting a concern with the range of interpretations that might be sustained by the "utterance," where this depends not only on properties internal to it but also on its categorization. Where the concern is an aesthetic one, the intentions are the servants of the conventions and not vice versa. Such is the intimacy of the relation between conventions and intentions that artists' intentions always will be of critical importance in suggesting ways in which their works are best to be interpreted. But such is the nature of an interest in art that interpretations are answerable to conventions—conventions promoting the functionality of art as well as fixing the range of a work's contents—rather than to artists' intentions.

Back to the Intentionalist's Approach to the Definition of Art

In this chapter I have considered the way in which artists' intentions are relevant to our understanding of their artworks, as regards both the categorization of those works and the presence in those works of aesthetically important properties, such as that of representational character. My aim has been to show that the nature of our interest in art suggests that conventions, rather than intentions as such, set the constraints in terms of which we appreciate and interpret artworks. At the same time I explain the undeniable importance and relevance of artists' intentions as reflecting the intimacy of the relationship that holds between the conventions in terms of which art is appreciated and artists' deliberate use of those conventions.

This discussion bears on the issue of the autonomy of the historicist/intentionalist approach to the definition of art. In Chapter 7 I pointed to ways in which plausible versions of such a theory appear to lean, depending on their detail, toward functionalism or proceduralism. If that tendency is to be checked short of collapse, short of reducibility, it must be the case that artists' intentions, at one level or another, take primacy over conventions structured in terms of functional or procedural considerations. It must be the case that such intentions determine the range of proper interpretations of artworks, either at the level of their contents or, more likely, at the level of their categorization. I have argued that this is not the case (since the nature of an aesthetic interest denies primacy both to first-order and second-order intentions). Accordingly, I conclude that the intentionalist approach to the definition of art fails to establish itself as an autonomous rival to the functional and procedural approaches and, to the extent that it represents itself in such terms, I also conclude that it fails to provide a definition of art.

CHAPTER 9

Functionalism, Proceduralism, and Intentions

The discussion in Chapter 8 invites a final return to the comparison between the functional and the procedural approaches to the definition of art—does the account that I have offered of the critical relevance of artists' intentions sit more comfortably with the one than the other? At first glance it would appear that a functionalist might be happier with my reply to Walton's argument than would be a proceduralist because of the emphasis I placed in that discussion on the functional importance of art as guiding the search for a categorization in terms of which the work in question might best be appreciated aesthetically. Moreover, at least one critic has perceived a tension within the insistence of the institutional theory, in Dickie's version of the theory, that status conferral necessarily involves artists' intending to confer art status. The tension is perceived as following from the fact that such intentions seem to arise outside the institutional limits of the conventions that govern art-making practices. I have been inclined throughout this book to favor the institutional/procedural approach over the functional one and, in order to remain faithful to that theme, it is necessary that I consider these matters.

The Reply to Walton, Again

To summarize briefly the argument presented in the previous chapter: Walton denies that mere similarity with established artworks, in combination with a desire to maximize the value of some given piece, sets an acceptable standard for the categorization of that piece as art. He suggests this because he thinks that any work might be a masterpiece in any number of artistic categories, each of which is continuous with the past history of art making. Accordingly he looks for some other determinant of an artwork's proper category and, without further argument, gives that role to artists' intentions. Against this view I have suggested that, while it may be true that any piece could be a "masterpiece" of its type, not just any piece could be a masterpiece of art, because by no means all categorizations of a piece could facilitate its meeting the point of art, in terms of which it is to be evaluated as an artwork.

Both the functionalist and the proceduralist on the definition of art can allow that artworks are to be evaluated as such in terms of their efficiency in meeting the point(s) of art, so both the functionalist and the proceduralist can reply to Walton with the argument I have just sketched. The functionalist differs from the proceduralist, however, in believing that only those categories the members of which might meet the point of art to some minimal degree could be categories of art. By contrast, the proceduralist accepts that the categories of art might come adrift from the function of art, so that a category might be a category of art without its promoting within its members the function of art. This difference in their positions leads to different continuations of the objection against Walton.

The functionalist might argue that not all categories could be categories *of art,* because not all categorizations would be such as to determine in their members properties that might (minimally) allow those members to meet the point of art. So the functionalist might go so far as to claim against Walton that he fails to show not only that there are any number of categories within which a given piece would be an artistic masterpiece but also that all of those categories could be categories of art, and hence he fails to show that the piece in question is an artwork at all. The functionalist might doubt, for example, that GUERNICAS could be a category of artworks. Within what form of life could an interest in a member of GUERNICAS as a GUERNICA (that is, "for its own sake") be enjoyably rewarding? What could there be among the variable properties of a GUERNICA to find worth understanding and appreciating aesthetically?

If, perchance, those questions might be answered to the functionalist's satisfaction, she might argue for the view that not all categories of art are categories in which the best member is an artistic masterpiece. Light opera, novellas, farces—all might be categories of art in which it is not possible to produce an artistic masterpiece of the first rank. This could be so just because the properties standard to the category—that is, the properties by virtue of which a piece belongs in the category—limit its potential to engage with the point of art. For example, the brevity of the novella might make difficult the sustained development of character which, in the novel, provides scope for the exploration of the more subtle and complex aspects of the human personality and the variety of contexts in which such aspects are revealed.

By contrast, the proceduralist separates questions of aesthetic evaluation from those of definition and so must take a different line. Three strategies seem to be available. (1) The proceduralist might allow that the categorization of an artwork is a different matter from its attaining art status and then allow that the categorization of the artwork pays heed to functional issues in a way that the initial attainment of art status does not. In taking this line the proceduralist would have to concede that, on some occasions, we can know that something is an artwork without also knowing how best to categorize it into an art genre. Such an entailment need not be difficult to live with, since it seems to accord with a common perplexity that arises often in dealing with revolutionary works. The appropriate classification of a piece can be difficult to discern—and may not become clear until the passage of time has led to the creation of many new works—without its following that one need be in doubt at any time about the art status of the piece in question. (2) Alternatively, the proceduralist might allow that a category of things can be a category of art just as long as it is consistent with the history of artworks and their categorizations, and as long as it is taken up within the institution of the Artworld.

That is, the proceduralist might regard the conventions of categorization as institutionalized, so that it could come to be the case that they operate independently of functional considerations. In taking this line the proceduralist would move further from the reply I have offered against Walton in that he would describe the categorization of artworks as governed more by conventional practices than by reference to the function of art. (3) Finally, the proceduralist might combine the two strategies indicated here, perhaps by allowing that firmly established conventions of the institution settle the problem of categorizing nonrevolutionary works, but that, in altering such conventions to deal with revolutionary, difficult-to-categorize works, heed should be paid to the functional efficacy of the categorizations that suggest themselves. That is, in cases where the established conventions seem not to be suited to dealing with the case in hand, the modification of the relevant conventions might be made with an eye not only to institutionally and historically relevant factors but also to the manner in which different candidate categories determine in the work in question properties that suit it or not to engaging with the point of art.

Whichever of these strategies is adopted, the proceduralist is more likely than the functionalist to concede to Walton that there are any number of categories of art in which a piece is exemplary and is therefore an exemplary artwork. But the proceduralist, who sees classification and evaluation as distinct activities appealing to different criteria, can maintain against Walton's contrary claim that there is no reason to assume that a work that is exemplary as a member of its category is thereby an artistic masterpiece.

The proceduralist might deny that Walton's GUERNICAS is a category of art for a people whose art history is like the history of our art up to A.D. 1500. At that time it is difficult to see how GUERNICA-making could establish its institutional credentials as an art-making activity. On the other hand, if the people in question have an art history that is like our own to the present day, it would be possible for GUERNICAS to become established as a category of art. This, though, is not to say that a typical member of the category could be an artistic masterpiece, for there is no reason to believe that that categorization will determine in its members properties that would make them highly successful in realizing the point of art.

I have suggested above that the reply I offered to Walton's argument is available to the proceduralist on the definition of art, as well as to the functionalist, despite the fact that the proceduralist does not regard functionality as definitional of art status. Now it looks as if one might take the argument further by turning what at first appeared to be a possible fault of the institutional account into a virtue. Because the proceduralist separates questions concerning the categorization of a piece as (a type of) art from questions concerning its evaluation as an artwork, he can challenge directly the link assumed by Walton to hold between a piece's exemplifying the features of a category of art and its possessing artistic merit. By contrast, because the functionalist shares with Walton the assumption that links categorization and artistic merit, the functionalist must reply to Walton by denying that most of the categories in which a piece would be exemplary are categories of art.

Of course, Walton is right in his claim that a piece's mere resemblance to works that fall within a historically continuous artistic tradition is not sufficient as a basis for its categorization as an artwork, but, in view of the above argument, both the functionalist and the proceduralist might reject Walton's insistence on the overriding importance of artists' intentions. The functionalist would see the point of art as constraining and directing the classification of artworks. The proceduralist would more likely assign that role to conventions established and maintained within the informal critical practices of the Artworld (in which case artists' intentions as regards the categorizations of their works will derive what importance they have only from the power of the conventions that allow expression to such intentions).

Feagin's View

One writer who has outlined a view on the critical relevance of artists' intentions very like the one I have defended is Susan Feagin

(1982). She detects within this view a certain "tension" between the place it gives to artists' intentions and the role it assigns to the conventions of art. In this section I argue against Feagin's worry, suggesting that she undervalues the symbiotic relationship that holds between intentions and conventions. Because she takes the two to be autonomous and potential rivals (in that each might attain the same effect), she feels a tension (where none exists) in appreciating that they can and must interact.

Feagin argues that, while the creation of art and the interest we take in artworks presupposes the presence and importance of artists' intentions, in any particular case factors can compete with and override the artists' intentions as to the interpretation of their pieces. She explains that some intentional concepts, such as those of art and allegory, become institutionalized, so that whether a passage is allegorical depends not on artists' intentions but instead on the passage's similarity to other passages deemed by the institution to be allegorical. Some concepts (such as "art") can be institutionalized and others (such as "satire") cannot. She says that in the case of the former concepts, "the effect of the presence of an institution is precisely to defeat the necessity of there being any particular intention that the artist may have had" (1982, 71).

Feagin claims that intentional and institutional accounts come near to incompatibility—presumably she says this because she sees the conventions of the institution (often) as taking over from artists' intentions the role of determining the status, and the proper interpretation, of artworks. In light of this claim, she detects a tension within the institutional account in that it must appeal to artists' intentions (apparently in preference to appealing to institutional conventions) at three points: (1) the status of art must be intentionally conferred, yet the artist's intentions and the conventions within which art status may be conferred can be in conflict; (2) artists' intentions can alter and affect the conventions, both for conferring art status and for the interpretation of artworks, so sometimes there must be some intentions with an importance greater than that of the prevailing conventions; (3) Dickie allows that the artist's intentions are sufficient to determine the identity of the aesthetic object but that the same intentions are merely necessary, and not sufficient, to determine the identity of the artwork, and this leaves us with the possibility of the aesthetic object's being different from the artwork.

In her conclusion Feagin tries to accommodate all possible views and makes no attempt to reconcile their differences. She allows that different (and exclusive?) reasons might be given for interpreting various works allegorically, for instance. One work is allegorical because its artist intended it to be; another work is allegorical because it is similar (as determined by institutional conventions and criteria) to works that are allegorical; and a third work is allegorical because it has effects that are functionally similar to those of allegorical works (which is to say, I take it, that the work is aesthetically gratifying when treated as if it is allegorical).

While I support Feagin's recognition that the conventions of art making and art interpretation allow for approaches to art which, in the absence of those conventions, would be possible only on the presupposition that the artist had the appropriate intentions, I am inclined to defend the institutional theory against her charges and to reject the catholicism of her final solution. Indeed, I believe that the institutional theory is better suited than is the functional approach to accounting for the nondeterminative, but important, relevance of artists' intentions for the appreciation and understanding of their artworks.

It seems to me that Feagin may misunderstand the relation between intentions and conventions (Davies 1987c). In the first instance she fails to recognize the interaction between artists' intentions and the institutionalized conventions of art making and art appreciation. They interact in at least three important ways.

First, the conventions of art exist as the vehicle by which artists convey their intentions. Artists' intentions can be effective only if they can be "read off" the product of the artists' actions, and the conventions make this "reading off" possible. It is because artists use conventions known to their audiences that they can make their intentions plain. Equally, the conventions exist and are sustained only because artists regularly and intentionally use them. As the pattern of that use changes or is deliberately modified, so too are the conventions. It is no surprise, then, that there is interaction between the conventions and the ways in which artists try to put their intentions to effect.

Second, the existence of social practices and social institutions makes possible certain actions, and the intentions to which those acts give expression, because those acts are performable under the relevant description only within the context of the practice or institution. I can intend to write a check, and my signing my name can be understood as my authorizing a check, only within the context of a banking system that recognizes and deals with checks. In other words, the presence of social practices and social institutions, rather than defeating the necessity of someone's having particular intentions, makes possible one's having, and giving effect to, certain intentions.

Third, it is by no means always the case that the use of some convention is available to all. What I can achieve by what I say might sometimes depend not just on whether I can make my intentions understood, but also on whether I am authorized to achieve such effects. It is within the framework of social practices and social institutions that we can characterize actions as belonging to the occupant of some role (and not merely as belonging to the individual qua individual). It is only in terms of the authority that attaches to different roles that we can explain why the use of some given convention is available at a particular moment to some people and not to others. My saying, "Stand to attention!" can be understood as an order requiring obedience (as opposed to mere compliance) only where I might be seen as occupying a social role that carries with it the authority to issue such orders. So the possibility of my seriously and sincerely intending to issue such an order depends upon my being able to consider myself as the occupant of a role to which such authority attaches. If I do not believe myself to occupy such a role, I can intend to recommend, to exhort, to plead, to advise, and so forth—but not to order—someone to stand at attention. It is only by appreciating how it is that what can be intended depends sometimes on a person's place within a social practice or social institution that we can explain how it is that some people, and not others, can give effective expression to certain intentions.

In the second instance I believe that Feagin perceives a tension between intentions and conventions where none exists because she sees that, if an aesthetic interest is an interest in "utterance meaning" rather than "utterer's meaning," intentions seem to drop out of account. If they cease to be determinative because of the nature of the interest taken in artworks, how can their reintroduction at key points in the analysis fail to generate the tension that goes with inconsistency? If conventions become an alternative and an equivalent device to intentions for doing the same job as is done by intentions, it will be inappropriate to invoke intentions at points where conventions alone apparently are inadequate to carry the analysis forward.

The reply to these points is as follows. Even if artists' intentions drop out of account, in the sense that they do not determine a restricted meaning that the audience must grasp if it is to "correctly" understand artists' works, they do not drop out of account as sustainers of the conventions in terms of which artworks are appropriately to be appreciated. Previously I described the relation between the two as symbiotic. It does not follow from the fact that artists' intentions lose their primacy over artistic conventions that those intentions cease to count altogether. The conventions do not replace intentions in doing the same job as is done by intentions—that is, the job of fixing the meaning of the "utterance." Rather, the conventions are freed from their usual job of making it possible for the audience to consider what the "utterer" meant by her "utterance," so that now, what it is that allows them to perform that standard job also makes it possible for them to accommodate a different concern, an interest in "utterance meaning." If artists' intentions are ignored, the means by which the conventions perform the end of conveying those intentions continue to operate, but now to a different effect. The end becomes that of allowing for an interest in the interpretations that can be put on the artwork consistent with its conventionally determined content(s) and, in particular, with the interpretations that provide the most aesthetic gratification. The conventions do the job they always have done—that of presenting "utterance meaning"—but, because of the nature of an aesthetic interest taken in such "utterances," that job no longer is subsidiary. (Just as conventions can do that job in the standard case only in conjunction with their intentional use, so too they can do that job, when the interest focuses on that job alone, only in conjunction with their intentional use.)

The effect of the presence of the conventions (and of the institution within which they are established) is not to defeat the necessity of the artist's having any particular intention, any more than the conventions and practices of language render unnecessary speakers' intentions. Instead, the presence of the conventions makes possible an aesthetic interest in artworks "for their own sakes." That interest presupposes the crucial relevance of the part played by artists' intentions in sustaining the relevant conventions, even if the conventions cease to be mere servants of such intentions where the concern is an aesthetic one.

So I disagree with Feagin's view that there are three ways in which a work might be allegorical. It is allegorical only if it is intended as such (given that allegory is a property like that of representation). But it may be appropriate, where one's interest is aesthetic, to ignore the artist's intentions (or lack of intentions) and to consider instead if the work has (what I have called) an allegorical character. There is a point to our being interested in the allegorical character of a work if interpreting it that way leads to an appreciation and understanding of the work from which can be derived more, or as much, gratification as is available from alternative interpretations.

Indeed I would go further in my rejection of Feagin's position: it is a virtue and not a defect of the institutional account of the definition of art that it allows, as other theories do not, for an explanation both of the relevance and importance of artists' intentions and of the subservience of an interest in those intentions to a wider concern that allows for the multiple interpretability of artworks. One cannot explain how artworks might be understood and appreciated, when being considered in a way that does not treat their creators' intentions as determinative of their significance, unless due importance is given to the way in which art making and art interpreting are activities structured by social practices and conventions. More than that, one cannot explain how it is that some people, rather than others, can use and alter the conventions that they do use and alter, unless that social practice is viewed as institutionally structured. One cannot characterize the full gamut of artists' and critics' intentions except in terms of the institutional context from which those intentions take their significance.

To the extent that a thoroughgoing functionalist nods in the direction of proceduralism in allowing that art making and art appreciation are inclined to be structured as social practices, the functionalist can avail herself of many of these arguments. A functionalist need not dismiss artists' intentions as interpretationally irrelevant; neither need she regard them as necessarily determinative of the features, or range of features, which are to be appreciated in understanding the artwork aesthetically. This said, though, it is apparent, I hope, from the stress placed on the conventionality of art in the previous two chapters that the nod needs to be more than cursory.

It is by allowing that the function of art is to be realized (if at all) only within the context of a social practice, a practice that may be informally institutional, that a full account of the place of artists' intentions can be given. It is only by recognizing that art is necessarily, and not merely incidentally, social that the apparent tension between the importance of artists' intentions, on the one hand, and audiences' critical freedom in understanding and interpreting artworks, on the other, can be resolved. To accept that is to acknowledge, perhaps, that should the institutionalized procedures for conferring art status come to operate in a way conflicting with the function of art, then the definition of art must be given in procedural, rather than functional, terms. The point is this: the procedure can operate effectively (for a time) even if it becomes divorced from the function that once it was created to serve, but the function is met effectively only within an institutional context (or so I have implied), and thus, where procedure and function go their separate ways, to serve the function of art is to make something that does the job of an artwork but is not thereby to make an artwork.

Finally

In this book I have attempted to characterize, in the broadest possible terms, the strategies that might be adopted in the attempt to define art. I have concentrated on three approaches—the functional, the procedural, and the historical/intentional. I have tried to make clear that each of these approaches contains an important element of truth, so that a theory concentrating on any one of these views is bound, if it is to seem plausible, to find a place within it for elements important in the other two. I am critical of the historical/intentional approach on the grounds that it must accord to artists' intentions an importance that seems to be at odds with the nature of the interest taken in artworks qua art. Because I believe that the procedures of art making have parted company with the point of art, and because the functional approach is forced to challenge the art status of many contemporary works that seem to me to have established their credentials as artworks, I favor a procedural approach to the definition of art as promising the most convincing results. Whether or not art is as thoroughly institutionalized as is claimed in the institutional theory's version of proceduralism is not clear to me. Rather than settling the issue of the definition of art, my aim has been to demonstrate the usefulness of an approach to aesthetic issues—problems of ontology, evaluation, and interpretation, a well as of definition—which views the debates involved in terms of a distinction between functional and procedural conceptions of the nature of art.

I have no formulaic definition to offer. The arguments of the previous pages tempt me to characterize art in the following terms.

Something's being a work of art is a matter of its having a particular status. This status is conferred by a member of the Artworld, usually an artist, who has the authority to confer the status in question by virtue of occupying a role within the Artworld to which that authority attaches. The Artworld is an informal institution structured in terms of its roles. The Artworld has a history; it grew from (noninstitutional) social practices and has continued to develop through time. The practices from which it arose were ones that were concerned with what we now recognize as the point(s) or function(s) of art. At first the Artworld served that function directly, but through time the institution has altered in ways as a result of which it continues to operate sometimes without direct heed to that function (and sometimes in opposition to that function). Artworlds other than that of twentieth-century European culture could and do exist; that they are Artworlds is evident both from the structure of roles that they contain and from their having arisen historically from social practices such as those from which "our" Artworld developed. The practices from which the Artworld emerged, and the products of those practices, the *Ur* artworks, are important to us because the Artworld emerged from them. If we regard the *Ur* artworks as art, it is because the Artworld accords to them that status. Had the Artworld never arisen, there never would have been any artworks, though there might have been religious worlds, or other social institutions, in which items were produced with an eye or ear for their aesthetic character.

Any Artworld is bound to have a changing history. Although the point can be overexaggerated, it is true that many artworks can be appreciated fully as such only in relation to other artworks. As the art of the present becomes the art of the past, so the context of appreciation alters. In this way items of a type that once could not have fulfilled the function of art might come to do so. But it is difficult, if not impossible, to predict the direction in which art will be taken, and the forces at work here are hard to discern. In the case of our Artworld, technical skill in production has become less important than once it was. (The factors that have led to this might be ones applying across the entire culture.) As a result, the qualifications for occupancy of art-conferring roles have altered through time, as has the nature of the objects upon which art status may be conferred. One result of this has been a tendency toward the democratization of some of the "creative" roles within the Artworld. At the same time other kinds of skill may have come into prominence, so that not all the means for art creation are available for the use of all occupants of roles within the Artworld carrying with them the authority to confer art status.

The primary function of art is to provide enjoyment, but this is not to deny that an interest in art can have far-reaching social benefits. Good artworks, properly approached and understood, afford enjoyment. Standards for the proper approach to artworks are governed by interpersonal conventions of the Artworld. These conventions are grounded in the history of the practices of the Artworld and are not established by stipulation. One good reason for creating an artwork is that it is enjoyable when approached in one or another of the ways in which art has been approached in the past. The production and appreciation of art also serves wider social functions—providing employment, securing the value of investments, and so on. By being shaped and directed by such considerations (as well as by others that are internal to the Artworld and its history), our Artworld has come to operate in a way that often is at odds with the function of art.

Artworks are the product of the Artworld. They need not be artifacts, as that term normally is understood, but they must be public objects available (in principle, if not always in fact) for appreciation and interpretation by the Artworld audience. As public objects they come to exist only if they are physically instanced, or a specification for their creation is physically instanced. They need not themselves be material objects.

Most, but not necessarily all, conferrers of art status are artists; "artist" names a role (or the occupant of the role) within the institution of the Artworld. There are conventions by which art status is conferred, and there are limits on the occupancy of the relevant roles and the range of objects upon which, or the range of processes by which, art status can be achieved. A person may be authorized (by his occupancy of a relevant role) to confer art status, and may succeed in doing so, without this being apparent to other members of the Artworld, but as with authority in general, the successful and sustained use of the authority that goes with the relevant roles depends ultimately on the cooperation and recognition of others (that is, in this case, other members of the Artworld). In particular, attempts to expand or alter the conventions by which art status is conferred are likely to be successful only when the agent has a recognized, established position of prominence within the Artworld. The limits of the role of artist are to some extent flexible, in that one person may be more of an artist than another and may be able to use conventions for the conferral of art status which are not available for the use of "lesser" artists.

It is a general, perhaps even a necessary, condition for the successful use of the conventions by which art status is conferred that the art maker intends her product to be viewed in one or another of the ways in which art has been correctly viewed in the past. Once, something had to be *made* to be an artwork, or to be a specification for an artwork. This is no longer true in all cases; other conventions for the conferral of art status are available (for the use of some people, at some times, with respect to some items).

References

Aagaard-Mogensen, Lars. 1975. "The Alleged Ambiguity of 'Work of Art,'" *The Personalist*, 56, 309–315.

Aagaard-Mogensen, Lars (editor). 1976. *Culture and Art*. Atlantic Highlands, N.J.: Humanities Press.

Aldrich, Virgil C. 1963. *Philosophy of Art*. Englewood Cliffs, N.J.: Prentice-Hall.

1977. "McGregor on Dickie's Institutionalized Aesthetic," *The Journal of Aesthetics and Art Criticism*, 36, 213–215.

Alexander, Hubert G. 1976. "On Defining in Aesthetics," in Aagaard-Mogensen (editor), 110–118.

Alperson, Philip. 1987a. "Music as Philosophy," in Alperson (editor), 193–210.

Alperson, Philip (editor). 1987. *What Is Music?: An Introduction to the Philosophy of Music*. New York: Haven.

Anderberg, T., T. Nilstun, and I. Persson (editors). 1988. *Aesthetic Distinction: Essays Presented to Göran Hermerén on His Fiftieth Birthday*. Lund, Sweden: Lund University Press.

Bachrach, Jay. 1977. "Dickie's Institutional Theory of Art," *The Journal of Aesthetic Education*, 11, July, 25–35.

Barrett, Cyril. 1971/72. "Are Bad Works of Art 'Works of Art'?," *Royal Institute of Philosophy Lectures*, 6, 182–193.

Bartel, Timothy W. 1979. "Appreciation and Dickie's Definition of Art," *The British Journal of Aesthetics*, 19, 44–52.

Battin, Margaret, P. 1988. "Lessons from Ethics: Case-Driven Aesthetics and Approaches to Theory," in Anderberg, Nilstun, and Persson (editors), 13–24.

Baxter, Brian. 1983. "Conventions and Art," *The British Journal of Aesthetics*, 23, 319–332.

Beardsley, Monroe C. 1958. *Aesthetics: Problems in the Theory of Criticism.* New York: Harcourt, Brace and World.

1961. "The Definitions of the Arts," *The Journal of Aesthetics and Art Criticism*, 20, 175–187.

1969. "Aesthetic Experience Regained," *The Journal of Aesthetics and Art Criticism*, 28, 3–11.

1970. "The Aesthetic Point of View," in *Perspectives in Education, Religion, and the Arts.* Ed. Howard E. Kiefer and Milton K. Munitz. Volume 3. Albany: State University of New York Press, 219–237.

1976. "Is Art Essentially Institutional?" in Aagaard-Mogensen (editor), 194–209.

1978. "The Relevance of History to Art Criticism," in *History as a Tool in Critical Interpretation.* Ed. Thomas F. Rugh and Erin R. Silva. Provo, Utah: Brigham Young University Press, 1–18.

1979. "In Defence of Aesthetic Value," *Proceedings and Addresses of the American Philosophical Association*, 52, 723–749.

1982. *The Aesthetic Point of View: Selected Essays.* Ed. Michael J. Wreen and Donald M. Callen. Ithaca: Cornell University Press. Contains:

1982a. "Redefining Art," 298–315.

1982b. "Intentions and Interpretations: A Fallacy Revived," 188–207.

1982c. "Art and Its Cultural Context," 352–370.

1983. "An Aesthetic Definition of Art," in Curtler (editor), 15–29.

Berleant, Arnold. 1964. "A Note on the Problem of Defining 'Art,'" *Philosophy and Phenomenological Research*, 25, 239–241.

Binkley, Timothy. 1976. "Deciding about Art," in Aagaard-Mogensen (editor), 90–109.

1977. "Piece: Contra Aesthetics," *The Journal of Aesthetics and Art Criticism*, 35, 265–277.

Blizek, William L. 1974. "An Institutional Theory of Art," *The British Journal of Aesthetics*, 14, 142–150.

Bond, E. J. 1975. "The Essential Nature of Art," *The American Philosophical Quarterly*, 12, 177–183.

Bourdieu, Pierre. 1987. "The Historical Genesis of a Pure Aesthetic," *The Journal of Aesthetics and Art Criticism*, 46 (Analytic Aesthetics), 201–210.

Brand, Peggy Zeglin. 1982. "Lord, Lewis, and the Institutional Theory of Art," *The Journal of Aesthetics and Art Criticism*, 40, 309–314.

Brown, Lee B. 1969. "Definitions and Art Theory," *The Journal of Aesthetics and Art Criticism*, 27, 409–415.

1971. "Traditional Aesthetics Revisited," *The Journal of Aesthetics and Art Criticism,* 29, 343–351.

1989. "Resurrecting Hegel to Bury Art," *The British Journal of Aesthetics,* 29, 303–315.

Bullough, Edward. 1912. "'Psychical Distance' as a Factor in Art and an Aesthetic Principle," *The British Journal of Psychology,* 5, 87–98.

Bywater, William G. 1972. "Who's in the Warehouse Now?" *The Journal of Aesthetics and Art Criticism,* 30, 519–527.

Carney, James D. 1975. "Defining Art," *The British Journal of Aesthetics,* 15, 191–206.

1982a. "A Kripkean Approach to Aesthetic Theories," *The British Journal of Aesthetics,* 22, 150–157.

1982b. "What Is a Work of Art?" *The Journal of Aesthetic Education,* 16, Fall, 85–92.

Carrier, David. 1979. "Art without Its Objects?" *The British Journal of Aesthetics,* 19, 53–62.

1982. "Art without Its Artists?" *The British Journal of Aesthetics,* 22, 233–244.

1987. *Artwriting.* Amherst: University of Massachusetts Press.

Carroll, Noël. 1986. "Art and Interaction," *The Journal of Aesthetics and Art Criticism,* 45, 57–68.

1988. "Art, Practice, and Narrative," *The Monist,* 71, 140–156.

Cebik, L. B. 1990. "Knowledge or Control as the End of Art," *The British Journal of Aesthetics,* 30, 244–255.

Chambers, John H. 1989. "The Aesthetic-Artistic Domain, Criticism, and Teaching," *The Journal of Aesthetic Education,* 23, Fall, 5–18.

Charlton, W. 1974. "Is Philosophy a Form of Literature?" *The British Journal of Aesthetics,* 14, 3–16.

Cohen, Marshall. 1965. "Aesthetic Essence," in *Philosophy in America.* Ed. Max Black. London: Allen and Unwin, 115–133.

Cohen, Ted. 1973. "The Possibility of Art: Remarks on a Proposal by Dickie," *The Philosophical Review,* 82, 69–82.

Coleman, Earle. 1979. "On Saxena's Defense of the Aesthetic Attitude," *Philosophy East and West,* 29, 95–97.

Cormier, Ramona. 1977. "Art as a Social Institution," *The Personalist,* 58, 161–168.

Cox, Renée. 1986. "A Defence of Musical Idealism," *The British Journal of Aesthetics,* 26, 133–142.

Crawford, Donald. 1983. "Nature and Art: Some Dialectical Relationships," *The Journal of Aesthetics and Art Criticism,* 42, 49–58.

Crowther, Paul. 1981. "Art and Autonomy," *The British Journal of Aesthetics*, 21, 12–21.

Curtler, Hugh (editor). 1983. *What Is Art?*, New York: Haven.

Danto, Arthur C. 1964. "The Artworld," *The Journal of Philosophy*, 61, 571–584.

1973. "Artworks and Real Things," *Theoria*, 39, 1–17.

1974. "The Transfiguration of the Commonplace," *The Journal of Aesthetics and Art Criticism*, 33, 139–148.

1976. "An Answer or Two for Sparshott," *The Journal of Aesthetics and Art Criticism*, 35, 80–82.

1981. *The Transfiguration of the Commonplace*. Cambridge: Harvard University Press.

1983. "The Appreciation and Interpretation of Works of Art," in *Relativism in the Arts*. Ed. Betty Jean Craige. Athens: University of Georgia Press, 21–44.

1984a. "The End of Art," in Lang (editor), 5–35.

1984b. "Philosophy as/and/of Literature," *Proceedings and Addresses of the American Philosophical Association*, 58, 5–20.

1986a. "Art, Evolution, and the Consciousness of History," *The Journal of Aesthetics and Art Criticism*, 44, 223–233.

1986b. *The Philosophical Disenfranchisement of Art*. New York: Columbia University Press.

1987. *The State of the Art*. New York: Prentice-Hall Press.

Davies, Stephen. 1982. "The Aesthetic Relevance of Authors' and Painters' Intentions," *The Journal of Aesthetics and Art Criticism*, 41, 65–76.

1987a. "The Evaluation of Music," in Alperson (editor), 305–325.

1987b. "Authenticity in Musical Performance," *The British Journal of Aesthetics*, 27, 39–50.

1987c. "A Note on Feagin on Interpreting Art Intentionalistically," *The British Journal of Aesthetics*, 27, 178–180.

1988a. "A Defence of the Institutional Definition of Art," *The Southern Journal of Philosophy*, 26, 307–324.

1988b. "True Interpretations," *Philosophy and Literature*, 12, 290–297.

1988c. "Kripke, Crusoe, and Wittgenstein," *The Australasian Journal of Philosophy*, 66, 52–66.

Dempster, Douglas J. 1985. "Aesthetic Experience and Psychological Definitions of Art," *The Journal of Aesthetics and Art Criticism*, 44, 153–165.

Devereux, Daniel. 1977. "Artifacts, Natural Objects, and Works of Art," *Analysis*, 37, 134–136.

Dickie, George. 1964. "The Myth of the Aesthetic Attitude," *The American Philosophical Quarterly*, 1, 56–65.

1965. "Beardsley's Phantom Aesthetic Experience," *The Journal of Philosophy*, 62, 129–136.

1966. "Attitude and Object: Aldrich on the Aesthetic," *The Journal of Aesthetics and Art Criticism*, 25, 89–91.

1968. "Art Narrowly and Broadly Speaking," *The American Philosophical Quarterly*, 5, 71–77.

1969. "Defining Art," *The American Philosophical Quarterly*, 6, 253–256.

1971. *Aesthetics: An Introduction.* Indianapolis: Pegasus.

1973a. "The Institutional Conception of Art," in Tilghman (editor), 21–30.

1973b. "Defining Art II," in Lipman (editor), 118–131.

1974. *Art and the Aesthetic: An Institutional Analysis.* Ithaca: Cornell University Press.

1975a. "What Is Anti-Art?," *The Journal of Aesthetics and Art Criticism*, 33, 419–421.

1975b. "A Reply to Professor Margolis," *The Journal of Aesthetics and Art Criticism*, 34, 229–231.

1977. "The Actuality of Art: Remarks on Criticisms by Cohen," *The Personalist*, 58, 169–172.

1979. "An Earnest Reply to Professor Stalker," *Philosophia*, 8, 713–718.

1980. "Review of Weitz's *The Opening Mind*," *The Journal of Philosophy*, 77, 54–56.

1983. "The New Institutional Theory of Art," *Proceedings of the Eighth International Wittgenstein Symposium*, 10, 57–64.

1984. *The Art Circle: A Theory of Art.* New York: Haven.

1987. "Why Not the Both?" *The Journal of Aesthetics and Art Criticism*, 45, 297.

1988. *Evaluating Art.* Philadelphia: Temple University Press.

1989a. "Reply to Stecker," In Dickie, Sclafani, and Roblin (editors), 214–217.

1989b. "Reply to Ryckman," *The Journal of Aesthetics and Art Criticism*, 47, 177.

Dickie, George, Richard Sclafani, and Ronald Roblin (editors). 1989. *Aesthetics: A Critical Anthology.* 2d ed. New York: St. Martin's Press.

Diffey, T. J. 1969. "The Republic of Art," *The British Journal of Aesthetics*, 9, 145–156.

1973. "Essentialism and the Definition of 'Art,'" *The British Journal of Aesthetics*, 13, 103–120.

1977. "The Idea of Art," *The British Journal of Aesthetics*, 17, 122–128.

1979. "On Defining Art," *The British Journal of Aesthetics*, 19, 15–23.

1982. "Aesthetic Instrumentalism," *The British Journal of Aesthetics*, 22, 337–349.

Dipert, Randall R. 1986. "Art, Artifacts, and Regarded Intentions," *The American Philosophical Quarterly*, 23, 401–408.

Donnell-Kotrozo, Carol. 1982. "In Defense of George Dickie," *The Journal of Aesthetic Education*, 16, Summer, 55–64.

Ducasse, Curt J. 1929. *The Philosophy of Art.* New York: Dial Press.

Dutton, Denis. 1979. "Artistic Crimes: The Problem of Forgery in the Arts," *The British Journal of Aesthetics*, 19, 302–314.

Dziemidok, Bohdan. 1980. "Institutional Definition of a Work of Art," *Philosophical Inquiry*, 2, 555–564.

1988. "Controversy about the Aesthetic Nature of Art," *The British Journal of Aesthetics*, 28, 1–17.

Eaton, Marcia M. 1969. "Art, Artifacts, and Intentions," *The American Philosophical Quarterly*, 6, 165–169.

Eldridge, Richard. 1985. "Form and Content: An Aesthetic Theory of Art," *The British Journal of Aesthetics*, 25, 303–316.

Elgin, Catherine Z., and Nelson Goodman. 1987. "Changing the Subject," *The Journal of Aesthetics and Art Criticism*, 46 (Analytic Aesthetics), 219–223.

Ewin, R. E. 1981. *Co-operation and Human Values.* Brighton: Harvester.

Feagin, Susan L. 1982. "On Defining and Interpreting Art Intentionalistically," *The British Journal of Aesthetics*, 22, 65–77.

Fletcher, James J. 1982. "Artifactuality Broadly and Narrowly Speaking," *The Southern Journal of Philosophy*, 20, 41–52.

Forge, Andrew. 1971/72. "Art/Nature," *Royal Institute of Philosophy Lectures*, 6, 228–241.

Gallie, W. B. 1948. "The Function of Philosophical Aesthetics," *Mind*, 57, 302–321.

1956a. "Essentially Contested Concepts," *Proceedings of the Aristotelian Society*, 56, 167–198.

1956b. "Art as an Essentially Contested Concept," *The Philosophical Quarterly*, 6, 97–114.

Glickman, Jack. 1976. "Creativity in the Arts," in Aagaard-Mogensen (editor), 131–146.

Godlovitch, Stan. 1987. "Aesthetic Judgment and Hindsight," *The Journal of Aesthetics and Art Criticism*, 46, 75–83.

Goldman, Alan H. 1990. "Aesthetic Qualities and Aesthetic Values," *The Journal of Philosophy,* 87, 23–37.

Goldsmith, Steven. 1983. "The Readymades of Marcel Duchamp: The Ambiguities of an Aesthetic Revolution," *The Journal of Aesthetics and Art Criticism,* 42, 197–208.

Goodman, Nelson. 1968. *Languages of Art.* New York: Bobbs-Merrill.

1978. "When Is Art?" in *Ways of Worldmaking.* Indianapolis: Hackett, 57–70.

1984. *Of Mind and Other Matters.* Cambridge: Harvard University Press.

Grice, H. P. 1957. "Meaning," *The Philosophical Review,* 66, 377–388.

1968. "Utterer's Meaning, Sentence-Meaning, and Word-Meaning," *Fundamentals of Language,* 4, 225–242.

Grossman, Morris. 1983. "On Beardsley's Definition," in Curtler (editor), 33–47.

Haines, Victor Yelverton. 1990. "Refining Not Defining Art Historically," *The Journal of Aesthetics and Art Criticism,* 48, 237–238.

Harrison, Andrew. 1968. "Works of Art and Other Cultural Objects," *Proceedings of the Aristotelian Society,* 68, 105–128.

Hepburn, R. W. 1971/72. "Nature in the Light of Art," *Royal Institute of Philosophy Lectures,* 6, 242–258.

Hermerén, Göran. 1988. *The Nature of Aesthetic Qualities.* Lund, Sweden: Lund University Press.

Holtzman, S. H., and C. M. Leich (editors). 1981. *Wittgenstein: To Follow a Rule.* London: Routledge and Kegan Paul.

Hospers, John. 1967. "Problems of Aesthetics," in *The Encyclopaedia of Philosophy.* Editor-in-Chief Paul Edwards. Volume 1. New York: Macmillan, Free Press, 35–56.

Humble, P. N. 1982. "Duchamp's Readymades: Art and Anti-art," *The British Journal of Aesthetics,* 22, 52–64.

1984. "The Philosophical Challenge of Avant-garde Art," *The British Journal of Aesthetics,* 24, 119–128.

Iseminger, Gary. 1973. "The Work of Art as Artifact," *The British Journal of Aesthetics,* 13, 3–16.

1976. "Appreciation, the Artworld, and the Aesthetic," in Aagaard-Mogensen (editor), 118–130.

Jamieson, Dale. 1979. "A Note on Originality," *The Southern Journal of Philosophy,* 17, 221–225.

Karlen, Peter H. 1986. "Worldmaking: Property Rights in Aesthetic Creations," *The Journal of Aesthetics and Art Criticism,* 45, 183–192.

Kennick, William E. 1958. "Does Traditional Aesthetics Rest on a Mistake?" *Mind,* 67, 317–334.

1964a. "Definition and Theory in Aesthetics," in Kennick (editor), 86–93.

1964b. "Theories of Art and the Artworld," *The Journal of Philosophy,* 61, 585–587.

Kennick, William E. (editor). 1964. *Art and Philosophy.* New York: St. Martin's Press.

Khatchadourian, Haig. 1958. "Common Names and 'Family Resemblances,'" *Philosophy and Phenomenological Research,* 18, 341–358.

1961. "Art-names and Aesthetic Judgments," *Philosophy,* 36, 30–48.

1969. "Family Resemblances and Classification of Works of Art," *The Journal of Aesthetics and Art Criticism,* 28, 79–90.

1974. "Art: New Methods, New Criteria," *The Journal of Aesthetic Education,* 8, July, 69–85.

Kivy, Peter. 1979. "Aesthetic Concepts: Some Fresh Considerations," *The Journal of Aesthetics and Art Criticism,* 37, 423–432.

1984. *Sound and Semblance: Reflections on Musical Representation.* Princeton: Princeton University Press.

Kjörup, Sören. 1976. "Art Broadly and Wholly Conceived," in Aagaard-Mogensen (editor), 45–53.

Kolak, Daniel. 1990. "Art and Intentionality," *The Journal of Aesthetics and Art Criticism,* 48, 158–162.

Konstan, David. 1983. "The Object of Art," in Curtler (editor), 51–61.

Korsmeyer, Carolyn. 1977. "On Distinguishing 'Aesthetic' from 'Artistic,'" *The Journal of Aesthetic Education,* 11, October, 45–57.

Kovesi, Julius. 1967. *Moral Notions.* London: Routledge and Kegan Paul.

Kripke, Saul A. 1982. *Wittgenstein on Rules and Private Language.* Oxford: Blackwell.

Krukowski, Lucian. 1980. "A Basis for Attributions of 'Art,'" *The Journal of Aesthetics and Art Criticism,* 39, 67–76.

1981. "Artworks That End and Objects That Endure," *The Journal of Aesthetics and Art Criticism,* 40, 187–197.

1987. *Art and Concept: A Philosophical Study.* Cambridge: University of Massachusetts Press.

1988. "The Embodiment and Duration of Artworks," *The Journal of Aesthetics and Art Criticism,* 46, 389–397.

Kuhns, Richard. 1984. "The End of *Art*?" in Lang (editor), 39–53.

Kuspit, Donald. 1988. "Review of Krukowski's *Art and Concept,*" *The Journal of Aesthetics and Art Criticism,* 46, 524–526.

Lake, Beryl. 1954. "A Study of the Irrefutability of Two Aesthetic Theories," in *Aesthetics and Language*. Ed. William Elton. Oxford: Blackwell, 100–113.

Lang, Berel (editor). 1984. *The Death of Art*. New York: Haven.

Langer, Susanne. 1953. *Feeling and Form*. London: Routledge and Kegan Paul.

1957. *Philosophy in a New Key*. 3d ed. London: Oxford University Press.

Leddy, Thomas. 1987. "Rigid Designation in Defining Art," *The Journal of Aesthetics and Art Criticism*, 45, 263–272.

Leich, C. M., and S. H. Holtzman. 1981. "Communal Agreement and Objectivity," in Holtzman and Leich (editors), 1–27.

Levinson, Jerrold. 1979. "Defining Art Historically," *The British Journal of Aesthetics*, 19, 232–250.

1987a. "Review of Dickie's *The Art Circle*," *The Philosophical Review*, 96, 141–146.

1987b. "Zemach on Paintings," *The British Journal of Aesthetics*, 27, 278–283.

1988. "Artworks and the Future," in Anderberg, Nilstun, and Persson (editors), 56–84.

1989. "Refining Art Historically," *The Journal of Aesthetics and Art Criticism*, 47, 21–33.

1990. "A Refiner's Fire: Reply to Sartwell and Kolak," *The Journal of Aesthetics and Art Criticism*, 48, 231–235.

Lipman, Matthew. 1975. "Definition and Status in Aesthetics," *Philosophical Forum*, 7, 90–102.

Lipman, Matthew (editor). 1973. *Contemporary Aesthetics*. Boston: Allyn and Bacon.

Lord, Catherine. 1977. "A Kripkean Approach to the Identity of a Work of Art," *The Journal of Aesthetics and Art Criticism*, 36, 147–153.

1980. "Convention and Dickie's Institutional Theory of Art," *The British Journal of Aesthetics*, 20, 322–328.

1985. "A Gricean Approach to Aesthetic Instrumentalism," *The British Journal of Aesthetics*, 25, 66–70.

1987. "Indexicality, Not Circularity: Dickie's New Definition of Art," *The Journal of Aesthetics and Art Criticism*, 45, 229–232.

Lyas, Colin. 1973. "Review of Dickie's *Aesthetics: An Introduction*," *The British Journal of Aesthetics*, 13, 81–83.

1976. "Danto and Dickie on Art," in Aagaard-Mogensen (editor), 170–193.

McFee, Graham. 1980. "The Historicity of Art," *The Journal of Aesthetics and Art Criticism*, 38, 307–324.

1985. "Wollheim and the Institutional Theory of Art," *The Philosophical Quarterly,* 35, 179–185.

1986. "Review of Dickie's *The Art Circle,*" *The British Journal of Aesthetics,* 26, 72–74.

1989. "The Logic of Appreciation within the Republic," *The British Journal of Aesthetics,* 29, 230–238.

McGregor, Robert. 1974. "Art and the Aesthetic," *The Journal of Aesthetics and Art Criticism,* 32, 549–559.

1977. "Dickie's Institutionalized Aesthetic," *The British Journal of Aesthetics,* 17, 3–13.

1979. "'Art'—Again," *Critical Inquiry,* 5, 713–723.

Mandelbaum, Maurice. 1965. "Family Resemblances and Generalizations concerning the Arts," *The American Philosophical Quarterly,* 2, 219–228.

Manser, Anthony R. 1967. "Games and Family Resemblances," *Philosophy,* 42, 210–225.

Margolis, Joseph. 1968. "On Disputes about the Ontological Status of a Work of Art," *The British Journal of Aesthetics,* 8, 147–154.

1974. "Works of Art as Physically Embodied and Culturally Emergent Entities," *The British Journal of Aesthetics,* 14, 187–196.

1975. "Review of Dickie's *Art and the Aesthetic,*" *The Journal of Aesthetics and Art Criticism,* 33, 341–345.

1977. "The Ontological Peculiarity of Works of Art," *The Journal of Aesthetics and Art Criticism,* 36, 45–50.

1979. "A Strategy for a Philosophy of Art," *The Journal of Aesthetics and Art Criticism,* 37, 445–454.

1980. *Art and Philosophy.* Atlantic Highlands, N.J.: Humanities Press.

1988. "Ontology Down and Out in Art and Science," in Anderberg, Nilstun, and Persson (editors), 85–99, and in *The Journal of Aesthetics and Art Criticism,* 46, 451–460.

Mark, Thomas Carson. 1980. "On Works of Virtuosity," *The Journal of Philosophy,* 77, 28–45.

Matthews, Robert J. 1979. "Traditional Aesthetics Defended," *The Journal of Aesthetics and Art Criticism,* 38, 39–50.

Mendenhall, V. 1982. "Dickie and Cohen on What Art Is," *The Journal of Aesthetic Education,* 16, Summer, 41–54.

Mitias, Michael H. 1975. "Art as a Social Institution," *The Personalist,* 56, 330–335.

1977. "The Institutional Theory of the Aesthetic Object," *The Personalist,* 58, 147–155.

1978. "The Institutional Theory of Artistic Creativity," *The British Journal of Aesthetics,* 18, 330–341.

Mitias, Michael H. 1988a. *What Makes an Experience Aesthetic?* Amsterdam: Rodopi.

Mitias, Michael (editor). 1986. *Possibility of the Aesthetic Experience.* The Hague: Martinus Nijhoff.

1988b. *Aesthetic Quality and Aesthetic Experience.* Amsterdam: Rodopi.

Moravcsik, Julius. 1988. "Art and Its Diachronic Dimensions," *The Monist,* 71, 157–170.

Morton, Bruce N. 1973. "Review of Dickie's *Aesthetics: An Introduction,*" *The Journal of Aesthetics and Art Criticism,* 32, 115–118.

Mothersill, Mary. 1961. "Critical Comments," *The Journal of Aesthetics and Art Criticism,* 20, 195–198.

1984. *Beauty Restored.* Oxford: Oxford University Press.

Moutafakis, Nicholas J. 1975. "Of Family Resemblances and Aesthetic Discourse," *Philosophical Forum,* 7, 71–89.

Nash, Roger. 1981. "Dickie: Defining Art and Falsifying Dada," *The Journal of Aesthetic Education,* 15, July, 107–110.

Nathan, Daniel O. 1973. "Categories and Intentions," *The Journal of Aesthetics and Art Criticism,* 31, 539–541.

Novitz, David. 1989a. "Art, Narrative, and Human Nature," *Philosophy and Literature,* 13, 57–74.

1989b. "Ways of Artmaking: The High and the Popular in Art," *The British Journal of Aesthetics,* 29, 213–229.

Osborne, Harold. 1973. "Definition and Evaluation in Aesthetics," *The Philosophical Quarterly,* 23, 15–27.

1981. "What Is a Work of Art?" *The British Journal of Aesthetics,* 21, 3–11.

Passmore, John. 1951. "The Dreariness of Aesthetics," *Mind,* 60, 318–335.

Pepper, Stephen C. 1962. "Evaluative Definitions in Art and Their Sanctions," *The Journal of Aesthetics and Art Criticism,* 21, 201–208.

Rader, Melvin. 1974. "Dickie and Socrates on Definitions," *The Journal of Aesthetics and Art Criticism,* 32, 423–424.

Richardson, David B. 1976. "Nature-Appreciation, Conventions, and the Artworld," *The British Journal of Aesthetics,* 16, 186–191.

Ross, Stephanie. 1989. "Philosophy, Literature, and the Death of Art," *Philosophical Papers,* 18, 95–115.

Ryckman, Thomas C. 1989. "Dickie on Artifactuality," *The Journal of Aesthetics and Art Criticism,* 47, 175–177.

Sagoff, Mark. 1976. "The Aesthetic Status of Forgeries," *The Journal of Aesthetics and Art Criticism,* 35, 169–180.

Sankowski, Edward. 1980. "Free Action, Social Institutions, and the Definition of 'Art,'" *Philosophical Studies,* 37, 67–79.

Sartwell, Crispin. 1988a. "Aesthetics of the Spurious," *The British Journal of Aesthetics*, 28, 360–367.

1988b. "Aesthetic Dualism and the Transfiguration of the Commonplace," *The Journal of Aesthetics and Art Criticism*, 46, 461–467.

1990. "A Counter-Example to Levinson's Historical Theory of Art," *The Journal of Aesthetic and Art Criticism*, 48, 157–158.

Savedoff, Barbara E. 1989. "The Art Object," *The British Journal of Aesthetics*, 29, 160–167.

Saxena, Sushil Kumar. 1978. "The Aesthetic Attitude," *Philosophy East and West*, 28, 81–90.

1979. "Reply to My Critics," *Philosophy East and West*, 29, 215–220.

Schlesinger, George. 1979. "Aesthetic Experience and the Definition of Art," *The British Journal of Aesthetics*, 19, 167–176.

Schultz, Robert A. 1978. "Does Aesthetics Have Anything to Do with Art?" *The Journal of Aesthetics and Art Criticism*, 36, 429–440.

Sclafani, Richard J. 1970. "'Art' and Artifactuality," *The Southwestern Journal of Philosophy*, 1, 103–110.

1971. "'Art', Wittgenstein, and Open-textured Concepts," *The Journal of Aesthetics and Art Criticism*, 29, 333–341.

1973. "Art as a Social Institution: Dickie's New Definition," *The Journal of Aesthetics and Art Criticism*, 32, 111–114.

1975a. "The Logical Primitiveness of the Concept of a Work of Art," *The British Journal of Aesthetics*, 15, 14–28.

1975b. "What Kind of Nonsense Is This?" *The Journal of Aesthetics and Art Criticism*, 33, 455–458.

1976. "The Theory of Art," in Aagaard-Mogensen (editor), 146–170.

Shusterman, Richard. 1987. "Analytic Aesthetics: Retrospect and Prospect," *The Journal of Aesthetics and Art Criticism*, 46 (Analytic Aesthetics), 115–124.

Sibley, Frank. 1959. "Aesthetic Concepts," *The Philosophical Review*, 68, 421–450.

1960. "Is Art an Open Concept? An Unsettled Question," *Proceedings of the Fourth International Congress of Aesthetics*, Athens 1960, in Lipman (editor), 114–117.

Silvers, Anita. 1976. "The Artworld Discarded," *The Journal of Aesthetics and Art Criticism*, 34, 441–454.

1984. "The Rebirth of Art," in Lang (editor), 201–236.

1989. "Once upon a Time in the Artworld," in Dickie, Sclafani, and Roblin (editors), 183–195.

1990. "Politics and the Production of Narrative Identities," *Philosophy and Literature*, 14, 99–107.

Simpson, Alan. 1986. "Art and Games," *The British Journal of Aesthetics*, 26, 270–276.

Sircello, Guy. 1973. "Arguing about 'Art,'" in Tilghman (editor), 65–86.

Snoeyenbos, Milton H. 1978a. "Vagueness and 'Art,'" *The British Journal of Aesthetics*, 18, 12–18.

1978b. "On the Possibility of Theoretical Aesthetics," *Metaphilosophy*, 9, 108–121.

1979. "Saxena on the Aesthetic Attitude," *Philosophy East and West*, 29, 99–101.

Sparshott, Francis. 1976. "Some Questions for Danto," *The Journal of Aesthetics and Art Criticism*, 35, 79–80.

1980. "What Works of Art Are: Notes toward a Homespun Ontology," *The Pacific Philosophical Quarterly*, 61, 346–367.

1982. *The Theory of the Arts*. Princeton: Princeton University Press.

1987. "How to Define a Work of Art," unpublished paper.

Stalker, Douglas F. 1979. "The Importance of Being an Artifact," *Philosophia*, 8, 701–712.

Stecker, Robert. 1984. "Aesthetic Instrumentalism and Aesthetic Autonomy," *The British Journal of Aesthetics*, 24, 160–165.

1986. "The End of an Institutional Definition of Art," *The British Journal of Aesthetics*, 26, 124–132.

1990. "The Boundaries of Art," *The British Journal of Aesthetics*, 30, 266–272.

Tatarkiewicz, Wladyslaw. 1971. "What is Art? The Problem of Definition Today," *The British Journal of Aesthetics*, 11, 134–153.

Tilghman, Benjamin R. 1973a. "Wittgenstein, Games, and Art," *The Journal of Aesthetics and Art Criticism*, 31, 517–524.

1984. *But Is It Art?* Oxford: Blackwell.

1989. "Reflections on Aesthetic Theory," in Dickie, Sclafani, and Roblin (editors), 160–170.

Tilghman, Benjamin R. (editor). 1973. *Language and Aesthetics*. Kansas: University Press of Kansas.

Todd, George F. 1983. "Art and the Concept of Art," *Philosophy and Phenomenological Research*, 44, 255–270.

Tolhurst, William E. 1979. "On What a Text Is and How It Means," *The British Journal of Aesthetics*, 19, 3–14.

1984. "Toward an Aesthetic Account of the Nature of Art," *The Journal of Aesthetics and Art Criticism*, 42, 261–269.

Tormey, Alan. 1974. "Transfiguring the Commonplace," *The Journal of Aesthetics and Art Criticism*, 33, 213–215.

Von Morstein, Petra. 1986. *On Understanding Works of Art: An Essay in Philosophical Aesthetics.* Lewiston, N.Y.: Edwin Mellen.

Walhout, Donald. 1986. "The Nature and Function of Art," *The British Journal of Aesthetics,* 26, 16–25.

Walton, Kendall L. 1970. "Categories of Art," *The Philosophical Review,* 79, 334–367.

1973. "Categories and Intentions: A Reply," *The Journal of Aesthetics and Art Criticism,* 32, 267–268.

Weitz, Morris. 1956. "The Role of Theory in Aesthetics," *The Journal of Aesthetics and Art Criticism,* 15, 27–35.

1973. "Wittgenstein's Aesthetics," in Tilghman (editor), 7–19.

1977. *The Opening Mind.* Chicago: Chicago University Press.

Welsh, Paul. 1981. "George Dickie and the Definition of a Work of Art," *Acta Philosophica Fennica,* 32, 248–262.

Werhane, Patricia H. 1979. "Evaluating and the Classificatory Process," *The Journal of Aesthetics and Art Criticism,* 37, 352–354.

Wieand, Jeffrey. 1980. "Defining Art and Artifacts," *Philosophical Studies,* 38, 385–389.

1981a. "Quality in Art," *The British Journal of Aesthetics,* 21, 330–335.

1981b. "Can There Be an Institutional Theory of Art?" *The Journal of Aesthetic and Art Criticism,* 39, 409–417.

1983. "Putting Forward a Work of Art," *The Journal of Aesthetics and Art Criticism,* 41, 411–420.

Wimsatt, William K., Jr., and Monroe C. Beardsley. 1946. "The Intentional Fallacy," *The Sewanee Review,* 54, 468–488.

Wittgenstein, Ludwig. 1953. *Philosophical Investigations.* Trans. G. E. M. Anscombe. Oxford: Blackwell.

Wolfe, Tom. 1976. *The Painted Word.* New York: Bantam.

Wollheim, Richard. 1973. "Minimal Art," in *On Art and the Mind.* London: Allen Lane, 101–111.

1980. *Art and Its Objects.* 2d ed. Cambridge: Cambridge University Press.

1983. "On the Question 'Why Painting Is an Art?'" *Proceedings of the Eighth International Wittgenstein Symposium,* 10, 101–106.

1987. *Painting as an Art.* London: Thames and Hudson.

Wolterstorff, Nicholas. 1987. "The Work of Making a Work of Music," in Alperson (editor), 101–129.

Wright, Crispin. 1981. "Rule-following, Objectivity, and the Theory of Meaning," in Holtzman and Leich (editors), 99–117.

Zangwill, Nick. 1986. "Aesthetics and Art," *The British Journal of Aesthetics,* 26, 257–269.

Zemach, Eddy M. 1986. "No Identification without Evaluation," *The British Journal of Aesthetics*, 26, 239–251.

Zerby, Lewis K. 1957. "A Reconsideration of the Role of Aesthetics—a Reply to Morris Weitz," *The Journal of Aesthetics and Art Criticism*, 16, 253–255.

Ziff, Paul. 1951. "Art and the 'Object of Art,'" *Mind*, 60, 466–480.

1953. "The Task of Defining a Work of Art," *The Philosophical Review*, 62, 58–78.

Index

Library of Congress Cataloging-in-Publication Data

Davies, Stephen, 1950–
Definitions of art / Stephen Davies.
p. cm.
Includes bibliographical references and index.
ISBN 0-8014-2568-9 (alk. paper). — ISBN 0-8014-9794-9 (pbk. : alk. paper)
1. Art—Philosophy. I. Title.
N71.D38 1991
701—dc20 90-55756